THE
SCALLYWAGS

MEMORIES OF A RASCAL'S
1950s CHILDHOOD

PETER STOCKLEY

JOHN BLAKE

Published by John Blake Publishing Ltd,
3 Bramber Court, 2 Bramber Road,
London W14 9PB, England

www.johnblakebooks.com

www.facebook.com/johnblakebooks
twitter.com/jblakebooks

This edition published in 2016

ISBN: 978 1 78606 016 7

All rights reserved. No part of this publication may be reproduced, stored in a retrieval system, or transmitted in any form or by any means, without the prior permission in writing of the publisher, nor be otherwise circulated in any form of binding or cover other than that in which it is published and without a similar condition including this condition being imposed on the subsequent purchaser.

British Library Cataloguing-in-Publication Data:

A catalogue record for this book is available from the British Library.

Design by www.envydesign.co.uk

Printed in Great Britain by CPI Group (UK) Ltd

1 3 5 7 9 10 8 6 4 2

© Text copyright Peter Stockley 2016

The right of Peter Stockley to be identified as the author of this work has been asserted by him in accordance with the Copyright, Designs and Patents Act 1988.

Papers used by John Blake Publishing are natural, recyclable products made from wood grown in sustainable forests. The manufacturing processes conform to the environmental regulations of the country of origin.

Every attempt has been made to contact the relevant copyright-holders, but some were unobtainable. We would be grateful if the appropriate people could contact us.

DEDICATION

I would like to dedicate this book to John H. Conlan for keeping me at it during those faltering times and to Our Logger (Larry Riley), Joe Keaney, Mike Kinsella, Billy Vaughan, Robby Tully and Mick Furlong. Those lads helped me live my young life to the fullest. Times were hard but enjoyable. We learned that the world had a lot to offer, but nothing to give.

The men of our time were true men and tried to pass on their principles of fairness, toughness and most of all, the need to face up to the consequences of our actions: to say sorry when needed, to give when necessity calls and, most of all, to spend time with those who need comfort – for time is all you have to truly give.

As for the remarkable women of that area, this is my tribute to them: *When God made woman he took the hardest working bone from Adam and began to carve it. The bits that fell to the earth became beasts of burden.*

CONTENTS

PROLOGUE

As a child, did you ever . . .

. . . Run across vast swathes of railway line, some carrying enough electricity to zap your leg off, should you earth yourself solidly while touching them?

'"Long John" Phil has got a boss-new leg now!' – 1954

. . . Teach yourself to use a warehouse hoist relying on centrifugal force to lift the weight on the delivery rope and then have your friends lifted and lowered on it – even have a go yourself, with only your grip to keep you safe while being hoisted thirty feet up in the air?

'Wil-Wil slipped one day, then became known as "Wil-Wil No-balls"' – 1956

. . . Climb over the top landing of a five-storey block of flats and shimmy down to the fourth, with nothing below you except a freefall that would end in a crash-landing onto solid concrete?

RIP Robby Jackson – 1957

. . . Sneak onto a busy industrial site, such as a thriving dockland, and play around with the bogies and solid-wheeled cranes used for carrying and lifting cargo, only to have one wheel run over your right foot, reducing your big toe practically to a pulp?

'Wow, that hurt!' – Peter Stockley, 1957

. . . Tread the boards of bombed-out houses, ripping out the old planks to take them home, then chop and sell them for firewood?

'We all made money out of that' – Joe, Mick, Robby, Mike, Billy and Peter, 1949–59

. . . Swim in the putrid waters of a busy canal, where you could often see a rat taking to the waters, or feel the carcass of a dead animal floating just below the surface as you dived for bits of coal off the muddy bed?

Danny Doran's favourite pastime, 1949–59

. . . Hang onto the back of a speeding lorry for one mile, having been told, 'Not far now, Nylon, hang on!'? So you do, but that mile seems more like ten as your muscles begin to lose their power until – finally – there is nothing left to keep those fingers tight. So you let go and bounce along, like a bouncing bomb, on those granite cobbles before coming to rest almost at the rear of the – now stationary – vehicle. Meanwhile, you have a coggy the size of a duck egg on your forehead, which your companions watch grow before their very eyes.

'What a horrible experience that was!' – Peter Stockley, 1955

. . . Jump onto the back of a half-loaded lorry and let it take you wherever it may, before you disembark and make your own way home via instinct and recollection alone?

'Oh yeah, and the number of times the local bobby would pull you in merely for being there!' – 1950–9

. . . Bunk in to see a movie at one – or all – of the local picture houses during the week?

'One of our favourite pastimes' – 1949–59

. . . Bunk on a train for a day trip?

'Yes, it was exciting and fun' – 1949–59

. . . Play pranks on your pals, some so scary they would soil themselves – and the more they filled their pants, the funnier it seemed?

'Only those without nerves escaped that mess!' Robby – 1949–59

. . . Go where most wouldn't, do what most don't, and smile when things don't work out right?

'We all did it often, but sometimes the smiles were lacking' – 1949–59

No? Not to worry. Not a must for life's travels, but they fill your cart with tales – and our carts are full. But, then, we were 'the Scallywags', from the Melrose Road tenements, known locally as 'the Buildings' in Kirkdale, Liverpool. The docks, warehouses and canals became our playgrounds, which we trespassed on and plundered almost every day between the ages of six and sixteen before we formed our wings and flew out into the world of work, which had once been our playground.

We learned our skills from the older lads, who had done it all before us, but sometimes we came up with original ways to be Scallywags. And we all had nicknames bestowed on us by my cousin Logger, eighteen months our senior and the best of mentors, but most of all we had lots of fun along the way. These pages are dedicated to those stories, and to exploring the paths I walked on the journey from boyhood to manhood on the streets of Liverpool in the 1940s and 1950s.

However, by the time I had reached thirty I was serving a seven-year sentence for attempted murder. I'd beaten up a bent police sergeant, given a well-known detective a stiff talking-to in the doorway of the Ascot club, sent some hot gangsters fleeing for their lives, away from Liverpool to their hidey-hole on Cantril Farm, and single-handedly whupped most of the bullies of Liverpool's gang-torn clubland. Then I got out of prison and did it all over again. A bad outcome for me, I freely admit, but not for any of my Scallywag friends, nor my mentor, our Logger. They grew up to lead wholesome, uninterrupted lives as hardworking, decent and honest people. Yet we trod the same path, went to the same school and faced the same dangers together. So where the hell did it all go wrong for me?

Mother and father, yeah, I had one each of them: Mum was a Scouser, Dad was a cockney. Sisters, two: one died from cot death. Brothers, none. Other, one: Mum died having it, I don't know what it was, never been told. By the time I really wanted to know, there was no one alive who could tell me. They call me Peter Stockley – Dad's surname. Perhaps, given the choice, I would have chosen Riley, my mother's name. But, then, it was also her father's name – a man who, for some reason, hated me. I ended up loathing my own father, but I stuck with Stockley because choosing between a man who hated me and a man I grew to hate was no choice at all.

My other family, the Scallywags, were six in number: Robby Tully, Mike Kinsella, Mick Furlong, Joe Keaney, Billy Vaughan and me, Peter Stockley. We all had mentors, and mine was my cousin Logger. He talked like a Tommy gun being fired, was quick to smile and always ready to give advice or guidance. He was a great help to me during the period of time I suffered from rheumatic fever, which left me battling a bad heart for a long, long time.

A final note: at times, I've had to assume some things in order to tell this story in its fullest. . . the things people said when I wasn't there, the thoughts in their heads. I've represented these as best I could, in keeping with their characters and according to the situation at hand. I hope you'll bear with me during these occasional passages of what you might call 'artistic license'.

Well, enough filling in. Let me tell you the story of those times, how it all began. You might call this a history book, without the boring bits. If you don't like it, sue me. My defence will be: 'You moved, I only meant to wound you!'

Ladies and gentlemen, read on . . .

CHAPTER 1

GETTING ACCEPTED

While my mother was alive I had two homes: one at 61 Scarisbrick Crescent, Norris Green, and the other six miles away in the Buildings (known locally as 'the Billogs') in Kirkdale. Number 8a Stanley House was my ninny's (grandma's) three-bed flat, where she lived with Granddad, Uncle Frank and Aunty Mary.

In those days Norris Green was a softer, quieter area than the docklands. The houses had gardens back and front, with privets as borders, not walls. They also had toilets upstairs and down, as well as bathrooms with hot running water fed from the back boiler of the fire. They were good – but *freezing* in the winter.

The docklands was a much grimier, bustling place, where the houses were not far from, or sometimes mixed in with, the industrial throbbing of Liverpool's heart. There were streets and streets of up-and-down terraced houses – some two-bed, others three – all without hot running water and only an outside loo, which often froze up in winter, from where you dangled your legs. Some had the blessing of electricity while others made do with gas mantles, but those Buildings, built within the confines of three roads and a large washhouse on Melrose Road, Owens Road and Fonthill Road, were like an oasis within a huge desert of outside-loo jobs. Each had an indoor toilet, a bath and hot running water so long as the fire was lit. They even had a form of central heating if you count the open storage boiler in the kitchen as a radiator. Compact but comfortable, they were a blessing to those who had moved from the slums and bombed-out buildings.

Every weekend and almost every day during the school holidays we would go to Ninny's and it was magical. To me the most meaningful things were: our Logger (my cousin and mentor), my Scallywag pals (Joe and co.) and our playground, the dockland. Of course I loved my ninny, my aunties Ann, May and Mary, and my uncles John, Larry and Frank, but that Liverpool-to-Leeds canal, the warehouses, the vast, busy, rail network and those docks just did it for me. However, without our Logger and the lads from those Buildings, even that wonderful playground would not have been the same. On their own everything was ordinary but, when you put it all together, it was bloody magical, exciting and often extremely dangerous.

By my sixth birthday I'd travelled the distance between those two homes so many times that my mother began to let me go on my own. Mainly it was by tram, which ran down the middle of the dual carriageway on the East Lancashire Road. I boarded it by the Crown pub and would pay a penny return. I liked to sit near the driver and watch as he pushed the lever that would apply the electricity to the wheels. You could hear the power being increased by the whirling sound of the motor as it strove to drive us along. Then I would often wonder if the driver could wind his brake on fast enough to get us to halt at the fast-approaching stop, where crowds of people were waiting to board. That was when the screeching would start and the engine would decrease its whirring and whining to signify all was in hand and those waiting would soon be aboard.

Sometimes I would choose to ride up top and mess about with the seats by pushing their backs across so that people would have to sit facing in the opposite direction; but, if the conductor caught you, he would clip your ear or, if we were near the terminus, he'd make you fix the lot and save him a job. It was good on the tram with the interaction of being able to see the driver, move those seats and feel the power as it surged to go forward but slackened to stop, then screeched to a halt. However, taking the tram meant almost a mile-and-a-half walk from Stanley Park down to those Billogs. Not bad if you had little to carry, but, when the laundry load had to be transported for its dirty date at the washhouse, we had to get two buses: one from the Crown pub to Seaforth, seven miles, and then the other from the dockside bus terminus at Seaforth to Melrose Road, a distance of another six miles. It more than doubled your journey, but, then, you only had to carry the huge bag of washing for less than a hundred yards to Ninny's house once you got off the bus.

If I had to choose between the tram and the bus I would always say the tram, although the bus was a smoother ride and had soft seats compared with the tram's solid wooden ones. The latter had a curious kind of mystique to it as it rattled along, swaying as if unsteady on its tracks, and made each rail joint echo our crossing as it sped along with a clickety-clack. It made you feel as though you were somehow a part of it.

Consciously or inadvertently, my mother gave me a whacking great free-roaming spirit by letting me travel alone from an early age. One time, at the age of four, I was sent to London by train with my name-and-address tag pinned to my top jacket pocket. I was put on the train by Mum and met at the other end by my cockney grandfather, having spent the whole journey sitting on mailbags in the luggage car. Then there were the times when she would allow me to travel on the tram down to Ninny's. Except for one time, when I was attacked by three boys my own age on a piece of waste ground within sight of our Buildings, I had no problems with that journey (I managed to stand up for myself well during that attack despite having my head split open by a brick and needing stitches, for which I had to go to Stanley Hospital). However, after a few more uneventful solo journeys, Mum allowed me to take my little sister Diane with me – which I did, somewhat reluctantly, due to her constant moaning. But one day her moaning helped us make a tanner (sixpence in old money, two and a half pence in new). Diane tripped while getting off the tram and she really hammed it up crying, so much so that a lady stopped and offered her a silver sixpence, which I quickly pocketed. I then made Diane stop crying by saying, 'If you don't stop crying, the lady will want this tanner back.' As much of a moaner as she was Diane knew pennies bought sweets – and six of them bought loads.

Due to that incident, and the resulting shiny sixpence, I tried tripping my little sister up a few more times, especially when there were lots of ladies around, but that soon stopped after a few abortive attempts ensuing in nowt but her howls and tears and a few tuts from those disapproving women who felt I should be more caring.

The *coup de grâce* of my mother's attempts to make me into a self-sufficient traveller came when she asked me to take the washing to Ninny's because she had things to do, but not the time to take the longer route with the large bag of washing. I must have been getting on her nerves or something, so she nominated me and I jumped at the chance.

Two long bus journeys later, I disembarked on the corner of Stanley Road and Melrose Road, waltzed over to the Buildings on Owens Road and crossed the first square over towards the washhouse, where I turned into Ninny's gate and skipped into a welcome from my lovely grandmother, who was peeling spuds in her kitchen.

'Hello lad,' she greeted me happily. 'Where's your mum?'

'She had something to do,' said I, chirpily, 'so she sent me down with . . . the . . . washing.' Those final words dribbled out due to the horrifying realisation that I didn't have the washing with me: I'd left it on the first bus, all the way back at Seaforth. My face said it all as I thought, It'll be bloody well gone now!

Ninny was at first aghast, but soon pulled herself together and helped me to regain my confidence by explaining that they had a lost-property office at every terminus, especially at Seaforth because so many buses stopped there. Then she packed me off to collect the washing. My main worry during that return bus ride was the fear of someone having taken it, but it all turned out well – as my Nin said it would – and soon I was on my way back to her with the washing, having suffered a barrage of ridicule from some of the bus personnel, who had laughed and taken me in the staff canteen. Once there, they made me stand next to the bag of washing, which was almost the same size as I was. These words were ringing in my ears nearly all the way back to the Buildings: 'Look at this, boys. How can something so little forget something so bloody big?'

The imminent arrival should have been a happy occasion – I may even have had a proper brother but something went wrong during the delivery. And so, tragically, my mother died in June 1951.

At first Dad tried a few substitutes to 'mother' us. One was Kate, the other was Nell. Kate's was a smoker, drinker and (sadly) a robber. So she did not last long. Nell, however, was a proper, loving type of person, who reminded me a lot of my Aunty Mary, who married an army redcap by the name of Tommy McAvoy. That wedding was a disaster for my backside, since our Logger and me snuck off to Ford Canal (the Liverpool-to-Leeds canal, which passed through an area named Ford), where we spent most of that day fishing for jacksharps. Needless to say, lying on the canal bank waiting for those jackies to suck in the worm gets your best clothes really dirty, hence the need for a walloped arse on our return.

Once again, Ninny's best intentions were not to my advantage as Aunty Nell grabbed a strip of boxwood and began to use it like a slipper to whack my bottom. It didn't really hurt but I yelled blue murder just to let her think it did. My acting convinced Ninny that the wood was too much, so she took it off Nell, telling her to use her hand instead. Wow, my cries after that were real, believe me! Nell's many years as a skivvy spinster had toughened those hands good and proper, as my poor bum will for ever testify.

All the same, Nell was an unpretentious good 'un – kind, righteous, hardworking and a good cook, too. She soon had our house once more back to being a home and snugly filled the gap that my mother's death had left. I began to feel contented again as Nell made it her job to more or less carry on as my mum had done, even down to going to the washhouse. She looked freakish in the washhouse gear of rubber aprons and wellies! She made us all laugh in those out-of-character clothes as she put on the show of having been born into them. However, I think that God fella had it in for me because he put a wedge in that relationship by allowing my dad to meet Hilda, who turned out to be the snake in the long grass of my life. Poor Nell – used and abused after being promised our world and working hard to prove her worth. It really broke her heart and I was so sorry for the loss of her.

This time the bonus of going to Ninny's while Dad took Diane and made plans for a future with Hilda was not the same because we all missed Nell – even Ninny, who had grown to love her as if she were an incarnation of my mum, Claire.

By 1953 my father married Hilda, who turned out to be a witch. I was left at my ninny's house until after the wedding. Dad took Diane with him, as he always did whenever I had to go to Ninny's. She was easy to handle, being only three, whereas I took a lot of looking after. By the time he came to collect me three months later, they had moved from Norris Green to Gillmoss (a new estate three miles further out from the city) because Hilda felt a new start in a new house was needed. Presumably, this was so that she could make a new person out of me, away from the familiar surrounds of my previous life, which she felt had been too lackadaisical, short on house rules and, most of all, discipline. She even tried to curtail my trips down to Ninny's, which I missed terribly and rebelled hard against, often resulting in my being allowed to go there again. Seeing that as a win for me, she tried a different tack: the introduction of ruthless and petty house rules. She tried hard, but she couldn't break the free spirit that my mother had left me with. In retrospect, it was as if Mum had foreseen the need to instil in me that spirit and set it in granite. And so, after eighteen months of fruitless effort, Hilda gave Father an ultimatum: I was to go, or she would. That ultimatum swung wide open the gates of his wrath: he began to come down on me harder than ever in a bid to pacify the Witch, but it served only to turn me against him little by little.

Having run away to Ninny's twice after experiencing periods of morale-breaking attacks designed to crush my spirit and transform me into an obedient lap dog, I ended up in care. Once Hilda realised that Father was on her side completely, he was fed lies about things that I had supposedly done. Only Hilda and I knew that I was innocent, so it was impossible to disprove her accusations, which often resulted in my arse being strapped. For example, she would say that I had refused to clean my shoes when I had not been asked, but such an excuse is futile to a tired man who has just finished a twelve-hour shift amid the noisy hubbub of a busy power station down on the docks and was scared of losing his new wife.

Eventually, at the age of ten, and after a most traumatic twelve hours in that house, I rebelled in such a way that I scalded her with hot tea and then hightailed it for seven miles in my pyjamas, my bare feet strapped to a pair of roller skates. I went all the way down to my ninny and those beloved Buildings. Father turned up some weeks later and took me to a courthouse, where he handed me over to the authorities after telling them lots of lies about me. They then placed me in a remand home called Woolton Vale, owing to a mix-up and the lack of places in any of the available orphanages. This was much to the dismay of Ninny, who set the wheels in motion to retrieve me.

Woolton Vale proved to be a pure hellhole and I got into a lot of trouble there, most of it down to the fact that my peers refused to believe that I had not stolen anything or broken the law in any way, but some of my troubles were due to the guards, who thought us all to be fair game for their abusive ways.. It certainly helped me to stand up for myself against some of life's tough nuts and nature's cretins. Within a four-week stay there I had fought with five tough lads, been badly knocked around by a 'master' (or guard), whose finger I bit after he had dunked me in a freezing-cold bath, and been thrown in a cupboard no bigger than the one beneath our stairs in Norris Green for twelve hours one night with the promise of a full week in there should I ever bite another member of staff.

The twelve hours in that cupboard felt like a week. It had a large metal door that slammed noisily and seemed to shake the bare floor I was lying on each time one of the masters closed it. I was more mad than sad during that time, but missed my family ever so much, especially my ninny and those Buildings. As for my sister, I knew she was OK and, being so young, she would have found it hard to understand my current predicament anyway, especially against the backdrop of Hilda's lies.

Ninny persuaded Aunty Ann to adopt me – her sister Claire's son – by using sisterly love and affections as a crowbar. Fundamentally, she blackmailed her daughter by reminding her of a fact they both knew to be true: 'If the boot were on the other foot, Claire would take you two under her wing.' And that is how I ended up as a full-time resident in those Buildings instead of merely being a very frequent visitor. Now I felt as if I had arrived and could be fully accepted by the lads who lived there instead of simply jogging on as an occasional friend.

However, being a regular visitor to the Billogs meant you were a nonresident and, as such, a lesser person. Even though the fact didn't really surface, it was always in the air and I felt I had to do something to become totally accepted – but what? I put myself forward as the skivvy, the daredevil, the mug to test if the water was too hot or cold, the one to shout, 'Dodge the army!' at the patrolling policemen and the one to take the crack across the ear for it because the others had run a bit earlier than I had, knowing full well the bluebottles would give chase.

'That's life,' my uncle John Boylan, and *de facto* new dad, would say whenever I came in with a thick ear. 'You'll learn!' He would then add, 'Why don't you just do what your mates do? If they stick their necks out, so do you. If you stop sticking your neck out and that results in them not wanting you as a mate, find some others who want a mate and not a gofer or a pet knobhead!'

Sounds about right, but I wanted those guys as friends. They were not the bad ones in the area, but neither were they the goody-goodies: they were the in-between ones, which made me feel at ease in their company.

So I took my new dad's advice and tried others as friends, but, in the company of the goodies, I felt somewhat restrained, and being with the ones who often got into trouble made me want to be somewhere else, due to the unease on seeing them turn into octopuses whenever we walked into shops.

Their place of learning was now mine too: St Johns RC School in North Dingle. Often there were fun things and pranks being played, but somehow I always seemed to be the one who got caught and caned because I stuck my neck out too far in an effort to impress. Bit by bit, I drew that neck in and got caned less, but then came a problem for us to share. For most of us in the Junior School, this was the year before the final twelve months; it was the time when the teachers began to sort out those pupils with any chance of passing the upcoming 11-Plus. A pass would send us to grammar school, while a fail meant we would be back at St Johns, only this time at the Senior School, which lay a mile away in prefabricated buildings known as 'the Huts' in Latham Street, just off Stanley Road. As my new friends and I spoke about the prospect of the 11-Plus we found common ground: none of us wished to go to grammar school. If we did, we would be forced to attend school until we were sixteen, and for us that was a giant no-no.

The playground of North Dingle Juniors was on the roof of that four-storey building and gave a view of all the rooftops, not that it fazed us in any way: living in tenements, we were all accustomed to heights. Even so, to me it was still a bit strange looking over row upon row of rooftops during playtime after the playing fields of St Swithin's in Gillmoss, where I used to go.

The teacher who ran St Johns football team, Mr Thomas, had a ton of hair protruding from his nostrils and a half-ton from each ear – he looked like a bear, and sounded like one suffering a painful ailment, too. Unlike my previous school, St Johns did not have its own playing fields and so, after alighting from the bus, which took us to the playing fields we used, I stood with most of the others in my class, shivering in my PE kit and wishing I was in the baths or somewhere more pleasant when the Bear walked over, a case ball tucked under his arm.

'You play football, son?' he wanted to know.

I was just about to deny any knowledge of the game when this previously lovely red-haired lad, John Sweeny, whom I had known for some time, chirped up, as he was the school scout: 'Yes, he can, sir. Remember when we played St Swithin's last season?'

Remember? How could I *forget* being in that St Swithin's side? St Johns had kept up a clean sheet until that game, almost a full season without being beaten, when the loose ball was caught up by the baying eighteen or so chasers and the kicking match started. The ball had been booted a number of times but kept rebounding back into the middle, and I'd been kicked hard a couple of times by gozzy-eyed miskickers. I was so livered, I took one almighty boot at the ball to get it away from me and sent it spinning off into the centre of the field, only for it to get picked up by our resident goal-hanger and slotted into the net.

We won 1–0. Everyone in our team was jubilant except for me: my legs were bruised, I was cold, wet and pissed off because I had not enjoyed playing at all. Football was just *not* my game!

Sweeny and I saw Mr Thomas's lip curl as he seemed to recall that unpleasant defeat by what he regarded as a rather inferior team; and then Sweeny pointed at me, saying, 'He was the lad who passed that ball upfield to be picked up and scored. He's why we lost!' I felt like kicking 'mouthy' in the balls as Mr Thomas nodded and said, 'I'll be keeping my eye on you during this session.'

Keep your bleeding eye on who you like, mister, I thought as I took up my position near the back of the pitch for ninety minutes of shivery hell. You'll get no fireworks out of me!

What a game! As we divided the group into two teams, it began to drizzle and that cold wind caused an icy, intermittent spray. I was in no mood for being there, let alone chasing after a stupid ball and getting kicked to shit merely trying to offload it somewhere else and not knowing where it was going anyway. Every time the ball came near me, I toe-punted it as hard as I could in the direction of the other end. Some silly bugger in the opposition must have had the same idea, because often the bloody ball came flying up into the air and headed my way, with that galumphing bunch of players chasing after it, like a pack of baying dogs after a fox. Not wanting to get caught up in a kicking, I would just hurry and kick the bloody thing back from where it had come from and then smile as the baying mob turned and went yelping the other way.

This went on for most of the game until, for once, everyone was spread out as if in their proper positions, waiting for their goalie to take a goal kick. By this time I think the marrow in my bones had just about frozen up: if one goal could have been the decider, I would have kicked the bloody thing into my own net. Their goalie took a whopping great walk back to the goal before turning and beginning his run to kick the ball upfield.

The knobhead! I thought, as the wind seemed to worsen and bit its teeth even deeper into me. The goalie seemed to be wasting time, for which I cursed him.

It was a great kick – up, up, up, it went, high into that grey-clouded sky that was tipping freezing rain down upon us. Then the ball began its descent, causing orderly members of both teams to once more turn into a baying mob and head for the ball, which was coming down to land, right by me.

No way! I thought, as it homed in on my patch with that pack of heavily shod feet running like the blazes to pounce on it. I met it with an almighty *thump*, thus rescuing myself from being in the middle of a free-for-all, and sent that leathery nuisance hurtling off on its way back.

Oh, it was a lovely feeling, watching that pack skid to a halt as they did an about-turn. But the smile soon slid off my face when I watched in horror as their goalie trotted back to his space, only to be turned goggle-eyed at the sight of that bleeding thing bouncing off the turf just in front of him and sliding along the muddy ground before going into the net.

Shit! I thought to myself. This is just not fair!

'Well done, Stockley!' Mr Thomas beamed at the end of the game. He then thrust an icy spear into my frozen soul with his next words: 'You're in my team.'

What with my mam dying, my father putting me in an orphanage and now this! I was beginning to feel that I had pissed in the font during my christening or been fathered by a heathen.

Of course I did my best to play badly at every game but always messed up by doing something right; and so, out of sheer desperation to get out of the team, I began to miss training and even twice failed to turn up for a match. The second time got me thrown out of the team but also landed me six of the best for – ha, wait for it – 'denying somebody else the chance of getting into the team'.

Six of the cane for that? I thought after apologising to my hands. Cheap at double the price!

Denying somebody else the chance of getting into the bloody team? I thought to myself afterwards. I'd have paid anyone to take my place.

And that was just after Christmas, 1954.

By the time Easter arrived, we'd done the walking on thin ice on the canal at the back of Tillotsons' cigarette-carton factory, made a few bob shifting snow from people's doorsteps and paths, peppered others with snowballs from the landings of our tenements, sold tons of chopped-up firewood, which we took, plank by plank, from the bombed-out buildings waiting to be demolished, and torn a fair bit of lino from behind the couch to fit into our shoes and cover the holes that had appeared due to our clambering and rummaging through the docklands and scouring the warehouses and derelict buildings. I'll bet that the shoe manufacturers never envisaged the kind of wear and tear we gave their footwear but, then again, neither did our parents, poor souls.

Occasionally we would go into town or to the pier head and be entertained by the street buskers who broke paving stones on one another's chest using a sledgehammer, or performed an escape routine using chains and a sack. Then there were the men who looked terribly deformed, as if they had two heads due to the enormous growths protruding from their necks. There were a few in the Kirkdale Homes – what had been a Victorian workhouse, now used to house ex-servicemen with various injuries, both mental and physical – but those fellas in the town seemed to be the worst-afflicted and yet they didn't hide away. Often, they could be spotted sitting on park benches as if displaying themselves for the public, something we cruelly took full advantage of whenever we passed by.

Now was the time for frogs and newts at Formby sandhills, a kind of Mecca for the kids of the Buildings to visit at that time of year. The journey consisted of a train ride from Bankhall and then a long walk from Formby station to the sandy foothills of the shore. I'd had the pleasure of this before with my cousin, our Logger. He had shown me how to remain still while standing on an old tree stump – or some other form of natural flotsam clogging the many ponds – until a newt came up for air, and how to swoop with my special net made from a bit of wire covered by an old nylon and somehow tied on to a piece of stick or cane. Catching newts was always fun and filled me with excitement – I just loved to watch them close up and would pretend they were dinosaurs.

As for the frogs, well, they were everywhere, and frogspawn was so abundant in those days that there always seemed to be much more of it than the water it was in. When the tadpoles hatched, those ponds resembled puddles of writhing tar. Goodness knows where the frogs got to because they could never be found once they'd produced and laid their eggs. Perhaps somewhere among those sandhills was the amphibian equivalent of a pub.

While running around on that hilly foreshore we always kept a wary eye open for Tasker, an old tramp who supposedly had a hut hidden among the dunes. One day, Mike Kinsella, one of the Scallywags, made the humongous mistake of saying, 'Tasker's my uncle!' So, when this was recounted to Logger, 'Tasker' was used as a nickname for Michael and remained with him for the rest of his youthful days, just as the one Logger christened me with did ('Nylon': derived from my name, 'Stockley', meaning stocking, meaning nylon).

Much as I enjoyed the company of Joe, Robby, Billy, Mick and Mike, as yet I had still had not been fully accepted to the extent of their calling for me whenever they went on their jaunts and my being part of whatever plans they had for that day. If I wanted to be a part of those plans I had to listen carefully for them calling one another from the square via a yodel or one of their names being shouted. Ha, the shout always began with, '*Now*!': 'Now, Joe Keaney!' or 'Now, Billy Vaughan!' – the 'Now' being a prefix to the name, even though it was mostly barely audible as a word, more like a grunted catcall: '*Neeow!*'

Anyway, my ears were attuned to this sound and my feet acted like springs, which propelled me to the root of that call whenever it sounded. Needless to say, I was not always greeted with a smile, but I was never rebuffed either, so I got to tag along and enjoy the day's adventures, wherever they led us.

At least when I went out with Robby, Joe and co. we would all return similarly blackened by the day's efforts of climbing and exploring, carrying and searching, and I was thankful because at least my new mum, Hilda, could not say, 'How come you're like a scrag end and they're all clean?' Not like when I palled up with a lad called Jimmy Mitchell.

Blond and blue-eyed Jimmy was slim-built with a softly spoken and very respectful manner when I first took him home. I swear Hilda made an on-the-spot wish for a swap. (If the truth be known, I think she made hundreds of such wishes from the day she adopted me until the day I left school and began work, but that first meeting with Jimmy lit a wish up in her eyes, like neon headlines.) Anyway, Jimmy and I got together as pals and I was eager to show him all that I had learned about my playground and the dockland, a place he himself had never trespassed on. I took him everywhere – through the dripping, soot-filled Seeky tunnel, around the huge coal yards, where the coal men loaded their coal into sacks from out of open-topped rail cars, over Joe Dodds's horsebox stables, fishing for jacksharps (little red-breasted tiddlers) on the canal, through acre upon acre of wood yard and down to the Tate & Lyle sugar factory in Love Lane, where we pinched a few handfuls of taygo (what we called raw brown sugar). Mine went straight into my pocket, but Jimmy scouted around and found an old copy of the *Liverpool Echo*, in which he wrapped his.

We hit the docks, where I showed Jimmy how to work a bogie and how to get a crane to move. I left no stone unturned in my efforts to make him understand that I was sharing my beloved world with him. No matter how many of my favourite haunts we visited, or how many walls we climbed over, Jimmy would always look pristine. It was as if he had just come out of his house – even his shoes were unscathed. It was my mum who made that connection, cracking me over the head one day to my surprise when we had just returned from our gallivanting.

'Ow! What's that for?'

'Look at Jimmy, look!' she told me.

And so I looked. To me it was just Jimmy, pristine Jimmy – so what?

'What about him?' I wanted to know.

Another crack came my way, followed by yet another.

'Ow! Ah, hey, Ma, what's up?' I said, seeing the exasperated annoyance on her now reddening face, but still wondering why.

'Look at him, yer daft prat! Look how clean he is. You look like you just fell down the bin chute from the top landing!'

'I work harder than he does,' I explained, meaning that I was more of a moocher and, if I didn't mooch around, he wouldn't get to see half the things we did.

One more crack she gave me before shaking her head.

'Fuck off!' she said, before taking another wild swipe at me and missing as I dodged, wise to it by now. 'Look, now you made me swear. God forgive me!'

She made the sign of the cross before heading indoors without further ado. I nodded to Jimmy to follow me away from the house – right now indoors would be dangerous for me. She had never taken off on me so badly after my days out with the other lads because we were all as dirty as each other.

Much as I liked Jimmy, he had to go. I'm convinced he went home sad that night but his mother must have lit a candle and thanked the Lord for having answered her prayers.

Back to my original plan . . .

Once more I was back to running when the 'Neeows!' sounded and permitted to jog on for whatever journey they had planned. Each time, as we all bade one another goodnight, I kind of begged myself to hear them asking me to join them for their adventures the following day. But there was an escapade and a strange episode off before this eventually happened.

The escapade was the latter part of a trip to Crosby. We were walking up from the park on the foreshore. I don't know what really went through my mind as we all stood at one of those pavement kiosks, spending a penny each on sweets. A box of Rollos stood alongside other boxes of sweets; right on the end, it was, just beckoning to be taken. So, while the man turned to get an Arrow bar from behind him for Robby, I duly obliged. I soon had it cradled in my coat like a stray puppy as I hightailed it to the station, some two hundred yards away, and waited. I'd become an octopus myself, but I was with the wrong group of guys for an ovation.

'You're fucking mad, you are!' pronounced Robby.

'Yeah, it's a sin, you know. You'll have to tell the priest,' Joe added.

'Yer daft cunt, yer coulda got us all inter trouble!' Billy (known as Rip Van) rapped.

'Yer mad, and, like Rip Van said, you could've got us all into trouble!' Mike added.

Of course this all made me feel a bit lousy, but they were right: I really could have got them all into trouble. It was a fact that I had not even thought of, but then a light shone out of my gloom as Mick smiled and put out his hand, saying, 'Give us some, then!'

By the time we got home, we had shared half the box and I tossed the remainder into the square from the top landing, much to the joy of the many kids who seemed to come out of the woodwork once the first tube of chocolate had been tossed down to young Tommy Jones, whom I liked owing to his tenacious attitude, despite the leg irons he had to wear due to his polio.

Later that night, the lads bade each other goodnight as the first of the drinkers began to emerge from the entry that led from Orwell Road through to Owens Road. It was always the cue for running home before our fathers (who had been drinking in the Orwell pub) came through into our road. Mick Furlong ('Fishcake') had been explaining something to me as the others began to leave, then he too walked off but he called back, 'See you tomorrow, Peter.'

Those words made me feel like a million dollars.

Although my name was not called the following night, I wasn't met like an intruder as I hurried over towards the lads after that first 'Neeow'. The couple of half-nods thrown my way were a little more welcoming. However, it was when Johnny Butler, the cripple with the hand-pedalled trike, persuaded us to go a-wandering in the ghostly Kirkdale Homes that I was truly accepted by the gang. Johnny B had twisted legs, as if someone had tried to knot them when he was a baby; he was a sort of teacher to us all inasmuch as he knew lots and lots about all things, especially sex, and answered any of our enquiries on the subject openly and without a flinch. He could con us out of money for a loosey (a single cigarette) merely by getting us involved in one of his yarns, then stopping at an exciting part while he pretended to look for ciggies, saying he was gasping for a fag. If none were forthcoming from his audience then he would beg a penny ha'penny off someone in order to buy a loosey from the Sassbar.

At the top of Owens Road, just before the entrance to Fonthill block, the Sassbar was a kind of meeting place for us all. It had a jukebox and sold sweets and soft drinks. Crippled Johnny used it like a fruitful welfare office, owing to our regular presence there.

'Yeah,' he said, as he blew out a blast of smoke from the ciggy that Robby had given him three ha'pence to buy. 'The old air-raid shelter by the cabbage patch in the Kirkies is where Split-Kipper hides his money. Half a crown [12.5p] every week he puts down there, and in a different place every week.'

We'd all seen Split-Kipper. He was really weird: big, big as Joe's dad, Jack (and he was six-foot-odd). We often saw him sitting in the 'rec' (recreation park, with bowls, swings and a roundabout), watching the bowls being played out. He walked by throwing one foot forward, then dragging the other one after it. Then came a slight pause while he got his first foot solid before moving the next one; the one foot did nearly all of the work.

'Got blown up in the war,' Johnny once told us. 'An', just like me, he's bloody lucky to be alive!'

His face looked as if a tram wheel had gone right down the middle and left a wide ridge between his right and left sides; both his lips looked cleft. With a huge, dark, staring eye either side of that wide scar, Split-Kipper would give you the willies simply by being in the vicinity.

'How do you know?' Fishcake butted in. 'I mean, you couldn't get down them steps that you have to go down for the air-raid shelter.'

'Yeah,' said Joe, now that Mick had pulled a Sherlock on that point. 'How do you know?'

'Yer fuckin' disbelievers!' Johnny B countered gruffly. 'He's me fuckin' mate, innee? Confides, confides he does. I'm his mucker, got blown up in the same war an' all that, you know what I mean?'

'What yer grassin' on yer mucker for, then, Johnny?' Billy asked in a somewhat accusing way.

'Not grassin' on me mate, I'm grassin' on the money. Shouldn't be there, it's doin' no one any good, is it?'

'He might need it one day,' said Joe, thinking of his own little hoard of sixpences hidden underneath the wardrobe in his bedroom and shuddering at the thought of that going missing.

'What's he need it for, eh? We all live in the Kirkies, it's our home. We get our clothes when we need them and three solids a day. He only smokes five a week an' he's got no one to give it to. All he's doin' is givin' those spider-ridden bricks a bloody silver necklace with all them half-crowns.'

'So,' said Mike, 'get to the point. What do you want us to do?'

'Don't have to take them all, just a few. And one for me, for ciggies.'

And that was how we came to go into the grounds of that old

Victorian workhouse, the Kirkdale Homes. Unlike in the ghostly stories of the movies, there were no claps of thunder, no fog or rain. It was a lovely moonlit night but we were all apprehensive due to the inmates that lived there – the forgotten, shell-shocked old soldiers, the homeless, hapless and now mentally deficient men who had once been fighters for the British Army but were mentally burned out due to that service, leaving only the wreckage of the men they had once been. Some slobbered as they spoke; others jerked their heads or wriggled uncontrollably as they sat or stood around; some had only one leg or one arm; and a few merely sat and stared as if in a film that didn't move. They looked truly pathetic, forgotten people but scary as anything, with their big leather belts pulled tight and their hobnailed boots scuffing the floor as they tramped or dragged themselves around the grounds during the day – which was mainly what kept us out of there. However, because a fair few of our mothers worked there, we knew the rules: 8 p.m. was suppertime, and then it was lockup for the night. It was a firm rule of that place, since even the grownups would feel apprehensive when bumping into one of the more disturbed men in the shadows of nightfall and street lamps.

We were soon by the cabbage patch, where the old Kirky-Homers, as we called them, dug and planted their homegrowns, and the outline of the shelter looked ominous, as if it were half-sunk into the soil. We had shelters under Fonthill block that had been almost like a home from home during the war years for our families but were now unused rubbish dumps that smelled like filthy toilets. I'd been to this one in the Kirkies with our Logger – it wasn't as smelly as those under Fonthill block but it was dank due to the years of seeping water from the nearby hose used for watering the veggie patches.

It was ten steps down, then you turned right and went down

another five steps into the first chamber, which was very dark, but a light from one vent slightly lit the passage leading from it to the next room. That first chamber was about fifteen by fifteen feet and led into another of about the same size via a three-foot-wide, six-foot-long passage with a small room in the middle (Logger said it was used as a bathroom, with buckets for toilets).

After a hubbub of 'Who's going first?' I led in an effort to once again ingratiate myself, but I don't think anyone took it as being toady because I had used the fact that I had been there previously with Logger. We lit a couple of folded papers to proceed. I nearly fell down the second lot of stairs due to the sudden blackness because I hadn't screwed my paper up tight enough, causing it to burn out too quickly. Someone lit more papers, creating shadowy flickers, which added to the eeriness, but the burning smell helped kill the dank aroma that prevailed.

And so the search began for those trinkets of silver that Johnny B had forecast would be there. But where had Split-Kipper put them? As hands began to scrape along the various ledges, Robby let out an almighty scream: he had moved his burning torch too close to an immense spider's web, where a glimmer of what he thought was a piece of silver exploded into life by expanding to three times its normal size, legs sprouting from everywhere. It jumped just as he went to grab it and then disappeared into the darkness, which now engulfed Robby as he dropped his paper. There followed some really choice explosions of F words as adrenalin surged through everyone's veins before the search resumed.

Nothing was found in the first room, so we edged our way along the narrow corridor until we came to the little bucket room – minus the bucket. Mick Furlong went in there with a fresh piece of paper while we carried on into the next room, but we had to shoulder the door to gain entrance due to the damp expanding the wooden casing and the door itself. There were more beams of light shining through some busted air bricks at the top, giving the atmosphere of the room a kind of night-sky look – the light beams came from the floodlighting on the walls of the Homes. At least we could now save what little paper we had left and begin our search for those elusive half-crown pieces. Fishcake (Mick) came in and said: 'Psst, come and see this!' So we followed him back into the bucket room.

As we crowded into that small room, Mick stood to the side of a thin, old, wooden cabinet on the wall. It reminded me of a bathroom mirror box that my father would use for shaving or my mother might keep talc, pills or plasters in. He opened the box to reveal that it was being kept up by two six-inch nails protruding from the wall, and between the sides of the frame an old landscape photo was stuck to the brick, showing four military men sitting on or leaning against a field gun. Underneath that there were four half-crowns stuck to the bare brick as if they were wheels for that photo. The bottom of the box formed a shelf and at each end of that stood a used night-light, which appeared to make up a shrine. We were held rapt – until the sound of someone coming pricked our ears. Who could it be? Whoever it was didn't care about being quiet. Then, as it became obvious that someone was struggling to get down the stairs, we all realised that it had to be Split-Kipper.

I suggested we go into the moonlit room where the door had been closed and we could all lean against it to prevent him from getting at us. It was basically the only way we could go, so we did.

'What if he's got a knife?' Billy Vaughan asked.

'He might even have an axe,' Joe whispered, as we all leaned heavily against the now-closed door, forcing it to wedge back into place.

'I've just shit!' said Robby.

I think Mick Furlong wanted to say the same but decided to let Robby take the blame for it. After an unbearably long time, there shone a light beneath our door and through the various small holes in the wood of the barricade. We could hear Split-Kipper as he dragged that almost dead leg of his into a holdup position before moving his other leg forward again. For the first time since I had known these lads there was complete silence as all ears strained for any noise that would give a hint of what was happening. Then our door suddenly lost its silhouette.

'He's gone into the little room!' Billy pointed out as he glanced through one of the holes in the door.

'Shall we all make a run for it?' Mick Kinsella suggested.

'Yeah, let's – by the time he turns, we can all be well gone. Open the door, Nylon!' Joe ordered me, so the obedient me tried, then realised it wouldn't open.

My hoarse cry of 'Can't!' almost reduced the gang to tears, now that we realised we were well and truly trapped, because there wasn't a handle on this side of the door, and nor were there any grips with which we could pull the thing open. Just then the silhouette at our door reappeared: Split-Kipper had emerged from his little room and was holding up a lantern as if to try to see beyond it.

'I think he's gonna come this way,' Billy whispered as he peeped through a small crack.

'Oh, shit!' squealed Robby, as he let another one go.

'Your undies must be chocker by now, Robby,' said Joe.

'He's comin',' Billy observed and then moved back from the spyhole, pushing us all back as he did so.

Suddenly, it happened in the order that we had retreated, with Little Billy in the front, his arms out, as if protecting us from what was to come. The door shot open to reveal the sight of a gruesome-looking Split-Kipper. At this point, I think we all near soiled ourselves as the light shone onto Kipper's face, shrouding it in shadow and seeming to blow up his ruined lips to twice their size. It was a frozen moment, with six wide-eyed and horrified kids backed up against a wall and an old veteran holding up a lantern, grimly gazing down on them. Our faces absolutely mirrored the fear that broiled within our hearts, but, as we were to discover, his gruesome visage offered the exact opposite of what was in his.

'You kids all right?' he gently asked.

It turned out that Kevin (Split-Kipper) and his friends had been known as the 'One Pounders' in their unit during the 1914–18 conflict but he had been the only one to survive a direct hit on their position – 'If surviving is what you call this!' He had no family that he knew of and consoled himself with the only thing he loved: that photograph, which he spent at least an hour a day looking at as the candles flickered. 'Sort of makes them come alive, does those flame flickers'.

As good-looking and normal as any man, we all thought on seeing his rather foggy form sitting on the edge of a large wheel as he pointed out the man he once was in the photo. As for the half-crowns, there were only eight of them and they made up a pound to represent those 'One Pounders' and added a medal-type decoration to his shrine.

The next day I jogged on as usual but made a suggestion to the lads. Later, we went to the rec facing the Kirkies and played on the swings until Split-Kipper came hobbling by to sit and watch the bowls club play their game as he often did. We left the swings and went over to sit on the bench next to him. Robby pulled out a five-pack of Woodbines and gave them to him.

'Here, Kev, we got them for you!' He went silent for a while, then looked at us with glazed eyes and smiled. He never spoke but we all knew that he couldn't for fear of bursting into tears.

And guess what. The following evening I heard this: 'Neeow, Peter!'

It was the best of best sounds, ever. I got a kick out of that call, just as I got a kick out of being one of those Scallywags during my youthful days.

CHAPTER 2

OUR MOULDING

Now I felt that I truly belonged. I'd arrived, so to speak, and yet I had never really been away. Our Logger had always been there for me; the lads were still my friends, just as they had always been, only now I felt we had truly bonded.

What can I say about my neighbourhood that will help you to understand some of the trials and tribulations of our upbringing? The Buildings, big as they were, sheltered us with a comfort that our parents really appreciated, but that we certainly didn't at the time: electricity at the flick of a switch, a bath and inside toilet, together with constant hot water so long as the fire was lit and no freezing of pipes when the temperature dropped.

For us this was the norm but our parents knew only too well the difference between this and gas mantles, bathing in a tin bathtub and frozen winter pipes, coupled with that walk down the yard to the freezing throne of the outside loo, where winter made it a tossup as to whether you wiped or chipped. Logger was forced to continue that way of life because his house was No. 44 Owens Road, a two-up, two-down mid-terrace with a backyard and a leg-swinging outside loo. Their gas-mantle lighting system was still catered for by the local shops – I know because I often ran over to Joe Hills's shop for mantles at the request of my lovely Aunty May, Logger's mother. She would say, 'Here's the little man who's always having a busy day. Here, lad, go to Joe Hills's for me, will yer?'

Aunty May's home in that group of eight terraced houses stood as a constant reminder of how it used to be for everyone, and especially for us kids, to know the difference between a hard and easier way of living., just as our grandparents knew the difference between all that and galloping inflation: their tuppence a pint was now elevenpence and their tuppence for ten ciggies was now a shilling (5p). We had progressed – if that's what you want to call it – but what progress had to do with those prices going up was beyond our comprehension. Because more means more, if the prices go up then surely incomes must also go up in order to live. To us kids it just did not make sense to raise prices and then wages so that you could raise prices again and again and again. Mum might earn a million a week only to pay a million-plus out in expenses. It all seems so stupid. Where's the 'plus' going to come from once the million wages have gone merely for survival? However, what was not beyond our comprehension was the offerings of this world that we had been brought into, sometimes fraught with danger but nevertheless inviting us with the thrill of temptation. Johnny Butler, our resident funny (if creepy) old guy, with the hand-propelled trike, often said, 'Kid, this world has a lot to offer but *nothing* to give.'

Take 'the Brew', for instance – that cobbled slope which brought you down onto the level of the Buildings from Fonthill Road via its one-in-three gradient. A very sharp left at the bottom, more like a hairpin turn, led to Fonthill and Owen blocks' square. Bearing left ahead took you into the Owen and Stanley blocks' square (we called them 'squares' but in actual fact they were more oval- or pear-shaped).

Then there was 'dead ahead' at the bottom of that Brew. It led smack bang into the green doors of the boiler room. Those huge, sliding green doors at the bottom of the Brew took you into the coal storage and boiler room of that very long wash- and bathhouse.

At the other end of that conglomeration stood the square between Stanley and Melrose blocks. Each square was the domain of the surrounding inhabitants and was fiercely protected, especially around Bonfire Night or during street parties, when, instead of being friendly neighbours, people became adversaries due to healthy competition. However, the Brew belonged to no one in particular. It was the only incline within the vicinity that would allow good propulsion for the steering carts, which kids knocked together now and then by stealing a pram from the washhouse and stripping it of its wheels and axels. With a good push from the top, a decent rolling 'steery' would travel as far as the washhouse windows in the centre of Owen and Stanley square, or at least reach the side stairwell, which fed all of the landings, including Joe Keaney, who lived at 6c.

No one ever really turned sharp left in Fonthill/Stanley square for fear of tipping their cart over. Even the delivery vehicles came in from Melrose Road and followed the service road through due to the tightness of that turn.

One day Mike Kinsella received a good heave-ho from Robby Tully and went tearing down the Brew on their steery. The big green doors were open because a wagonload of coal had just been delivered; it all got tipped in a pile in the middle of the hall-type room, just in front of the big boiler, waiting for the stokers to shovel it over into its side storage place.

Most people do not really understand the level of skill needed to control a speeding cart with only two bits of string attached to the front crossbeams for pulling on in order to steer, especially if those beams are a bit short of foot space. Some kids just made it look easy because they had done it a lot of times or they were naturals; it had been from such kids that Mike Kinsella had taken his methodology. All of a sudden, what he had witnessed was nothing like the true happening of such a ride: the cobbles whizzed by at such a rate that it unnerved poor Mike and set the panic tap running at flood level, especially when he tried to put his foot on the crossbeam only to have it pushed violently upwards by the spinning wheel, almost throwing him off. Luckily, the cart kept a true, straight course and took him flying into that freshly delivered mound of coal.

Dishevelled and blackened, he emerged with the steery, which had been a little damaged by the collision (it needed urgent attention to the front wheel). To Robby's 'Shall we get another pair of wheels and fix it?' Mike replied, 'No, it's not fair on the women whose pram gets took. I'll ask me Ma to buy me some for Christmas. Let's go and call for the others and we'll go for a swim in the canal or summat instead.'

'What about the cart?' Robby persisted, thinking eight months was a long way off to wait for new wheels.

'Someone'll find a use for it,' Mike called back, so Robby let the string go and hurried after him.

'Ha, yer arse go, did it?' Joe asked, after we had joined up and Mike revealed the truth about it all.

'Not 'arf! Don't know what I would have done if that big door had a been closed.'

'You'd have ended up with a big green flat nose instead of that dirty black face!' Rip Van (Billy) told him, causing everyone to laugh.

'At least my legs would still be straight!' Mike retorted.

'Oh, startin' early, are yer? Yer Tasker bastard!'

The skitting (in common parlance, taking the piss) had stopped by the time we had finished a drink and listened to some records in the Sassbar, but more laughs were brought about at my expense due to a certain rag-and-bone man, who had made it as far as the Brew a few years earlier.

'Remember the time your ma battered that ragman on the Brew after tipping his cart up and she gave away all of his balloons?' Joe reminded me.

'Oh, yeah, I remember that as well. Didn't Tommy Conner's ma run down from the second landing to throw a few digs as well?' Robby Tully said, as his version of that event surfaced. 'I got a balloon out of that as well. God, we were only six, or was it seven?'

I was four or five at the time Robby was five or six. For me it had been an unforgettable experience, being exposed to a lot of emotions all within the space of about ten minutes. First, being asked by Mum to stand by her washing while she ran around to Joe Hills's shop on Owens Road for some washing powder. Then to hear the ragman make me an offer I couldn't refuse: 'I'll give you *three* balloons if you let me take that bag.'

Done!

'Where's the washing, lad?' asked Ma when she came back. She had a puzzled expression on her face. Perhaps she was thinking one of her mates had seen me and had taken it in for her. When I told her, she flew into a rage: '*Who? What* man with the cart? Which way did he go?' And off she tore after him, rubber apron flying and wellies clomping the floor. Thank goodness for the Brew: the man was struggling to push his cart up it when Ma caught up with him. She tossed up the cart and was beating the stuffing out of him when I finally caught up with them both.

As other women took over the punishment side of things, my mother took his box of prizes and doled them out to the big crowd of kids who had been attracted to the commotion. It made me feel really proud: after all, it was my mum who was giving out all those balloons and making the kids happy.

I took a bit of ribbing as the lads laughed over that one.

The Brew and Mike's steering cart came back to haunt us later after we had been down to the wood yards, playing on top of and among those huge piles of imported timber. We had the medals of a few bruises and splinters from climbing onto and occasionally falling off those enormous mountains of timber. But we were hardly ever chased because it seemed the thinking of those wood-yard men was: They can't rob nothing and, if they fall and hurt themselves, it's their own fault. They know they shouldn't be there. It was so very true of those days. In fact the only time the men actually gave us any gyp was if we made a noise during their lunch hour when they were trying to snatch forty winks.

It was really weird on the docklands during the lunch hour when everything fell silent. It was as if a magic switch had been pressed, causing the thousands of cranes, bogies and wagons to become frozen. During working hours you had to shout in those big, busy sheds to make yourself heard, whereas in the lunch hour a whisper would cut through the quiet like an empty tin can being kicked in the dead of night. Often we sneaked into those docks to play on the bogies and cranes, which were abandoned during the lunch hour.

Or we would climb up onto the high stacks of cargo and try to reach the pigeons' nests high up in the rafters.

The one o'clock gun of Birkenhead shot life back into the dockland, injecting movement and sound as thoughts turned to the ticking clock. Time was of the essence because tonnage had to be swapped to make space so that more tonnage could take its place. One shed would be filled with cargo from the belly of a ship amid the scurrying cranes and toiling men, while another shed, one berth away, would be visited by many wagons hurrying to offload their goods from the industrial areas so that they could reload with recently discharged raw cargo. As in beehives, those docks, warehouses and wood yards swarmed with workers toing and froing from one sling to another, fetching and sending, storing and loading, with not a thought as to where it would all end up, nor a care. For those dockers the only aim was to have a full wage packet at the end of the week. They must have worked hard, because Liverpool frequently topped the charts for tonnage in those days.

Five o'clock began the trudge away from the turmoil. Hail, rain or shine would bless or damn the dockers, for there were no buses servicing the dock road. If you were in a hurry, you had to give it legs, and, when those hobnailed feet began to scuff the footpath, we knew it was time to go home. We could, if we wished, stay out a bit longer and stand on the corner of any street, tapping the passing men for a sandwich left over from their carry-out (packed lunch). Monday was good for that, because the sandwich filling was nearly always beef, lamb or chicken. Tuesday was varied: it could be any of Monday's, or corned beef or Spam. Wednesday gave you Spam or corned beef, sometimes garnished with a bit of lettuce and tomato. Thursday, the day before payday, was known as Bally Ann Day (more precisely, Bugger All Day), so often you got something called 'sandwich spread', which didn't look as good as it tasted. And Friday was the day you didn't ever ask – bloody cheese, yuck! Nearly every docker had leftovers on a Friday, which they tended to throw to the pigeons or deep-throated gulls.

We had no idea what had transpired on the Brew during our trip to the wood yards as we called into Arthur's fruit shop for some 'bunking wire' before nipping home for our tea. The idea was to bunk into the pictures that night, but we needed the wire in order to manipulate the door – it was like having our own key.

'Thought it was one of youse,' Arthur said as he dragged the binding wire off one of the orange boxes and handed it to Mike. ''Cos I saw you going up to the Brew with your steery this morning.'

'Yeah, we saw you. What's happened, then?' said Mike.

Starting with 'Don't know for sure,' Arthur went on to explain that two lads with a crippled steering cart were messing about on the Brew when a wagon that had been delivering furniture to one of the houses headed up towards Fonthill Road, causing the kids to back into Fonthill Road to let the vehicle out. 'Anyway, when the wagon drove off, the lad pushing took one big run at the Brew and let it go. The front wheel fell off, there was a big tumble and the one on the steery went flying into one of those iron railings, head first.'

'Is he all right?' Joe asked.

'Who was it?' Robby wanted to know.

Arthur shrugged. 'Cracked skull as far as I know, but whoever it was has lost a finger as well – apparently got caught in the spokes or dragged by the steering rope as he tried to stop himself. I heard that the kid who was pushing was Paddy Dicko.'

'I saw Paddy Dicko with Tony Ward this morning,' Mick Furlong told us.

'They don't really knock around together,' said Joe, adding, 'Wonder if it was Tony who got hurt.'

'Don't know the kid's name but it was the younger one who got hurt,' said Arthur.

'Jesus, that's one unlucky bloody cart, that is!' Robby murmured and shuddered at the thought of fingers being ripped off.

As was usual we stood in Owens Road and chatted before going home for our evening meals. Of course the main topic was that terrible accident and who'd been hurt. Confirmation about the injured person came from our Logger – he'd seen the aftermath.

'It was terrible; the blood was everywhere. He only lost one finger, though – had the steering rope wrapped around his hand, so, when it went outta control, it sorta cut into his finger and wrenched it off. Tony Ward's grandmother was trying to hit Paddy.'

He laughed. 'Poor Paddy didn't know what to do. He kept on backing away from Tony's Nan, saying, "I only pushed him 'cos he asked me to." They all calmed down once the ambulance came.'

Mike Kinsella vowed not to venture onto the Brew with a steering cart again.

'Why, Mike?' Robby asked. 'It doesn't mean it'll happen to you.'

'It bloody nearly did this morning!' Mike returned quickly, only to get some stick from us all for being a shitty arse when it came to danger.

'Say what youse want,' he contested, 'but a wise man knows when to call it a day. What happened to me this morning was a little sign from Him up there.'

'Well, that "little sign" from Him stopped me from having a go on the steery,' protested Robby.

'Well, pretend it didn't, and you did, then go up to the 'ozzy [hospital] to swap your hand for Tony Ward's. An' swap your head as well 'cos he's got a cracked skull, yer cracked git!' Mike replied, doubtless thinking him dumb for not seeing the point.

Just then a stray ball came bouncing over towards us and Billy gave it a hefty kick back to the younger kids, but it was too heavy and instead went flying onto the roof of the haulage firm facing. The look of disappointment on the kids' faces caused us all to rib Billy to get it back for them.

'Piss off, I'm not getting up there for that!' he retorted

'Ha, who's got a shitty arse now, then?' Robby rebuked.

That started off another round of verbals, and so, as they slagged one another off, I nipped over and shimmied up the drainpipe to retrieve the ball. I threw it down to the kids, who shouted up their thanks and then ran off before Billy could kick it again.

A fierce cry caused me to turn as I slid down that pipe.

'What you doin' up there, Stockley, yer little cunt?'

A couple of the much older lads had just come from the Owen/ Stanley square. They were a year or so older than our Logger. Onk, Titch and Snake Eyes were the 'wide boys' due to go into the army – they couldn't see the sense in getting a job if they could live on their wits. Snake Eyes was an older brother of one of my friends, Bow Orourke, he had a nasty way about him rather like a growling dog that looked like it would bite you. The other older lads had a more respectful way about them.

'Just been getting a ball for the kids.'

'Yeah? Well, stay off that roof!' Snake Eyes ordered. 'I mean it!'

They were bothered about such an activity causing alarm within the company and having them put up security measures to prevent people getting on the roof and – eventually – getting into the storage yard. Their arrival meant our departure, because they didn't like us hanging around and knowing what they were up to, although we knew full well that they had only come round to watch the wagons coming in to see what they were loaded with before being garaged up for the night.

There were two haulage firms on Owens Road: J. A. Irvine and G. Lewis. Irvine's carried canned goods and general cargo, but Lewis's wagons seemed to concentrate on copper ingots and other heavy metals. We had often watched from the landings as the lads scaled the walls of the entry between the two garages by pressing their hands and feet against the walls and applying pressure, which kept them suspended. But we were a bit too short for that manoeuvre and could get up just as quickly by using the drainpipe. The downside of that route was that you were in full view of everyone on the street. Not that we wanted to get up onto either of those roofs because we would get a clip off the older lads, who acted as if they owned the place.

Their little fiddle was to chip away at the sides of those copper ingots – the bits that looked like drips left over from the smelting. Most of the smaller bits had been knocked off due to general handling, but the larger dribbles had to be chipped away with a hammer. They could knock a fair few chunks off in an hour and it made very little noise due to the density of those smelts. Consequently, the half-hundredweight that they did manage to nip off was not missed because they counted only the ingots when checking so their figures would tally.

Our Logger had filled us in with the blank spaces of that fiddle, so we knew all about it, except for how much they made. It was just one of those things that the older lads felt entitled to and we younger ones could look forward to doing ourselves someday.

Our ways of making money were varied and all of them had been hand-me-down tips. Collecting and cutting up planks of wood from the bombed-out and derelict buildings was a good one, but hard work. Another was gathering coal by first walking along the railway for a mile or so with an empty sack and judging when to return by how many pieces you had passed, then walking back and picking up the droppings that had fallen from the footplates while being shovelled into the roaring fires. If you wanted to work harder, you could go down to the marketplace and do some fetching and carrying for the street traders, who would be loading up their barrows and would let you push them until they got to their particular patch or had worked their round, but that paid little and really pulled the sweat out of you. Going on 'messages' (errands) or minding the prams in the washhouse brought in a little extra cash, too.

The favourite for us – and our parents – was the pea or bean picking in the summer. This was followed in the autumn by potato picking. It meant we were off the streets and away from danger or temptation – and earning half-decent money. You could pick up seven shillings and sixpence (37.5p) a day for pea picking and anything up to ten shillings (50p) a day for the beans. The best, however, was the spud picking: that paid fifteen (75p) if you picked a full-length (a length was usually a good fifteen strides long) and half that amount if you shared a length, which the farmer sometimes let us kids do if they were short on adult pickers.

Occasionally, something new would hit the scene, such as soap coupons. These turned out to be a big wallet booster in those days. They were stuffed through the letterbox and shoved under the door of every house in the city, all with offers of threepence (1.25p) or sixpence (2.5p) off for purchases of whatever brand was being advertised. At first we were not bothered, for it was a new thing, but our Logger had heard a rumour, so he took a coupon from his house to Frank's grocery store on the corner of Fonthill and Orwell. It was a sixpenny coupon for Persil washing powder.

'How do these work, Frank?' he asked.

'How many have you got?' Frank wanted to know.

'Just the one,' Logger replied.

'Well, if you get me ten, I'll give you half a crown [12.5p]'

That was it – free money! Those delivery ladies were followed everywhere. They walked up and down almost every street, marking the pavements with chalk as they went so as not to do the same street twice and to prove to their bosses that they had been there. We followed in their wake with a thin stick that could be pushed under the door and used to flip out the posted coupon. Sometimes we would sag school (play truant) to follow those women. After all, it was a chance to get good money for those coupons and no one seemed to give a damn.

Collecting jam jars was another trickle to the wallet. Everyone had them because jam butties were the most common form of snack and breakfast meal. We used to take them to the rag shop, where the man would give us a ha'penny each – a good day's collecting could fetch you a pound or more and that was decent dough, but you had to walk a fair distance and knock on many doors. The school used to ask us to bring them in, especially during 'Good Shepherd' week when extra effort was made to help the church-run charity, but in the end the sight of all of those ha'pennies going into the coffers of an already-rich church meant our empty pockets took precedence as we collected for the 'Good Shepherd' but ultimately decided that we were the best shepherds around.

Bunking into the pictures was a money saver but also an adventure. It was an art Logger had learned from his elders, then passed on to us. A noose of thin wire taken from an orange or apple box was key to the whole manoeuvre. First, the noose would be bent over your knee and rubbed from side to side, as if you were drying your leg after a shower. This would cause the wire to take the shape of a banana, which was then inserted into the crack between the fire doors of the picture house. Once in, the wire would be hovering beyond and above the centre push-bar and then, with a little manipulation and gentle pulling, the wire would catch on to the push-bar and 'click' it open, presenting us with free access for that show.

Once in, we would have to dodge around some so that any snitches already in there would be confused as to our exact whereabouts. Sometimes we would get caught and that meant a boot up the backside or a thick ear, along with an unceremonious ejection via the front door, where, much to the enjoyment of anybody queuing to get in, you would land on the pavement like a limp rag doll. A bit peeved and sorely remorseful, we would hobble home while the others were enjoying their ill-gotten gains and no doubt sniggering away at our capture and expulsion. I reckon we got away with at least 50 per cent of our attempts to bunk into the picture houses, which, at two or three tries a week for at least five years, wasn't too bad an average.

And finally came that all-important evolving period in everyone's life: sex. At eleven to twelve years of age we had all begun to boast about the odd hair that appeared around our nether regions. We had also noticed that some of our female friends were sprouting bosoms and often we lied about touching one or two of those, which sometimes meant we had to hide from the furious girl in question. Our Logger was something of a know-it-all but sometimes skitted us for wanting to find things out. However, the one to whom we could pose any question was Johnny Butler. Much of a talker as he was, Johnny never gave anything away: we had to pay him. And so it was always with a loosey in our pocket (pilfered from Mum's or Dad's packet) that we would walk up Owens Road to the Sassbar and get talking to the old crippled guy in his hand-propelled trike-chair. He smelled a little, but being out in the fresh air kept our nostrils from being fully assaulted. And he had some intriguing stories to tell, which we would try to get him to spill before taking the conversation into the arena of our true request.

I loved listening to tales of his time in the army, especially the one about his near demise. He hadn't always been a cripple, he would tell you, before laying out the time when they were in France: 'A batman I was, and a bloody good one. Ha, it kept you away from the bullets and let you get decent grub, and all you had to do was be a creep for the officers. I was the best creep that you ever clapped eyes on; I used to crease their uniforms so good they could almost cut their fingers just by running them along the creases down their legs and they could shave just by looking into their footwear. Being in charge of their billet meant that I had a soft mattress as well. Ha, sometimes I had the thickest and softest 'cos I picked them! A creep I may have been, but I was no mug.'

I liked Johnny; almost everything he said appealed to me because he was a give-and-take man. We gave and he took, but he enlightened us as to the ways of the world in a way that our parents couldn't or wouldn't, or never had the time for. Johnny always had time for us because he saw us as a means to an end. The story he told about his body being smashed up and how he got saved has always stayed with me, and made me realise my father's view of life – that destiny rules us – was correct.

Johnny's story took us through more of his service as the batman of that billet, of how he nicked the odd bit of tobacco and few cigarettes, of how he was given the odd bar of chocolate, and the occasional tot of fine brandy or whisky he got to savour while his peers were soaking or freezing in those trenches.

'Ha, even them officers had to go into those trenches, but I didn't!' he would proudly boast. Then his face would change to a scowl. 'Bloody trenches, I had to work treble hard to get them uniforms spit-off, I'll tell yer! The best time was when we took over a farmhouse – bloody hell, it was great! What with them bringing in pictures, lamps and mirrors, I had it like Buckingham Palace in no time. That's when it happened . . .'

He often paused at this point but acted as though he were collecting his thoughts. I always knew what was coming and guessed that his having to relive it caused the stall.

'There I was, making this uniform pristine again, fit for a parade in front of the King, it was – the boots all shiny, the fire lit and warming, pictures on the wall and . . .' He would smile through the pain of recounting this, his brown and crooked teeth glaring. 'I'd just nicked a double tot of brandy, I think that's what caused me to do it . . .' Often he would stop and gaze down at the floor, then up again and he would smile. 'Wanted to see what I would look like dressed up as an officer. Always fancied myself as an officer, but I couldn't talk like one so I kept my mouth shut as I looked into that big mirror: head up and shoulders back, could've been made for me, that uniform could. I remember wishing my mum could be seein' me like that, she would've been so proud . . .'

At this point there would always be the hint of a tear in his eye. 'Then it happened – the bloody world fell in. The next thing I heard, and it was like I was dreaming, was, "Can't just leave him, he's an officer. Get him to the hospital – quick!" Then everything went black, and this is the way I woke up, all bent and twisted.'

I, for one, never tired of hearing that story. Then again I never tired of hearing anything from Johnny Butler – he always entertained and never pulled any punches. If he had to answer our questions we got it as it would happen, regardless of everything usually taboo between adults and kids. It was normally after a story that we would give him the ciggy and then pose our question, which was mainly about the intertwining of bodies.

'Knew you wanted to talk dirty,' he would say, then he would light his gift and ask, 'What do you want to know about? Tits, fannies, dicks or arseholes, yer can suck three and block the other! What's it to be?' So we would tell him of our curiosity and he would explain the pros and cons as he knew them to be. We would think we were learning, but it was like Mike Kinsella and his steering cart: the *doing* is the learning, not the seeing or being told.

On the factual side of that subject we relied on a couple of the more liberal girls in our neighbourhood, Betty and Ethel. Mike Kinsella and Billy Vaughan were the leaders in our group in that direction. One day, while we were chopping firewood and hawking it via bundles in our arms from door to door, Mick had enlightened us all to the teachings that were available from those two girls. With empty arms and threepence in our pockets, we ran back to deposit the money with the kitty keeper before taking another armful. But Mick came down with his threepence and a face as red as a beetroot.

'Just been stopped on the stairs by Betty and Ethel,' he said, shaking his head. 'The bitches!'

'Why's that?' asked Joe as he threw the money into the kitty tin.

By the time I returned they were all laughing because the girls had cornered Mike with his arms full of wood, then took his todger out and laughed as they called him 'Pencil Dick', after which he – involuntarily – proved them wrong due to the sudden surge in blood brought on by their fondling. Mick shook his head, saying, 'I'll drop the wood next time, the bitches!'

'I'd a given them one!' Billy boasted.

'One what, a bit of wood?' Robby ribbed.

'Hey,' Billy replied, 'this is like a plank when it has its angry head on!'

After that whenever the lads saw Betty and Ethel they visualised having an armful of wood, but were glad they didn't. The older lads, however, had no such reserve with those girls, who appeared to be more submissive when met by them. We had often seen the likes of Tommy, Joe's brother, walking up to the likes of Betty, stopping to talk for a few seconds before walking off with her, as if she were his girl or something. Once we saw that, we knew where they had gone and sometimes followed them to Joe Dodds's horseboxes, if only to listen to the carryings-on from them. If we ever got caught, we would get a thick ear.

One such night I had to go and shout Logger because his mother was looking for him and she had told me to go and fetch him urgently. As I called out his name, he shouted back, 'I'll knock your head off, Nylon, if you're messing us!'

It turned out that he had to go down to the ship at the Alexandra Dock because his father, my uncle Larry – Big Lar – couldn't come home due to his night watch, but Aunty May urgently needed money to pay for the school meals the following morning. Larry had said he would ask the purser for an advance, but Logger had to go down there and collect it. I'd been forced to accompany Logger to see his mother just in case I'd been kidding him but, when it turned out where he had to go, he asked me to go with him to get the money from his dad.

He thirteen and I just eleven, Logger had shown me everywhere on those docks, but that had always been in the daytime or earlier in the evening, never seven thirty at night. It was a whole new world down there, a deserted one in comparison with the day or early evening time. Those ominous warehouses seemed even more hairy in the dim-lit areas of the docklands as we walked the cobbles towards the overhead railway, where we would turn right – and that was the only directions we had. Each of the many huge uprights holding up that overhead railway seemed to hide a ghoul behind itself as we followed the ground-rail tracks north, squelching the soggy, carpet-like mess of the ground coca berries or palm kernels from the trees underfoot as we went.

It got really scary when we saw three or more dark figures of Asian seamen gathering round an upright, smoke rising from between them. Logger grabbed my arm and led me from the umbrella of the overhead railway and out onto the road. We began to walk in the middle, but kept a sharp eye out for those creepy figures who were chatting away and laughing as though they were drunk. I grabbed Logger's arm as we walked by the group, who appeared to be sniffing at some burning rope. One of them turned and then sharply said something to the others, who all stopped talking and laughing and doing what they were doing to stare at us; that was hairy. My grip on Logger's arm really tightened as I kept my eyes on those men. I would have run like blazes had they made any move towards us.

'What were they doing, Logger?' I asked when I could finally move my tongue again.

'Fucked if I know, Peewee. You nearly severed my bloody arm, yer little fat fucker!'

'Sorry,' I said. 'It looked like they was burning rope and sniffing its smoke. What do you think?'

'I think me ma's a bleeding nuisance sending me down here at this hour of night!' Logger pointed over towards the umbrella and dock wall. 'Let's get back over to there and walk along the lines again.'

After ten minutes or more we arrived at a dock gate further up that creepy dock road; it was open. Logger popped his head inside the bobby's hut.

'Hey, mister, where's the Alexandra Dock?' he asked, then had to explain everything for the sleepy policeman to have his curiosity fed.

'It's a long walk, son. Only the Gladstone Gate is open at this hour, then you'll have to walk back towards the Alexandra Dock. You could come in here and walk up to it, I suppose, but you'd have to be careful.'

'If you had to go there, which way would you go?' Logger wanted to know.

'I'd go this way!' the bobby said, nodding his head into the dock gate and towards the north end.

So we did. And there we were, in that strange world of lights from the various boats reflecting on the still waters, while the distant sounds from various working sheds skimmed our ears, causing a weirdness beyond anything we had experienced to become enlarged, triggering our imaginations into running riot.

'Shoulda stayed out on the road, Logger,' I said as I grabbed his arm.

''Ere, let go of that bloody arm for starters! Either way, we have to walk on this side of the dock, so best we get used to it now, innit?' he told me sternly, before adding, 'If you have to grab a hold of something, hang onto my sleeve – that doesn't bruise.'

The numerous varying shadows and different docks we had to walk by just to get to the ship were haunting. Blue Star and Elder Dempster boats, Maru ships, tugs, dredgers, fireships and barges . . . Then there were the Indian Jala boats, with live animals huddled on part of their decks, giving off an occasional bleat or grunt, which carried on the wind, adding still more mystery. Each dock or basin, as they were called, threw their own shadows. Some had huge swan-neck cranes towering over their sheds while others had stubby towers that stood on railway tracks, which travelled the whole length of those quays. To us, with their various lights flicking and reflecting on the waters, they resembled massive spaceships, while the throbbing of the big ship's engines seemed to buffet the air and added to the reality of our impressions. It was so different from the daytime, when the combined noises of everything, including wagons, cranes, bogies and trains, became nothing more than a kind of silence. Darkness adds mystery, which turns the obvious into the obscure and causes nervous twitches in the uninitiated. We were both first-timers to this strangeness and as such felt the apprehension that goes with the not knowing.

Two men stealing a smoke break must have almost had a heart attack when Logger suddenly appeared and tugged at one of their sleeves.

'Hey, mister, is this the Alexandra Dock?' he asked, then repeated his story.

The gangway of the big ship was steep and wiggly as we climbed up and up and then some more until we reached the top. Now the throbbing of the engine could be felt in our feet as we popped their heads through a big iron door and peered down the long, white companionway. Suddenly one of the doors to that alley opened and a man with an oily face came out. Once again Logger repeated his story, but this time he had to shout above the din. The man smiled and signalled with his finger for us to follow him. He had a pair of jeans on, just like Logger's dad wore, and his boots left a black mark on the deck as he walked. The neckerchief he was wearing reminded Logger of Wild West films when they were doing hold-ups – but this fella was no cowboy, he was much too fat. He stopped and opened a door; the noise grew louder as it opened.

It was the loudest confinement of noise that we had ever heard. We stopped, the man turned and beckoned for us to approach him. Suddenly, we were enveloped in a cavern of throbbing vibrations as we entered the engine room and suddenly realised why the man had been using signs when asking us to follow. He went over to a switch, which he flicked on and off a few times, then he stood there with us. Together we scanned the massive engine nestling in its huge room of pipes and more pipes. Then we saw him: Big Lar, singlet, dungarees, boots, and a bandana round his forehead. Uncle Larry was holding a long oilcan in one hand, an enormous oily rag in the other. He looked up, the man up top raised his hand and then pointed at us. Uncle Larry raised the oilcan in acknowledgement, then spun his oily cloth round in upward circles, causing the man to tap us on the shoulder and indicate that we should follow him out.

It wasn't long before we were sitting in a mess room and being served up with a huge chunk of ice cream each, which we quickly gobbled up, feeling we had earned it. Big Larry came in, dirty sweat streaks adorning his huge body.

'Have trouble finding it, lads?' he wanted to know.

But we shook their heads as if it had been nowt and certainly didn't tell him how scared we had been during that epic journey. He laughed, then gave Logger the money before escorting us to the gangplank, where he stood until we were back on the quay and heading for home.

Both Logger and I had scary dreams that night and, although he hadn't said so, I think Logger was glad that I'd been there with him, but not so glad as I'd felt having him around. Once again, the older lad had given me a first to add to my CV of life, a moulding that would serve me well in the years to come.

CHAPTER 3

THE HUTS, 11-PLUS AND THE MILKMAN

Our Logger and Joe's older brother, Tommy, had long since done it. Mick Kinsella, Robby Tully and Mike Furlong were about to do it at the end of this summer. But Joe Keaney and I would have to wait until after the coming Christmas. Meanwhile, poor old Billy Vaughan had to wait until the following Easter for that long-awaited move to the Huts of Latham Street. It was the final leg of our journey into the promised land of work and wage earning, the stage between pimples, shaving and the sprouting of a useless clump of hair above the nether regions that couldn't even be used to make a face for a long-nosed dwarf because there wasn't anywhere to draw the mouth.

The Huts! Almost a mile from where we lived in the middle of Latham Street stood three double prefabricated buildings; two settled into a playground on the right-hand side of that steep street, which ran down from Stanley Road, and one was on the opposite side but without a playground. That was the leavers' hut for those in their final year. Mr Daybell and Mr Thomas were the keepers of that anxious lot as they champed at the bit of freedom for the whole of their final twelve months, which led to increasingly rebellious acts as they neared their release dates on the very first holiday after they reached their fifteenth birthday.

Throughout the pea-picking season of 1954, Robby, Mick and Mike had taunted us with things like, 'Well, we'll be goin' up to the Seniors when we go back, kids. Don't know if we can mix with youse juniors then, know what I mean, like?' We laughed it off, but felt envious at the thought of being left behind in the North Dingle section of St Johns. To us it seemed like a lifetime, but to poor Rip Van Billy it must have seemed like an extra sentence because he had to stay in the Juniors until the following Easter.

I remember the first day the three of them went. I was sauntering down the stairs after calling for Mike Kinsella, having been told that he had already gone. Then I heard laughter as I hit the second landing.

'Fuck off!' said Joe.

I looked. There was Robby and Mike walking behind Joe. They were in their long trousers; Joe was ahead of them wearing his short greys, like mine.

'Here's another junior, Robert. Doesn't he look cute in his short trousers?' Mike taunted, which was followed by another burst of laughter. Then, to add to our dismal feelings, we met up with Rip Van (Billy), who was being similarly leg-pulled by Fishcake (Mick) in Owens Road. As if that weren't bad enough, our Logger came over.

'Welcome to the Big Boys' Club, lads! How come youse are talking to those kids?' he asked with a laugh. 'If you new lads want to wait, we'll show youse the way, won't we, Tommy?' he called to Joe's brother, who had just followed us onto the road.

'Yeah, cost youse a loosey, though,' Tommy said.

'Loosey?' Robby questioned, then added, 'We know our own way to the Huts.'

'Yes,' Tommy replied, as he leaned into Robby's face before lowering his tone. 'But you don't know the nuts and bolts of the place, do yer?'

Like I said, I remember that day, seeing them walk off, laughing at our expense and me thinking, They'll give them a loosey, and we will have to give someone a loosey, then someone will have to give us a loosey – one day. However, those thoughts were short-lived because the teachers were on the 11-Plus search path. Those they picked were expected to dive into the pool of learning and swim in it until their eyes popped out, but for us that was not the problem. The problem was its prize: grammar school. Again, not a problem in itself, but the fact of having to stay on at school until you were sixteen was. *Sixteen?* One whole extra *year?* No, thank you – thank you, but *no*! We had so often spoken about the fact that the school-leaving age had only been raised in the last eight years, which made us feel somewhat hard done by, so the thought of an extra one on top just did not sit well. Although we did not express that thought to the teachers, equally we did not try hard when those pre-exam papers began to circulate; but what we didn't know then – but were told later – was that our previous schoolwork played a big part in the decisions our teachers made about us.

So, how I came to be picked for the 11-Plus was a mystery to me because I just knew that I had not done the work in St Johns. Add to that my previous school report from St Swithin's and there was no reason to pick me, even for a dunce's class. They had not taught me enough about fractions to enable me to cover the subject well enough to pass an exam, while decimals were nothing but orphaned dots and numbers to me. Although I could write a good poem, I was really crap at dissecting speech and putting it into prenamed boxes such as 'verb', 'noun' and 'adjective'.

Of course, in large measure my educational negatives were due to the difficulties arising from my mother's death and the resulting number of times that I had off school, being bounced from Ninny's then back to Norris Green before the eventual arrival of Dad's new wife. Hilda had shunned our old house in Norris Green and had taken us to a new home in Petherick Road, Gillmoss, where she promptly turned into a witch. She had established this new house, with its stringent rules, and was determined that I should follow them to the letter, but at nine years of age I had been moulded and set in the cast of my mother's ideas and attitudes, which was a mighty free-willed and roaming boat filled with determination.

Overnight, things I had never been forced or asked to do became law: enter only from the side door; shoes off, cleaned and then left in the side hallway; the settee is for sitting on only, so no lounging, no feet up, no standing on it and no tossing over on it; no touching the larder door without permission. Mealtimes were the only times to eat and the servings then were extremely meagre, so scanty in fact that I always felt hungry. Bedtime meant just that: bed – to sleep! Breaking any of those rules resulted in a belt: Dad's leather belt across the rump, which was held up for him by the chair I was made to lean across (up to this point my father rarely hit me).

For a boy who had been brought up by a tough but very liberal mother, these new rules were impossible to adhere to. Diane, on the other hand, was merely going along with everything. Being so young, she was not hit as hard by the changes I struggled so badly with. Almost unconsciously, more out of habit than devilment, I broke those rules, although I sometimes purposefully jumped on the couch, just to annoy Hilda. Consequently my arse became so acquainted with Dad's belt that it took on a leathery tone all of its own and pain became a way of life. I began to reach out to anything or anyone who could make me feel good.

The first escape I turned to was the enormous estate of Lord Derby, which surrounded my new area of Gillmoss. Almost every evening and weekend I trespassed those woods, sometimes with a Polish friend, Hugo, whom I had palled up with due to a bullying incident at school from which I had saved him. As far as I was concerned it was a great relationship because his mother used to give me a bowl of goulash, which, to my famished stomach, tasted so lovely. However, I always made sure that I arrived home for the allocated time and never, ever, told Hilda of that food, which supplemented her starvation diet.

One day I got a kind word from my teacher for my writing, so I took to it vigorously and eventually produced a poem from the first-hand knowledge I had about a fox and some sheep from the fields and copse that I frequented on Lord Derby's estate. Much of it was written from the standpoint of what I wished those animals would do as I watched, mostly on my own but sometimes with my friend, while some of it resembled a report on their antics as they ran and frolicked about in the field. I felt so proud when that lady teacher called me over to her desk and praised my effort. Eagerly I nodded when she asked if she could read it out loud to the class.

My one real friend in that class was Hugo, whom I'd rescued from bullying. After the many hidings I had received from my father, those puny kids meant little, so when I said, 'Leave him alone!' they could tell that I meant it and let it be; but it had always been clear that they held a grudge due to that intervention. All the same, it was a grudge that I ignored because my ninny always said, 'Be glad when someone shows a dislike to you because it gives you more time to find a true friend.'

So there I was, sitting attentively while that lovely teacher brought the class to attention with a tap of her ruler on the desk. How I wallowed in the following quiet as she spoke my name and then began to bring my poem to life simply by reading it aloud. It was as though I were seeing it all over again as that fox came out of the thicket, then stretched as if to say, 'Ah, this lovely sun is warm, bet those sheep are hot today.' If foxes thought in the same way as we do, then that is what it would say, because it was what I was thinking as the hot sun beat down on me. As she read, I felt a warm glow, just as I had that day. Just like then, I felt good, barely noticing that she had finished.

'What do you all think of that, then?' she asked, which made me feel embarrassed, especially when one of the girls from our road spoke out.

'It was good, miss, I liked it,' she said.

I remember that day vividly. As I felt my face begin to brighten, the leader of the little gang of bullies spoke out: 'Miss, he copied that, miss – he told me in the playground. Look, he's going red!'

He then pointed at me, causing everyone to stare, and *that* caused my face to brighten even more. However, I contented myself with the thought that the teacher, that very clever person, would kill the accusation once and for all by saying, 'No, he didn't'. But no rebuttal came from her lips. Instead she turned and glared at me, then shot a bolt into my head with, '*Did* you?' That brought a heap of loud laughter from my accuser and his cohort and this, in turn, allowed her accusation to detonate within the chasm of my mind, where all of my ills were stored, just waiting to be retaliated against.

From then on, what happened was totally beyond my control. I was hitting my father, the Witch, God (for taking my mother from me), that teacher, who should have known better, and the flat-nosed, bullying bastard who had shoved a lit match inside my keg.

First up was my chair crashing down on his desk as he flung himself backwards to avoid it, then the inkwell hitting him on the forehead. His desk ended up being pushed over onto his splayed legs, as I lay on top of them punching away at his face and shouted obscenity after obscenity until I was lifted up into the air by one of the male teachers and carried out into the playground, kicking and screaming. Finally, exhaustion overtook me and then I cried and cried as, through watery lips, a runny nose and clenched teeth, I sobbed out my hatred for everyone.

Up in my bedroom I could hear all the voices and I knew they were deliberating on me. My Polish friend had told his mother, who had turned up to verify the authenticity of that poem (for I had corrected a lot of it in her house while being treated for a head wound that her son had caused, after my head got in the way of a brick being thrown at the fox (he thought it was going to attack a sheep). That truth still didn't absolve me of the outburst, though, and consequently I received a leathering when Dad came home.

After that my schoolwork became almost nonexistent except for the mess on almost every page of my books as each lesson turned into a doodling session of scrawls and blob upon blob of runny ink from the bronze-coloured nib of my pen.

It wasn't long afterwards that things came to a head, as I increasingly turned into myself by ignoring almost everyone, especially when I found a photo of my mother in my dressing table drawer. It was a lovely photo, a head-and-shoulders portrait with her dark hair piled high. It made me remember how she took time combing it to make it sit up in that way, often making me laugh if it wouldn't stay just so. Her eye seemed to be twinkling and – to me – alive. For the next couple of weeks, each night I would take her out of that drawer and tell her of my troubles as if she were there with me, feeding me with the strength to ignore everyone in the house and at school. It was a weird feeling, looking at people and totally ignoring them; looking straight through them as if they were not there at all. That picture was all I wanted. I began to go straight to my room and would sit talking away for hours, coming down only for those measly meals but not caring that I was hungry, and rushing back up to talk to my mother. I found myself missing my ninny and the Buildings terribly but was determined to shut myself away from this persecution. For a while I even ignored Hugo. At first it hurt me to do this but it became easier as the days came and went. I had almost cocooned myself mentally when it happened . . .

One night I forgot to put Mum away and Hilda – the Witch – came into my room for a nose by way of telling me that my tea was ready (which she never did before: she always called up the stairs). She then saw my mum's photo. That led to a confrontation like we'd never had before, as I cursed her for touching the photo and snatched it off her when she tried to put it back in the drawer. That I had spoken after such a long period of not talking to people surprised her but it was my staring, wide-eyed defiance that prompted her to turn and leave, saying, 'Just wait till your father comes home, we'll see if you can keep it there then!'

I waited, expecting the worst and apologising to my butt for what was to come, but what came not only shook me out of the state I was in but restarted me completely, putting me back firmly where I belonged, with the doors of my mind flung wide open and in total charge of myself.

No doubt exasperated from the continual flow of complaints that he received daily from the Witch in her attempts to keep me in his bad books, I heard Dad say, 'For God's sake, Hilda, it *is* his mother!' I could scarcely believe my ears, listening to that wafting up the echoing stairwell as I stood on the landing outside my bedroom earwigging. He was actually sticking up for me. This was a first.

Then her voiced rose. 'If you think for one moment that I will stay in this house with *him* shoving *her* in my face every day then you have another think coming. It's me or her, make your choice!'

A silence followed that ultimatum, then the roar of, '*Right*!' sounded just as the door handle of the living room rattled. As the door swung open to signal that someone was on the move, I hurried back into my bedroom. I guessed it was Dad and then he roared, 'We'll sort this, once and for all!'

Uh-oh! I thought, because I had never heard him roar like that before. Then I listened as the stairs began to thump to the tune of his stomping up them. I sat on my bed, looking at the punishment chair, then at my mum on the dressing table; in a few minutes it would all be over and I would be yelling as if I was hurting terribly bad but in fact I would be yelling a false yell now that I was used to being strapped. As he stormed out of the bedroom I would raise two fingers in an 'Up yours!' defiance at the closing door and whisper, 'You bastard!' It was something that I had become good at. How I wished for the day when I could say it to his face.

Here it comes, I thought, as the door swung open.

He stood there looking at me, then glared at the photo. Then he took me completely by surprise.

I wasn't the target: he went for Mum – my mother's lovely photo. Up until that time I had disliked my father for taking Hilda's word, but in my own way I understood that I had no real proof of the lies said about me and my supposed actions or indiscretions. As he began to smash that photo across his knee, however, my dislike for him turned into a volcanic eruption of pure hatred.

With flaying arms, clenched fists and volleys of foul language I went on the attack by jumping on his back in a desperate attempt to stop the destruction of my beloved mother. With one hefty push I was flung off and landed heavily against the upright of my bed, which knocked the wind right out of me. By the time I had recovered my stance it was over. I remember a bubble bursting from my mouth as 'You bastard!' shot from it. It seemed to hit him hard, so I fired another and then another as we faced each other for the last time as father and son. I severed that relationship with a final 'Fuck off, yer cockney bastard!'

Slowly, he let the remaining pieces of my mother's photo fall to the floor. There was then a frozen moment filled with a telling tense silence as we faced one another, one pair of eyes blank and staring, the other wild and glaring as the engravers in my mind worked away feverishly, hacking it all onto the granite walls of my memory.

Edward Stockley then turned and left the room as I bent down to start picking up the pieces of glass, frame and torn photo I'd been using as a contact point during a period that could have taken me into the abyss. Each of those broken and torn pieces of my mother's photo that I collected acted as a fan, blowing away the mist that had recently clouded my mind, causing me to hide from a world that I thought was so unfair in so many ways. As I slid between the sheets in my striped pyjamas, clutching those bits of photo, frame and glass that had set me free, I felt restored.

The following morning, although I was still there in that house, I felt free, freer than I'd ever felt as, bit by bit, I replaced the photo of my mother on the dressing table. I then went over to the bed to collect the pieces that had slipped from my grasp during the night.

It was then that I noticed the dried blood on my fingers, the bedclothes and my pyjamas from the many cuts due to my grasping hold of those glass shards during a topsy-turvy slumber. My reflection in the mirror told a worse story, with the smeared blood making it look as though a massacre had taken place. The clip-clop of the milkman's horse told me that it was very early, so I slid back into bed, where I was consumed by a peaceful sleep, the first in a long time.

Whenever I had been chastised it was the norm for me to be kept in bed all day, with only an evening meal for sustenance. Hilda always made a point of bringing me up a cup of tea to show that she was the good one because she was breaking the rule that stated, 'Nothing at all to eat or drink'. Sure enough, she arrived with that steaming hot cuppa, saying, 'Don't tell your father but— *What?*' The sight of my massacred hands did shock her but not so much as the tea, which I had taken charge of. Somehow it got sloshed into her face, making her yell and drop to the floor, holding her head and screaming, 'Help me, help me!'

With that sound ringing in my ears I strapped on my skates and left via the front door, which I purposely left open as a final 'Fuck you!'

So that's how it came about that I was to be seen roller-skating along the East Lancashire Road in my bare feet and blooded pyjamas, attracting the strangest of looks from people as I sped on and on to Ninny's house in my beloved Buildings. I was given refuge, but missed school again for another six weeks or so while I was first put in a remand home because there were no places in the orphanage. Then, eventually, I went into an orphanage while all the rules and regulations of the adoption were sorted out before it was finally agreed for me to go and live with my Aunty Ann and Uncle John. However, those rules and regulations put my aunt and uncle through a real life-changing experience before the authorities allowed them to adopt me properly. Uncle John had to stop going to sea (he'd been a deckhand for years and loved it, often sailing with Uncle Larry) and they had to move from their two-bedroom home on Melrose block to a three-bedroom flat in Owen House: number 2e, next door to my friend Mick Kinsella.

For me it was great, but for poor Aunty Ann and Uncle John it meant hiking up eight flights of stairs each time they came home. It was worse for my new 'mum', because she came home from work twice a day, then had to pop in and out to go to the shops, not to mention the washhouse.

Apparently, there were bits of a smart kid showing through in my schoolwork as I dropped back into normality upon settling in at St Johns, causing me to be picked for the 11-Plus. I knew from those test papers that I was not ready for such an exam and, like my Scallywag friends, I had no desire to attend school until I was sixteen. My dismay at being chosen to enter the exam showed at home. When I told my new mother and father, I was bombarded with things that the future could hold were I to win a place in grammar school, but, no matter what was said, I did not wish to be a white-collar worker. Already the grease, grime and dirt of the dockland held the roots to my heart. Not even the promise of a new bike could make me change my mind, but the fact of their offer and concern did cause me to rethink what I myself wanted and to take into consideration their wishes and those of my ninny, too.

Reluctantly, I began to study for the exam with only a few weeks to go. It was an awkward few weeks that brought many skits from the lads, who were already planning their strategies for failure.

'I know how you can fail, Nylon. Just copy off Billy's paper,' said Joe.

''Ere, yer bullet-headed twat!' Billy retorted. 'He doesn't need any help from me to be soft: he's naturally thick. He doesn't even know where the dots go when we do decimals.'

The trouble with that truth was exactly that: I didn't know. Neither did Joe when I pulled him to one side and asked his advice. He just shrugged and told me, 'If you want a mate to fail this exam with, I'm it!' Our Logger didn't know either and neither did my former cousin, now new brother, Johnny. My new dad could tell you every point of the compass and name the whereabouts of any country, along with its ports, imports and exports, but, when it came to helping me with those flaming decimals, he too was lost. Mum and Ninny could tell you how to cook anything from fish to pigs' feet but decimals had never been a part of their kitchen, either.

Fractions I could do so long as they didn't go beyond a quarter, and even that sometimes had me twirling. Eight *half*-crowns made a pound, but one *half*-crown was an eighth of a pound. So how could a half be an eighth? The more I thought about it, the more confused I became and I truly began to regret those many, many months when I'd been off school due to the turmoil following my mother's death – nice as it had been at the time, staying at my ninny's house. Talk about the eventuality of having to pay the piper, I was certainly paying him during this period of my life.

Just as I'd feared, all of the things that I had worried about reared their ugly heads during that exam, so much so that I actually made a complete mess of it by trying to do those things I couldn't do merely by assuming what to do. Which made it worse because to the trained eye my papers had been deliberately messed up. In fact that was exactly what the headmaster, Mr Taylor, told me just before bringing me out in front of the whole school during assembly. He then gave me six of the best for 'denying another boy the chance to better himself'.

Although it hurt like the blazes I wasn't so disgruntled as I might have been because I should have swallowed my pride and made it abundantly plain that I really did *not* know those subjects. Then again there was a plus to it all: we had now reached the Huts with only four plain-sailing years before leaving school and no further exams to worry about.

As far as my education was concerned, all was not lost because I met a milkman by the name of Mac and began to help him deliver his goods. This began near the end of October 1955, immediately before my twelfth birthday, when he was at our house collecting the week's milk money and somebody passed by, saying, 'I've just chased some kids from your cart there, Mac, but they're still hanging around.' Mum nudged me to run around and keep guard and after that I began to help out every weekend. I would join him from Melrose block up until the finish of Fonthill and he would give me a pint bottle of orange juice for my troubles. Soon I grew to enjoy the responsibility and the trust that Mac placed in me and it wasn't long before I was hurrying to cross the quarter-mile railway bridge that ran along Stanley Road to Bankhall, where I would meet with Mac, load two hand crates (each held twelve bottles) with orders, then run on ahead with those crates and have them delivered to Melrose block before he hit Owen Road. What used to take him an hour and a half without my help now took only a half-hour as I zapped through those landings with enthusiasm and speed.

Sometimes Mick Furlong used to come and help but he felt it to be a bad deal and soon decided to stay in bed instead. After all, if he really wanted orange juice then he could ask his ever-loving mother to buy him a bottle. One day Mac gave me threepence, saying, 'Here, lad, you've earned that plus, but it's all I can afford 'cos I've got six kids to feed.' This would now be my daily 'wage'.

Mac smoked a lot and had horrible brown teeth, which suited his unkempt mop of dark hair, but, despite his appearance, he was a great guy. He made me laugh, but, more than that, he gave me a feeling of being worth something and he also knew about fractions and decimals, a skill he began to impart to me. The threepence a day was more of a token of his appreciation than a wage but I still managed to save a few of them each week. In fact I became so enthused about working that I began to hurry along Stanley Road early and would meet up with Mac as he delivered to the Shakespearian-named streets, past the Commodore picture house and along as far as Wadham Road, a distance of about a mile and a half from our Buildings – the Billogs. I would then help him to deliver as we went, but when we reached the Billogs I would leg it off to school, making sure to wash my hands in the toilets before going into class – those empty milk bottles really did make your hands dirty and smelly.

By the time winter crept in, I was getting up at five in the morning and walking that mile and a bit to Wadham Road, where I would load Mick's cart and have it ready for him. We would then start the round. It was an electric milk cart, with a long, swan-neck handle that you just pressed down on for it to move forward. You had to walk ahead of it but keep a hold of the handle to maintain control.

If you wished it to go faster, all you had to do was press the handle down further. You steered it by leaning the handle to the left or right, and, if you wanted it to stop, you merely let go of the handle. It was as simple as that; so simple a kid could do it – and I did.

Due to Mac's poor timekeeping I often ended up waiting for him to arrive in a morning. The depot manager, Johnny Parkes, had to load Mac's cart on those days when he was late and I always lent a hand. Sometimes Parksie would move the cart into place and leave me to load it up myself. One day I hurried to unplug the cart from its position at the charger for Parksie to move it but, instead of moving it, he waved me on instead. After it had happened for the second time I got up earlier and ran along that road just to do it all myself. It wasn't long before I had progressed to loading up the milk cart myself almost every morning before heading off along the round for two streets to Bianca Street, where Mac lived. He would then come out and join me.

I loved every minute of it, walking the mile-plus along the mainly deserted road and being acknowledged by the odd person going to work with a nod, a smile and sometimes even a 'hello'. It made me feel a part of the scene instead of being viewed as a possible young intruder. I also lapped up the attitude of the customers whose milk I was delivering: 'Morning, son' from the men and 'Thanks, lad' from the women. It was all so very, very different from the looks of suspicion that I got when merely walking down the street, heading for the dockland with the lads.

I had no idea that I wanted more out of life than I already had with the lads and the things we did, but this was a new feeling, a most welcome one at that. It warmed me in the same way as being with our group did, but this time there was a plus: the trust of the grownups, an acceptance from adults of being a part of the landscape, not a blot. It made me feel really worthwhile and so much so that I began to go home earlier just to be sure that I would not oversleep, which sometimes had the lads thinking I'd gone daft, especially when we were having fun, or mixing with the girls for the start of our A-levels in the field of sex.

Now my life was like this: 5 a.m., up, dressed, tea and a piece of toast, out into the morning air regardless of weather, sprightly walk along Stanley Road as far as Wadham Road, turn left, then walk down towards the distant Liverpool-to-Southport railway line and the docks. It was a longish road, full of bay-windowed terraced houses, their symmetry halted only by Queens Road as it sliced its cobbled path across from east to west: Wadham Road's tarmac. Immediately beyond that strip of cobbles on the left stood a noticeable break in the architecture of human occupation into one for animals. It was a stable block, which, until very recently, had been used to house that magnificent beast of burden, the carthorse, and was now a milk depot for the Reece's milk chain.

First job, unplug the cart and then move it out onto the street before waiting for the arrival of the big truckload of milk from the main depot. Load the cart straight from the wagon, start the round, knock Mac up and then carry on for two streets or so until he catches up. Eventually reach the buildings, help with the first couple of blocks and then meet up with the lads for the mile-long walk to our school, like the professional I was.

School, the Huts, Latham Street . . . Now we were all attendees, with new teachers, a fresh area, similar subjects but not so much effort due to our having little to achieve by working hard in those classrooms, Now there was light at the end of that dark school tunnel. It was a pinhole light that would get bigger and bigger as the four years passed until it became a huge screen playing the life which we clambered to get on board: the life of a wage earner.

The days spent in those huts were always a mixture of apprehension, bewilderment, fun, culture, searching and – sometimes – learning. Apart from the three Rs there was nothing those teachers ever pulled out of their bags to engage our minds and cause us to be distracted from the main focus: how to follow in our fathers' footsteps.

French – to us – was 'Fuck off' or other such swearwords, a fact often borne from the words of women shouting from the landings into the dark stairwells where we played cards when we let our language flow too loudly.

'Who's down there using that French?' they would demand to know, thus causing us to curb it.

We could, however, talk in 'back-slang', which was a form of adding various combinations of *A*s, *G*s and *O*s to every word. For example, 'yagou' means 'you', 'gago' is 'go', 'tagoo' is 'to' and 'theyge' means 'the'. We could speak it well but often forgot that some of our parents could do so too, which sometimes led to a crack over the ear from Mum, Dad or Aunty.

Geography had to be confined to the triangular perimeters of Liverpool, Rhyl and Blackpool. Everywhere else was basically a foreign country and not worth the effort of talking about for none of us had visions of ever going beyond those places. Science was gobbledygook – who on earth would want to say 'H_2O' when you could simply say 'water'? Oxygen was what we took into our lungs and it kept us alive so where it came from or how it came to be floating around was of no interest to us so long as it was free and plentiful.

As far as we were concerned scientists made monsters or were pals of the comic-strip hero Flash Gordon, and engineers were clever people who had been to university. But money, ha, that was different! Money bought us things; it paid the rent; it put food on the table and clothes on our backs. It would ensure that we could go to the pub or buy a packet of fags. But to get it we had to work, and that was our main aim. To do that, we had to leave school – hence our main objective.

Pea and spud picking helped us to earn a bit of money but, for me, helping Mac had a much better taste to it – it was as if I were part of something more special, where most of all I was needed and much appreciated, especially with the added respect that I got from his boss, Johnny Parkes, and others in the depot, who often tried to poach me for themselves by offering me more money. Sometimes they would even stoop so low as to tell me lousy stories about Mac in the hope that I would like him less and go with them instead.

I used to tell Mac whenever things were said about him but he would just laugh. Apparently he and Johnny Parkes were great pals and Mac expected those tall tales from him because of the rivalry between them: stealing me would be a jewel in crown of their relationship. The big guy would simply shrug and tell me things about his other accusers, making me laugh: 'Copy what the Good Book says, Peewack. Don't throw stones at sinners if you sin yourself!' It sounded about right, and I now knew how to do decimals and fractions thanks to Mac, but I still had no desire to continue attending school until I was sixteen, and neither did any of my friends.

I really was enjoying life then, but my poor ninny had no idea how much. Granddad used to tell her to shut up whenever she went on about my getting up so early. For some reason or other he hated my guts and, for as long as I could remember, had never said anything nice to me. Come to think of it, I cannot remember Granddad saying anything nice about anyone. Mum and Dad were content that I was doing the milk job; my being up with the lark did not disturb them and the fact that I came in early to ensure getting up was a bonus. But Ninny, grandmothers being what they are, thought she knew best and so she recruited the one person she felt sure would bring me to my senses: the parish priest, Father Hopkins.

Forever in and out of homes in the area – his broad-Irish, smooth-talking tongue consoling, pacifying and strongly hinting that we should live our lives according to the Good Book – the good father never refused a tot, if offered, which was often, but not in our house. Ninny was a fervent believer, who as such put her faith in the Good Book above the Pope himself. 'He is only a man who passes on the word of the Almighty,' she used to say. She would then add, 'Which is already in the Good Book, anyway. If the Son of God himself can come on this earth and be an ordinary man, what right has anyone got to be exalted?' Father Hopkins often called into Ninny's house for a cup of tea and a biscuit. He enjoyed her philosophy, which gave him respect but not adoration in any way.

It was after such a visit and an ear-bashing about my getting up early every morning that he collared me. Just as I was walking into Ninny's house, he was coming out. Unsure as to my identity but feeling it to be me, he turned and looked at Ninny, who nodded to him. 'Just the man,' he said as he turned away from that Judas nod and looked me up and down. He went off half-cocked with a totally unrehearsed, sermonic battering of Mac for more or less using me as a slave. It didn't sound right, it *wasn't* right, and it offended me greatly as he went on and on about youngsters being used by people while not once mentioning or asking about my feelings in all of this.

'What would yer sooner me do, go robbing for my coppers?' I blasted at him before I ran off.

It was over a week later that he bumped into me again, this time as I was coming out of the Sassbar. He was onto me like a flash with, 'Peter, just the man I have been looking for.' This time I sort of sidled out to give myself a chance to scarper should he be annoying once more, but his manner wasn't aggressive in any way, so I stood looking up at him with my back towards the Fonthill Road instead of the soft-drinks shop. 'I've been thinking of you a lot since our last meeting. Maybe I was a bit harsh with my opinion of your friend, the milkman. You may like doing what it is you do with him,' he went on.

'Delivering milk,' I replied firmly as if to denounce any inappropriate suggestions.

'Yes, delivering milk. You really should listen to your grandmother—'

'Ninny . . .' I again butted in, harshly.

'Ninny. Yes, I used to call mine "grandmother". Well, you should listen to your *ninny*, then. After all, it is not nice for her to see you missing your sleep to go out so early each morning for a mere threepence for all of that hard work. I mean, if you feel that you have to get up early and do something, why not think of serving God? I'm sure your ninny would be happy to see you doing that.'

'Doing what?' I asked with a sneaky suspicion of half knowing where all this was leading.

'Well . . . hrmph!' He cleared his throat. 'I've been looking for an altar boy for the early masses – very hard to get, you know . . .' He came to a halt as my eyes shot straight into their glaring position. 'Just an idea, y'know. It would please your ninny like nothing else could.'

He was certainly right about that. She would be over the moon if I were to do such a thing, but in doing so I would be letting her down because her main concern was always my fulfilment and happiness, which meant that I should stay with Mac because I really loved doing the work. But I had to get this sanctimonious prat out of my hair once and for all. After a short silence of discreet thought, I smiled at the good father and said, 'How much does it pay?'

At this his eyes almost popped and he seemed to take a step back due to the surprise. '*Pay?*' he demanded so loudly that the person being served in the Sassbar jumped, thinking the priest to be behind him and wanting him to hurry his transaction. '*Pay?* You don't get paid, you do it for the love of God, lad!'

'Well, I don't love him 'cos he took my mother. Now fuck off!' I told him. I then turned and ran like the blazes. For a few days afterwards I worried a bit, thinking he might come into the classroom and have me hauled out or something, but it didn't happen, so the worry sort of drained from my mind as I got on with life.

We Scallywags would meet in Owens Road to go to school and then stroll along Stanley Road, skitting one another, or others, as we went and then running if a skit were to go wrong. We had a song, something of a marching song or even victory chant, which we burst into now and then and even sang it loudly from off the spud wagon as it took us home after a day's work. It was a song passed down to us by our older kin, so I presume that it was concocted by an earlier group of scallywags similar to ourselves. It went like this:

Marching down Melrose road,
Do-ors and win-dows open wi-i-ide,
If you hear a copper shout
'Hey, put that candle out!'
We are the Melrose gang
We know our manners

We spend our tanners
We are respectful wherever we may be.

Depending on our mood, it could be repeated once or twice or during a journey, especially after a situation we'd made a clean getaway from or a precarious situation from which we had escaped injury-free.

Sometimes we would go up Wykeham Street and pass the rear of Stanley Hospital, taking a peek through the keyhole of the mortuary. Often we would see corpses laid out on trolleys, and one day we spotted a classmate at that keyhole for ages.

'Whatcha standing there so long for, Gilbo?' Joe asked this classroom clown, Gilbertson, as we caught up.

'Just tryin' to make out what that is in there,' he told us as he pointed towards the keyhole.

Joe took a peek and then stood up, puzzled.

'Dunno what it is,' he said.

Billy took a gander, then Robby and the others, before I myself had a go. It was definitely a trolley, but what was that white blob on it? Suddenly it dawned on me. Triumphant, I stood up and stated it to be a human skull with the end cut off, as if it had been scalped and was showing the inside: the brain. It had to be. Eventually everyone agreed with me but all that deducing had made us late for school. Mr Murphy (or 'Muff', as we referred to him) had an awful habit of putting us across his knee and slapping our thighs; if he could roll up the leg of our 'longies', he would slap the bare leg too. However, it was an effort for one boy to be punished in such a way, let alone four, and we could see him pondering the worth against the energy required to do so. He seemed to welcome the excuse that I blurted out when I told him about the topless skull and how it had fascinated us into being late – so much so that he made us all sit down and then took us into an unscheduled anatomy lesson, which made us feel glad that it wasn't the corpse's arse that had been showing!

When lunchtime came we'd had our fill of brain cells and how they work, look and, according to Muff, taste – if rumours of some tribes in Papua New Guinea were to be taken seriously. Our mile-long trudge to the dinner centre in Orwell Road took us past the hospital once more, but this time there were no more corpses for viewing. As usual the 'din-ee-o', as we called it, was full, with most being on free school dinners, and, despite its bad reputation for food, there were not many empty plates, including mine.

That day, however, I became the culprit who put people off the sweet – tapioca. With only the thought of mixing a blob of jam into my bowl of tapioca, I sat back down at our table and slowly stirred. Suddenly I got a flash. It was a keyhole flash of that sliced head we had seen through the hospital door, so I said so and everyone who had seen it too realised the similarity. Now there was a portion of that brain in our bowls, complete with the blood of jam stringing through the tapioca/brain matter. As the word spread, the other kids began to push away their servings, causing us to laugh. Then more followed suit and soon Mick Furlong and I were laughing fit to burst. Try as I might, I just could not stop laughing. Even when I was made to stand in front of the teachers' dinner table the uncontrollable urge to giggle carried on. Then Mr Thomas returned to the table with a bowl of tapioca and began to stir in his jam, causing the most disastrous thing to happen: while keeping my mouth closed in an attempt to suppress another outburst of laughter, the upheaval of wind sped from my tummy and out through my nose, causing a huge string of snot to pour out and dangle, which in turn caused poor Mr Thomas to retch violently. At this I just burst out laughing even more and then ran out of the building, forsaking the half-bowl of tapioca to which I could have returned, if only I'd managed to stem my fit of the giggles.

I don't know if the hospital management was ever informed of that incident, but, the next time we passed by the mortuary door, the keyhole had been blocked up. Just as well, I suppose – I really did like tapioca.

Laughter was a big part of our lives in those days and playing tricks on one another almost as common as breathing. Long before Hallowe'en became the spectacle it is today, we put on impressive performances that would have made Dracula hang up his cloak, or at least spit out his gnashers.

Then there were the horseboxes in Joe Dodds's yard that were mainly used for courting the ladies but also for frightening the life out of one another. In the crisscross of eerie shadows cast out by those boxes due to the way they were stacked, up to ten 8 x 10 x 8 boxes could be in that yard, some atop others, others standing alone in that dark, quiet brick-strewn yard – and each one a mystery as to whether or not it would be clean as far as horse muck was concerned.

If you knew that you would be taking a young lady there, you had to go sniffing for a clean box, but you also needed to be careful not to let anybody else know where you were going, because, when people knew, they hatched plans for devilment. Certainly, it was not unusual for the most amorous of moments to be spoiled by a bombardment of bricks as they crashed down on the roof or sides of the horsebox you were in, or for the sudden scent of horse shit to come up from beneath the carefully laid sacking with which you had covered the floor earlier. The worst one, though, was when the sacking you were sitting or lying on suddenly came alive because someone had been in and tied string to the edges, which they pulled once you had been given enough time to settle into titty touching.

No one was safe from those pranks, not even the toughest or meanest among us. The tough ones were respected, but still pranked. However the meanest were targeted without respect. Take, for example, Snake Eyes. He acted like one of the toughest and was a bit of a bully to us kids but more cowardly when it came to mixing it with the tough ones. Betty, the local boys' fitness teacher, once let it slip that Snake Eyes had commandeered her for that evening, therefore curbing our lessons, so we set about ruining their get-together as a payback for all the times he had robbed us soft by paying us buttons for collecting, chopping and selling his firewood. However, being the smartarse that he was, Snake Eyes made it look as though he was going to the horseboxes by visiting the yard early, as those with such plans would do, but he had other arrangements in place at the Sunshine Hotel.

The Sunshine Hotel was a derelict, three-storey house, with three-foot-high sandstone columns for gateposts, although the iron gate had long since been weighed in for scrap. It stood like the ghost of a better era than the one those terraced houses of Owens Road had seen. Taking the full brunt of the setting sun on sunny days, Sunshine took its name from the reflections blazing down from its broken windows on all three floors, through which we often viewed the docks, the Mersey and the Irish Sea. Especially in the evening, the attic room of that house was by far the best for two reasons: first, the top windows had never been broken; and, second, the shining sun had warmed the room by magnifying its rays. Snake Eyes was no mug: he knew the area well and would have had us fooled, had Fishcake (Mick) not seen him taking a duffle bag into Sunshine.

'But he set out a horsebox, I seen him do it. Didn't we, Mike?' Robby interjected.

'We saw him getting over the yard, yeah, but you know how foxy Snake Eyes is,' said Mike, as he stretched his grey matter to the limit.

'Tell yer what,' said Joe with a bit of enthusiasm, 'we'll trap the *two* places! Half of us go and do the horsebox, the other half go and set up Sunshine.'

While Snake Eyes was having his tea and Betty was putting on her makeup for the workout she was about to do, Joe led Fishcake and me into the Sunshine while Robby, Mike and Billy headed for the enclosed olla (a patch of waste ground, usually the result of a building being bombed or demolished) full of horseboxes.

Snake Eyes had chosen well, thought Joe, as he entered the attic room of the Sunshine, its warmth enveloping every part of him. Sure enough, beady-eyed Fishcake was right: there was the duffle bag set like a pillow at the head of an old blanket laid out like a welcome mat. Joe smiled as he bent down and picked out a small bottle of Scotch from the bag. At first we were tempted to take it but then decided that a good rude disturbance would be more pleasing to everyone. All we had to do was figure it out. Obviously, Snake Eyes would notice anything in the room, so we all squirmed up into the loft, taking care not to knock anything down through the holes in the ceiling. A few dead pigeons, the remains of a rat and a massive spider's web were about all we could find up there, but it wasn't enough to cause the earthquake we wanted to deliver – at least that was until I noticed the old water tank in one corner, still a quarter full of liquid. At this we looked at one another and then smiled.

By the time Snake Eyes met and escorted Betty to the Sunshine the lads (minus me) were on the top landing of Stanley block, looking down at the entry running from Owens to Orwell, the first door being the back door for the Sunshine. I'd volunteered to tip the tank over, pouring its contents onto the embracing couple when the time was right. To do this I had to clamber out onto the roof and climb in through the roof into next door.

I was careful not to make a sound as Snake Eyes introduced Betty to the room and then the Scotch before attempting to introduce her to his magic wand. Not having witnessed anything of this sort before, soon I began to forget what I was actually there for. Only recently had I become used to erections through stolen glimpses at discarded men's mags, and the sight of Betty writhing with one breast hanging out almost sent me over the edge, especially when her knickers ended up around one ankle. Soon the 'Gotta do it!' in my head became a mixed metaphor: tipping the water or tipping the scales of my mercury set, which had well overstepped the safety mark. Fortunately, a ticklish feeling on my hand brought me quickly back down to earth as I glanced down. A cockroach had run over it, and in the fading light I could see it heading for a big black ball of fluff, into which it disappeared.

A nest! I thought. I'd only ever seen one in a bombdy (bombed-out building) but my cousin Logger would not let me touch it. Instead we got some paraffin and then I held a lit paper underneath the nest as he poured the paraffin over the top of it. It was soon enveloped in flames and then the area became alive with cockroaches. There seemed to be hundreds of them but that nest was much smaller than this one.

Like a bomber in a Lancaster, I gazed down at the resting submarine of Snake Eyes, his periscope up, and the stretched form of

Betty, her cabbage patch on show and two nipples protruding amid dishevelled clothing.

Here's for all those times you conned us outta money, Snake Eyes! I thought, as I let the nest fall to land smack-bang on top of them. Wham! It burst open and became a war zone as creepy-crawlies scuttled everywhere. As the lads watched from the landings I emerged onto the roof amid the screams and cries of 'Bastard, *bastard*! Who the fuck? *Bastard!*'

I couldn't help but chuckle as I made my way across the tiles through to the next roof and I was still laughing as I emerged onto the street. Eventually, I ended up on the landing with the others, where I recounted what had happened but missed out on the fact of what nearly happened and how I came to see the cockroaches' nest.

There were some giggles as we watched Snake Eyes leave, pushing Betty away from him as she tried to link arms, saying, 'Piss off, soft arse! Don't want people to know we've been together.'

For Betty it must have been a lousy way to end the night, but as far as we lads were concerned, that was Snake Eyes through and through.

Mac laughed like the blazes when I informed him of the assault on Snake Eyes; it tickled him all the more because of the way he manipulated the lads in our area.

'All the same,' he said, once he had finished laughing, 'if Snake Eyes didn't use you lot then somebody else would – the world's full of users and doers. It's how we get on in life, a kind of learning curve. Betcha Snake Eyes has done some fetching and carrying before he cottoned on to getting someone else to do it. No doubt you'll have somebody working for you too one day, Peter.'

I argued the point on that one, for I could not visualise myself ever being a boss. A grafter through and through, I loved working and I said so.

'Well, stop moaning when someone gets you to work,' he replied with another laugh.

'I'm not moaning about the work: it's the lousy few pence he pays that I don't like,' I told him.

'But *I* only pay you peanuts,' said Mac with a look of slight apprehension.

'Yeah, but you're paying me out of your wages. It's not like you have all the money made from delivering the milk, is it? Besides, you've got six kids to feed. That Snake Eyes should share the money between us all 'cos we're all in it together, know what I mean, like?' I explained.

Mac laughed and nodded. 'I get your gist, kiddo. Just don't go communist on me – I can't stand them all-for-one-and-one-for-all eejits.'

The next couple of weeks had Mac explaining the ethics of communism to me, which at first seemed to ideally fit in my box of rights and wrongs, but, when it came to the bits about the state being the keeper of the wealth and the workers being those who shared the poorer way of life, somehow I went off that ideal and settled for the midfield position of 'wait and see what life has to offer'. In the meantime, I loved my work with Mac, my time with the lads in those Billogs, the diverse characters we met there and all this life had to offer.

CHAPTER 4

GRANDDAD

Old Sean Riley hailed from Cork. He had met and married Ninny early in 1901 after making the journey across the Irish Sea to the more promised land of Liverpool, where they lived in a two-up, two-down somewhere near to the docks – as most places were during the latter part of the 1890s and the early 1900s. My grandparents had six surviving children: John, Anne, Kate, Larry, my mum Claire and the baby of them all, Frank.

Like most men of his day, Sean was a labourer. He worked hard, played hard and, as was true of most men in those days, he ran the household with an iron fist. Sean was also a bit of a bully and became even more so as his lads grew older, bigger and stronger. He became especially reliant on Larry, who was strong and tough and doted on his father. However, that iron fist often smashed into poor Ninny's face during her younger years, causing Larry to begin to dislike his father, as he realised just how much of a brute the man was. Many arguments ensued, with the eldest lad, John, being the pacifier whenever words became heated.

It all came to a head one day just before my mother died in 1951, when Larry came home from sea to find his mother with a broken jaw. He picked his father up and rammed him against the wall, threatening to kill him should it ever happen again. John had stepped in that day, thinking Larry would kill Sean, but was strongly rebuffed, since he never really stood up to their father to prevent Ninny from getting hurt. Ninny knew it was not in John's nature to be violent because he truly took after her when it came to godly placidness. After that, John avoided Uncle Larry like the plague and rarely visited the family home except to occasionally call in and see Ninny.

Old Granddad seemed to hate everyone, especially Aunty Mary and me. Aunty Mary was the illegitimate daughter of Aunty Kate, who was a female double of the grumpy old Sean. Mary drank heavily, could curse for England and smoked in chain fashion. She had only to sit in the armchair by the fire and spit into the flames to become an exact replica of her father, who seemed to carry a permanent chip on his shoulder.

It was Kate who became my first substitute mother after the death of my real one, her sister. That arrangement was procured by Ninny, who felt it might be the turning point for her wayward daughter, having responsibility loaded onto her. Ignoring the fact that she had already abandoned Mary to her charge many years earlier, but still hopeful, Ninny badgered my father to give Kate the chance – which he did.

But that didn't last long due to a couple of things, one of which was her drinking and the other the death of King George VI on 6 February 1952. I was in the juniors at Leamington Road School,

Norris Green, at the time. That morning my teacher paused while writing on the blackboard and then burst into tears as she turned and broke the news of King George's death. To which I said, 'So what?'

She looked at me in disbelief, saying: '*What* did you say?'

The whole class looked on, too.

Silence blanketed the classroom as I repeated what I had said but added more: 'I said "So what?" Miss, because my mum died not long back and nobody even mentioned it. You didn't know the King, but you knew my mum.'

'You insolent little boy, you disrespectful little urchin! Get out of my class!' she shouted.

All the kids watched and then turned their heads to see what I was going to do; it sort of put me in a boat, which I had to row or let sink. But I had spoken the truth and so I stood by my words.

'I fuckin' won't!' I shouted.

Some of the girls began to scream because I had sworn.

'*What* did you say?' the teacher demanded loudly.

'I said, I fuckin' won't!' I shouted, and then upturned my desk to send it clattering to the floor.

Then there were more screams as the teacher just stood there and wet herself. The sight of that puddle appearing on the floor by her feet and getting bigger amazed me, but it must have scared some of the girls, because a few got up and began to run out of the class. That was when the teacher fainted, fell down she did, right into the puddle on the floor like a fat-arsed mop.

In the headmaster's office later, I was made to sit on a chair while things were said about me, which included my being a Catholic, although for the love of me I couldn't see what difference it made, even though I was in a Protestant school. I stood by my convictions, which stated the facts about my mother and King George. No one had said a word about my mum, but they expected me to feel sorry for King George – no remorse from me, mate!

Aunty Kate was sent for and I was promptly sent packing, running alongside Kate as she launched herself home with quick steps. No sooner were we in the house than a knock came on the door: it was a man. I had never seen him before. For a moment he and Kate spoke in whispers and then he left. Kate made a couple of jam butties then put them on a plate, saying she had to go out and that I would have to look after my little sister, Diane, who was playing upstairs. Then she left, just like that.

By the time Dad came home from his job at Clarence Dock power station, Diane was asleep in his armchair and I was listening to the radio with my back against the hearth and its roaring fire. The sink was laden with dishes from the previous night, along with all the breakfast things, and I had made a bit of a mess by making jam butties for most of the afternoon. There was no sign of anything for the evening meal and, as he bent to take off his bicycle clips, he said, 'Where's your Aunty Kate?' But before I could answer the sound of the front door being slammed shut echoed through the house, then Kate came stumbling into the front room, obviously drunk.

'Where've you been?' demanded Dad.

'Ask your son!' said Kate as she pulled off one of her shoes. 'He's bleedin' embarrassed me. I had to go and fetch him from school cos they've bloody expelled him. The little tearaway told the teacher to "Fuck off!"' With that she flung her other shoe to the floor. 'Here,' she told him, as she handed a parcel to my dad, 'here's some chips. I'm not gonna do any cooking now, I'm off to bed.' She then left him to go stumbling up the stairs.

I was shocked. Kate had screwed the truth of things in order to make me seem like the total cause of all that had happened, no clean dishes, no housework and no tea. To top all that, she had made it sound as though I'd instigated everything in school instead of – at least – adding the fact of how I felt about what had happened with that bloody King George dying. I glanced up at my angry father, who looked as though steam was going to come spurting out of his ears at any moment as he stared at the door through which Aunty Kate had gone. Then he turned and glared at me.

'*You!*' he roared. 'You little bastard!'

He then lashed out at me, catching me across the face with what felt like a hammer. That leathery smack woke Diane, who began to cry. Dad turned to her, so I seized my chance to run out. All I can remember then was running and crying as my face throbbed; just running and crying. It was dark and cold and I had no coat on.

A man was standing by his gate. I glanced up at him, catching him staring at me as I passed by – I felt embarrassed because I was crying, so I ran off when he asked what was wrong.

By accident or design I ended up among the bushes in the grounds of Leamington Road School, where I stood shivering but mad as hell, hungry and in pain as my face throbbed from the effects of that punch or whatever it was that he used to hit me. I needed something to take my feelings out on as anger took over. That school, it was all their fault, and that bloody King George too, but he was dead. So the school it was.

Within minutes the road was alive with people as doors opened and lights went on as the sound of breaking glass filled the air. With an armful of bricks I was walking along the school grounds, weaving in and out of the rhododendron bushes and lashing a brick at a new pane as the last one shattered. I don't know how many I broke before someone stopped me in my tracks, but it was a lot because half the street had come out to see what was going on. One of the kids recognised me, so they sent for my father.

Maybe it was that I looked like Quasimodo due to the swelling on my face that saved me from another smack. Maybe it was the looks people were giving me in my sorry state. I don't know. Nobody said anything, though – they didn't in those days. A family's business was a family's business, especially if they had a youngster who went around smashing windows. I was just very happy to snuggle down into my own bed. Even the hunger pains couldn't stop me from falling into a deep sleep.

The next day Dad had gone to work and Kate appeared to be remorseful. She cuddled me and bathed my face, then took Diane and me on a bus ride down to the pier head to see the ships and feed the pigeons and gulls. I was in bed before Dad came home, so I didn't get to see him that day. On the Saturday he had gone to work before we got up, as was the norm. Kate got us up at nine-ish but, strangely, she said we could bring our friends in to play – all of them (usually she didn't like them in because they made too much noise). I remember thinking she was making it up to me for having done what she did. We were allowed to go upstairs into the bedrooms and bounce on the beds. It was real pandemonium – lovely, uninterrupted chaos. I don't know who made the more noise, my friends and I or Diane and her screaming mob.

I don't know what time it all finished but it seemed to happen quickly and then Diane and I were left alone in the house. It was completely quiet and Kate was nowhere to be seen. I remember making a cup of tea and then scraping out the jam jar onto some butties for us to eat; we were munching on them as Dad came in.

He didn't even bother taking the cycling clips off his trousers due to the mess that met him. With glaring eyes that would put fear into a raging bull he walked towards me.

'Where's your Aunt Kate?' he demanded.

'Dunno,' I shrugged, but held up my hand to cover the sore side of my face just in case he was to strike out again – he didn't. Within an hour we were both in Ninny's house and tucking into her lovely beef scouse, a kind of stew.

It turned out that Kate had decided against rehabilitation, as she had done with every attempt Ninny made to change her, and wanted to show everyone that she never would change by stealing the money from the gas and electricity meters as well as taking our Sunday-best clothes, which she pawned before hightailing it to Manchester, where the police caught up with her and she got twelve months. I was thrilled when Dad announced that he was going to London for a while and taking Diane with him. It meant that I had to stay at Ninny's in my beloved Billogs. After the recent lows that had befallen me, this was one of the highs and it came with a bonus: no school.

Grumpy old Granddad continued to give me the Evil Eye whenever I was in the house –which was often, because I loved it there, despite his animosity. Besides, Ninny was always there to keep a check on his meanness. On Easter Day of 1954, I saw Aunty Mary rush out of Ninny's just as I was walking towards it. She was obviously upset, because she was crying, which puzzled me, but not for long. As I walked in, Ninny was having a real humdinger with the old drunkard.

'*You!*' I heard her say. 'You do nothing but pick on the nice people of this house. Our Mary is a lovely girl.'

'She's a bastard!'

'Aye, and whose bastard is she? Your favourite daughter, the one you encouraged to drink, smoke and swear as opposed to getting her to be godly!'

'God, that's your fuckin' trouble, woman . . .'

At this point, I was noticed and they stopped their rowing.

Why did they call Aunty Mary a bastard? I wondered. She's lovely – I love me Aunty Mary.

I remembered how she had sat me down and told me that my mother was dead before bursting into tears herself – just as that stupid teacher had done over the King's death that day, but I could understand Mary because she's our family.

Granddad slapped Ninny and barged past me, saying, 'Get outta the way, you little bastard!' Then he grabbed his coat and left the house, slamming the door hard as he left. I hurried over to Ninny, who had fallen to the floor but was just getting up as I reached her.

'I'm all right, son. Where's your Aunty Mary?' she said.

'Gone out crying, Nin,' I told her.

Ninny nodded.

'Go see if you can find her, please, lad,' she said.

So I did, but once I got outside I had no idea where to go. I knew she wouldn't be in our house because my ma was at work, and so were Aunty Ann's two children, Johnny and Annie, and Dad. I ran over to No. 44, Aunty May's two-up-and-two-down house on Owens Road. It was always Aunty May's house even though my Uncle Larry lived there when he was home, which he was, but home from the sea, not the pub. Fanny the cat, a loft full of pigeons, a daft black-and-tan Alsatian and of course Aunty May with baby Pauline and her older sister Ann, but no Aunty Mary.

'Try Nora's,' said Aunty May, so I hotfooted it up to the third landing of Stanley House, to No. 3d, where Nora Frost lived – she was Uncle Frank's girlfriend and Mary had become her friend. I felt there was a chance for her to be there, but her one-legged father said, 'No, not seen her.'

Now I was at a loss as to where to look next. There's nowt worse than wanting to help but not being able to due to lack of knowledge. Mary was good but not so holy as Ninny, so that ruled out the church, where some women went to kneel and pray for better things, or so I'd heard. Then I tried the shops just in case but got no joy there either. I never went near any of the pubs because she was just not a plonky woman (a drinker), unlike her ma. She did smoke, though, but you could do that anywhere, so that didn't help. So where could she be?

Where would I go if I was crying? I asked myself, but shook my head as the thought of smashing some windows crossed my mind. Naw, I thought, she wouldn't do nothing like that.

Just then I saw Ninny coming across the square, her familiar shuffle recognisable as she scuffed the ground with one foot due to her bunions.

'Couldn't find her, Nin,' I confessed as I walked up to her.

'She's home, lad. Here . . .' She handed me a half-crown. 'Go an' get a couple of shillings for the gas meter for me, will yer?'

So I did – at least I could do something to help.

When I got back, Uncle Larry was there.

'At it again, is he, Ma?' he asked angrily.

'No, lad, just mouthing off at Mary for nothing. Called her a bastard, he did. It's not fair!' she told him, and then began to cry.

Larry gave her a hug. 'Don't upset yourself, Ma,' he told her. 'I'll have a word with him.'

'Don't go causing trouble with him, lad. Promise.'

He gave her his word and then left.

That night, old Joe Mooney, janitor of those buildings, knocked on 8a. Ninny shuffled to the door.

'Better come, Misses, it's old Sean,' he said, as he pointed over towards Melrose Road.

As the story goes, Granddad left the Melrose pub just on closing and made his way along towards home. He'd got as far as the wall separating the entry of Saint Agnes Road and the open waste ground at the end of the washhouse facing Ninny's., so near and yet so far away from safety, when someone had given him a real terrible pasting and left him lying in a pool of blood, half on the olla and half on Melrose Road. Mary cried when she saw him and tried her best to comfort him until the ambulance came, followed by the police, then a late night as everyone crowded into Ninny's to debate what had happened. It was agreed that his attitude in the pub that night had opened the wounds of someone from his past bullying ways and whoever it was had waited in the entry for him to come rolling home. Even the police gave credence to the story after enquiries that backed up the horrid side of his attitude during that evening.

As for Granddad, he recovered sufficiently to be sent home from hospital, but he couldn't remember what had happened at all. His drinking days were over as he took to his sick bed in 1954, from where he worked Ninny to the bone as he got her to fetch and carry to his every whim. Up until then I had never really hated him but I soon began to do so as I would often hear him cursing her in the bedroom whenever she took his meals or medicine in.

About six months later, I walked into the front door and heard a faint cry coming from Granddad's room. I walked over and looked in. He was half in and half out of the bed, with his back on the floor, his legs on the bed and his nightshirt down by his throat so that all his crown jewels were on show to the world.

'Son,' he whispered in a low and strained voice, 'tell your Grandma . . .'

'OK,' says I before walking out and closing the door behind me. I walked into the back kitchen, where Ninny was tending to a pot of scouse.

'Hey, Nin,' I called out, but then a devil got me just as she turned to see what I wanted.

'What, lad?' she asked.

'Have you got a penny? I'm just a penny short for . . . for something I wanna get.'

So she gave me the penny and I left. I don't know why I did it, but I did and without any remorse, knowing he could be lying there till the cows came home – and even longer should Ninny put her scarf on and go to Benediction, which she might because it was a Wednesday. Well, I don't know if she did or didn't, but I do know that Granddad got worse.

On 19 July 1955, Granddad Sean Riley died. It was at his funeral that I heard the most alarming revelation, one that shocked mourners and the family alike.

The burial had been carried out in Anfield Cemetery, where he had been laid in the same grave as my mother. It caused me to remember her burial clearly. I had to be carried away, kicking and screaming that Mum was not to go down there because the priest had said she was going to Heaven: down was Hell, up was Heaven. Being a little bit older during Granddad's funeral helped me cope better as I recalled that moment, but, had I been of the same frame of mind, I would have thought him to be going in the right direction.

Ninny was a little upset due to my mum's grave being opened – it was as if her hurt was being uncovered. However, apart from that there were not many tears, except for Aunty Mary, who was genuinely sad.

Uncle Larry hadn't bothered to go to the funeral but back at the house his name was bandied around as everyone milled about. An argument began between Uncle John (Granddad Riley's eldest son) and Uncle Frank (his youngest son) and my uncle/dad (John Boylan). It became heated as John Riley voiced an opinion that he believed Larry to have been responsible for his father's hiding and subsequent death, but my dad and Uncle Frank defended the absent Larry to the hilt. As the crescendo of that row increased a voice spoke out; it was a quiet call, but it managed to reach everyone as if it were a scream. The speaker, Ninny, gazed down at the floor as everyone turned to look at her, and then, very slowly, she raised her head, high and proud like a queen dressed in black about to give judgement on an important matter. Her eyes were red as she looked at everyone as her confession rolled out.

'It was me,' she confessed solemnly, gaining everyone's attention. 'I'd had enough. He'd said some horrid things about our Mary and Peter and I just could not take it any more. I knew from his mood that he hadn't finished and would carry it on when he returned full of his stinking ale, so I took my dolly-stick and waited for him to come home. I waited in the entry over the road and when he turned the corner I just hit him and kept on hitting him until he was flat out.' She paused a second or so. 'Then I came home and waited,' she added, then cried, silently – no sobs, just tears as everyone stared. Mary hurried to her side to comfort her.

Who could blame her, who had the right to try? Everyone gave the only thing they could give to a person in such a predicament: blameless sympathy. After all those years of sticking by a man who had dominated her, ridiculed her religious beliefs, beaten and browbeaten her sons and bullied her daughters, as well as setting her daughter Kate on the wrong road, that night she snapped, but on this particular night none of us could see just how much of a relief her confession had given her, with not a priest in sight.

One out, one in! Uncle Larry's wife, my lovely Aunty May, gave birth to their final child, Stephen, not long after Granddad died, and I heard his first cries as I waited for our Logger to finish feeding his pigeons. To me and to most kids, something like that feels so strange – after all, it's just a new baby, just another baby to add to the billions already in this world. But when you hear it crying for the first time, especially when you know where it has just come from, like a comet it becomes a vivid memory, due to the drama of its passing.

Life, as they so often say, has to go on, and it did. As if following one another, Nora let it be known that she and my uncle Frank were going to tie the knot after Mary's wedding. Because Nora's father relied on her she decided to stay living there after they married. This would leave Ninny on her own, so Aunty Anne said we would move in, which we did. Oh, it was heaven for Mum and Dad not having to climb all of those stairs after work. And as for me, well, it was as if I had completed a full circle: 8a had been the very first house that I was taken to upon leaving Walton Hospital after my birth in 1943. It had also been my first home and many-times stopover, and now I was back after all that travelling and trauma.

The sleeping arrangements were a bit tight: Mum and Dad got Granddad's old room facing the front door, Annie snuck in with Ninny to the right of my parents' room and Johnny and I shared Uncle Frank's old room immediately to the right as you walked in. Although our dead had all been laid out in that house there were never any qualms about haunting or suchlike. I loved that move.

CHAPTER 5

ANNIE'S BIG WEDDING AND THE BOOKIES' WAY OF LIFE

We hadn't been staying at Ninny's long when our Annie planned to get married. Annie was the eldest of Aunty Ann's two children (Johnny was her junior by two years). When I became adopted, they were far older than I, so Johnny was more like an uncle. Annie hadn't really liked moving from Melrose House and – I think – because of that resented me a little, for it was indirectly my fault. She never ever said it outright but I could tell that I was, and always would be, only her cousin. Anyway, she had taken up with this fella from 'over the bridge' by the name of Davey Doran, whose father was a bookmaker. At that time bookies were an illegal bunch but very popular due to their being able to accommodate the wishful thoughts of punters.

'Over the bridge' meant on the dock side of the Liverpool-to-Leeds canal, which cut a line from Tate & Lyle's sugar factory all the way out of north Liverpool at a distance of approximately half a mile at the beginning, where it came out of the docks, up to two miles away from the docks at the Seaforth end, where it turned and veered out into the country via Litherland and Ford before heading off towards Yorkshire via Wigan and other coalmining communities before reaching Leeds. The saying 'over the bridge' was in frequent use by the dockers and dockland workers because they all had to cross the canal to get to work, so it became a main point of reference. There were not many houses on the other side of that canal but those who did live in the vicinity were always said to be from 'over the bridge' and were mainly of Irish descent.

The Steel Street Gasworks storage tanks were like ghouls rising and falling to give light or shadow to Davey's home and the constant smell of gas enveloped those streets just as much as daylight or nightfall did, but it was their home, and a happy one at that, as far as I witnessed it to be. I was there a lot after our Annie married that lad from over the bridge.

The run-up to the wedding certainly put a booster into our house. Every time I returned home there was something new going on or freshly wrapped parcels in the hallway.

Annie's brother Johnny worked at Lockwood's Cooked Meats, just around the corner from the Buildings on Melrose Road. It was there that he learned how to bone the meat before it got chopped up for making sausages. I found it fascinating listening to how they made sausages and black puddings and always wondered how the meat got into those skins. One day I asked Johnny to bring home some sausages as well as some bones so that I could make up a skeleton. At first the sausages didn't go down too well because he pulled them out of his trousers, where he had hidden them in order to get them out of his place of work. Mum winced at the sight of them being hauled out of that space where he kept his bits, but he merely smiled, saying, 'I've got me undies on!' Which, of course, made it OK, and, besides, they tasted good.

At first it was great fun playing with the bones but Mum soon put her foot down when they began to turn smelly, so the anatomy class was cancelled and Johnny was told to take them all back, but he put them down the bin tip instead. The poor bin men must've thought someone was cutting up bodies when they emptied the chute.

Johnny had also met a girl named Sheila, whom he was crazy about, but due to conscription he knew he was about to be called up for the army, so they were wary of progressing their relationship, even though they were still doing what came naturally.

About six weeks before Annie's wedding I walked into the house and saw Johnny and Sheila with her mother. Mum was in the back kitchen, making a cup of tea.

'Here, Peter,' she said, reaching for her purse. 'I want you to go to the pictures.'

'It's not open till tonight, Mam,' I replied, with a puzzled look on my face.

'No matter, here,' she ordered me, 'take this shilling and go to the pier head or something. Just bugger off till later, will yer?'

Those two final words were emphasised with a sternness that puzzled me even more, but had to be obeyed, so I took the shilling and walked out. With no one in the street I headed up to the Sassbar for refuge from the eviction. As usual, Johnny Butler was there, hanging around waiting for the likes of me to tap a ciggy from.

'Whatcha, Peewack, where's your mates today? What's wrong with your face?'

'Me ma just fucked me off – she seems to have a cob on over something. She just gave me a shilling and—'

'Get us a loosey, lad, will yer?' Johnny begged upon hearing that I had a shilling.

'You're a cheeky fucker, Johnny.'

'Yeah, and you're an ignoramus, but I'll wisen you up, yer rabbit!'

I came out with the cigarette but Johnny was already smoking. He could read the questioning look on my face, so quickly passed it off as a gift from a generous passer-by. After handing him the loosey I then restarted my tale, completing it with who was in the house when I left. I'd barely finished when Johnny fired off his diagnosis: 'She's up the duff, lad. That girl of your Johnny's is baby-bound. You're gonna be an uncle!'

And so it was, but wasn't: nothing was told and nothing said, just sad faces along with an atmosphere that you could cut with a knife. I felt our house to be one floor higher than it really was, as if everyone were floating. Annie felt zonked, her lovely wedding compromised by this seemingly pip-at-the-post movement, which would maybe take away the limelight of her big day. Meanwhile, Mum was devastated: her lovely son, she felt, had fallen into the marriage trap, the laws of which still had to be obeyed because it takes two to tango. The only ordinary one in the house was Dad but he – as usual – disappeared to go for a pint in the relative tranquillity of the Orwell pub.

Now I had experienced what lots of families in those days went through when re-creation dashed all hopes and aspirations of planning.

'At least they're getting married,' said Crippled Johnny Butler that evening when we met. 'Better than having a bastard to look forward to – that's when things really feel bad.' He looked skyward. 'Believe me, I know! Especially if you don't know if they're going to keep it or give it away.'

For some reason that brought Aunty Mary to mind – and myself too, as I'd been left with such lingering thoughts after Granddad's dying days. The following week I had no idea that Johnny and Sheila had been to the register office, when I arrived home to find lots of washed dishes stacked up on the draining board and a few empty ale bottles standing ready for the bin.

The room that he and I shared had been emptied of his things and, when I asked Mum why, she informed me of the happy event. As luck would have it, Sheila's mother had always been a thrifty person and made certain that her daughter got the money that would have been spent on her, had the wedding been a white one, by putting down a lot of cash on a house for them in Queens Road, just around the corner from Reece's milk depot in Wadham Road, Bootle, where I worked (as a matter of fact, their house became my first drop, and I would leave a free orange juice each morning for the expectant mother – without Mac's knowledge, of course.)

Johnny was called up into the army then, but, due to his scheming mother-in-law and his wife's excellent acting, he was granted a local posting because of Sheila's bad nerves. After his initial training, he was posted to the barracks of the 40th/41st Royal Tank Regiment in Park Road, Bootle, which basically became his workplace for the whole of his National Service.

That was the first time that I came near to falling out with Johnny Butler, who called my brother a lousy name because he thought *our* Johnny to be a dodger. However, it was our Logger who saved the day, as well as my relationship with Crippled Johnny. Logger came running up when he saw me arguing with Butler, incensed to the point of snatching his stick off him after he'd raised it to hit me with. Old Johnny was raging through spit-moistened lips as Logger tried to calm him: 'He must be a fuckin' dodger if he's doing his

National Service in bloody Bootle, when all the others are fighting those bloody Mau Mau in the jungle!'

'You've been in the army, Johnny. You know you don't have a say in where you're put – orders is orders, and you have to obey what the brass tell yer. Right? Besides, how many times have you bragged about fiddling the system and having it easy while "the mugs", as you put it, were being blown to bits in the trenches?'

'I got blown to bits, look!' Johnny protested.

'Yeah, only because that shell found your cushy job place. You said so yourself!'

With that, breached old Johnny looked down at the floor, his nonchalant attitude nowhere to be seen. Meanwhile, Logger carried on: 'This isn't you, Johnny. Something else is bothering you.' He put his hand on the older man's shoulder: 'What is it?'

It turned out there was to be a big shake-up for the Kirkdale Homes and it was looking like a lot of those Kirky-Homers were to be split up and dumped anywhere and everywhere around Liverpool. It was preying on Johnny's mind and he had become scared: those Kirkdale Homes had been his home for so long now. All of a sudden the angry words were forgotten and we were filled with sadness for this 'new' Johnny, who was sitting in front of us with tears in his eyes, looking vacant. Gone was the dictatorial Johnny who bummed cigarettes on demand and asked by ordering; to us it was a disturbing sight.

When the word got round about Johnny a lot of those hardworking mothers from the Buildings joined forces to badger the councillors, priests and vicars of the area. That got the holy, the righteous and the good-intentioned involved, but it was one of those whom Johnny had often decried who really helped him secure a special bungalow, which got him safely tucked into the norm of society and out of the helpful, couldn't-care-less grip of the Social Services, who ran those Kirkdale Homes.

It was a gay man known as 'Josie'. Real name Joe Dickinson, he was then aged twenty-three, a steward on the Cunard Line and a bit of a fighter when things became strained within the realm of human rights. For many years Joe had lived in the shadows of the Kirkdale area and he knew Johnny quite well – in fact it had been Johnny who had suggested making a career of going to sea rather than wait and be called up.

'The army don't really put up with poofs like yourself,' said Johnny on that day. 'And can't say I'm all for it myself, but your type are straight out as to what you are – you talk poof, you act poof, and leave no doubt in people's minds. It's them others I don't like – them poof bastards who talk to you like they're real fellas then try to hold your todger when you go for a piss. Can't stand 'em.'

Johnny didn't have the greatest of chat-up lines to win people over, but it was a form of camaraderie in the world of horrors and lies that Joe had to live in. Adhering to this advice, Joe looked to the sea for work. He was successful but stuck to those passenger Atlantic crossers that docked at New York, where he got to meet lots and lots of friends, but he never forgot the straight geezer with the bent body who had pointed the way for him.

His career at sea had brought him into contact with many people who had the same outlook on life, some by choice, some by chance and others who had been force-fed into that way of living as a child by corrupt officials who worked for people more corrupt than themselves. It was a chain of events that led a scared and harshly treated youngster into the clutches of a conniving, softly spoken official who was well versed in offering help, understanding and affection. Indeed, he was so skilled at it that the youngsters had no idea at the beginning that they had been trapped at all. Such entrapment had never happened to Josie, but, as time stretched its belt around his circle of friends, various stories began to collide and stick together, with the glue of truth binding them solidly.

A certain councillor's name began to emerge again and again until innuendo became a horrid picture of truth, a portrayal of the sickening violation of trust practised with impunity within the realms of those halls of power where the depraved councillors and MPs strutted their stuff.

In those days the fully initiated had no real meeting place, although there were various recognised pubs and clubs dotted about the city where supposed 'straights' could saunter in – and then show a look of alarm, should somebody be there who could point the finger at them as being a 'mixer'. One such place was the haunt of Josie when he was on this side of the Atlantic. It wasn't as plush as the dive he frequented in New York but it sufficed and gave him the refuge he liked when on Merseyside. That councillor (whom we'll call Eric), who had his sights set on becoming an MP, also liked the atmosphere of the place, and Josie knew him so well that the secrets he thought he had were like the pages of the local *Echo* to Josie, who had never spoken about vile deeds with him, but knew a lot of what he had perpetrated. When Josie heard about Johnny Butler's plight he felt himself to be in the right place and so he got in touch with a local villain from those Buildings: Snake Eyes.

Between them they arranged for Eric's home to be burgled on a night when the councillor was entertaining because this was a sure-fire way to have him flummoxed as to where he was and who he was with when the break-ins were reported. Consequently, the first few went unreported, although they were of great concern. Josie knew it was time to step in when Eric was at the bar showing all the signs of worry and depression that splitting couples usually advertise. Now the tables had been reversed and, instead of a harassed youngster being softly approached, now Eric was getting the treatment, something he fell into easily enough.

As Eric's tale of woe was poured out, Josie was loving it: this was a much better result than he had hoped for, especially when Eric asked for help. Josie was going to offer anyway but now there was no need; it kept whatever he had planned within the realms of natural progression.

'You scratch my back and I'll scratch yours' was the way that Josie put it when asked for help. In return for Eric's putting his weight behind a move for Johnny Butler, Josie would have a word with the bucks he knew from his youth to find out who had been behind the housebreaking. So, with the excuse of the pressure put on him by the women, priests and vicars of the area, Eric took up the cudgel for Johnny and came up with a prefab in the Kirkdale area, from where Johnny could still step out as he had always done, while Eric could settle back into his peaceful quagmire without the interruption of burglars.

As for Snake Eyes, he sent quite a few lewd photos of Eric with youngsters to various departments of the police, but nothing happened. He was really fuming because he knew that, if a photo had been taken of himself getting through Eric's window, he'd have been nicked with more speed than a bolt of lightning. It was a learning curve but a profitable one, because he got to keep all the jewellery and lumps of cash that he had snaffled during those break-ins. However, his dislike of policemen grew from that point on and his distrust for them expanded also.

As for Josie, he gained an ally who would be invaluable in his one-sided world where policemen had a free hand to plague those of his kind who did not come under the umbrella of protection that certain privileged people had. To some lawmen it was their only way of getting back at those they could not touch. It was a vicious, lousy merry-go-round that crippled the relationship between the public and the police, just as the enforcement of laws such as those against playing football in the street or a friendly game of dice or cards did. Then there were those like Annie's father-in-law: the bookmakers.

That way of life was a true cat-and-mouse affair because of the law. Some weeks Mr Doran would operate almost with impunity and would even take a bet from the local bobby as he passed while footslogging. Then there would be the days when he had to be on his toes and the 'Dixie' lads (or lookouts) he hired would really earn their half-crowns as the detectives tried hard to dodge the beady eyes and sneak up without being noticed. Despite my bad heart (more on this later), being a lookout was good because there were no strenuous moments other than having to shout as loudly as I could, '*Dixie!*' whenever a snoop appeared to be sneaking around.

Annie's wedding was like all weddings in the neighbourhood: the men would go out drinking the previous night while the women gathered in the house. There were last-minute preparations such as ensuring the house would be ready for the bride to be up and dressed in her room so that she could emerge like the glowing princess prior to the cars arriving. All of the borrowed chairs, benches and tables had to be organised. The tablecloths, serviettes, extra crockery, knives and forks that seemed to go to every house on such occasions had to be washed and polished up for the laying out by helpers who worked their magic while the wedding ceremony was being conducted at the church.

I particularly liked the various coats of arms and company emblems that adorned the cutlery, such as the Cunard crest and the insignia of the Canadian Pacific. People would comment on one motif or another and laugh at how it came to be in that collection. It was often said that the only one missing was a sample from Buckingham Palace itself.

The yard and street area had to be scrubbed and every bit of dog mess for at least a hundred yards either way must be cleared without trace. For this task the local janitor, Joe Mooney, was relied on greatly.

Once all was ready with clean curtains, polished windows, a perfumed toilet and a buffed-up bath, they checked the outside to ensure that the red paint around the border of the large inset doorway had been done properly. Then the wedding was deemed set.

I never gave our Annie many compliments but on that day she did look lovely as she walked out to the big, black car with my dad at her side, dressed in his smart suit. I'd never seen him so well dressed, as if he were going to meet royalty or something. The gawking gobs of the female onlookers were all yearning to catch a glimpse of the girl they had known for years but never envied until now as she walked out into the sunlight, the brightness of which caused her white lace and satin to glow.

A couple of years earlier my loving Aunty Mary had gone the same way but not so grand in the looks. That time I had dodged off with our Logger to do some fishing down at the canal, as I now planned to do once our Annie had gone. But Logger was bent on raiding the pigeon loft of one of the guests at the wedding, who rarely left his backyard unprotected and had a stock of prize Belgian Homers. And so, as the 'oohs' and 'ahs' softly wafted away in the breeze of the disappearing limo, Logger and I went on that mission because sitting in a church and having to be quiet while the drudgery of swapping vows and attending a non-Sunday Mass just did not appeal.

Logger only had one vice, and that was pigeons. Apart from girls, the odd beer and ciggies, they were his passion. He must have been responsible for half the break-ins of the local lofts, but this one was more than a mere dovecot: it was the local pinnacle of lofts and the birds were recognised – and spoken about – as top-bred stock. Often he stood and watched as they flew in large circles around the streets surrounding their home, which was facing the recreation grounds (the 'rec') by the Kirkdale Homes. The fact that the man who owned them was a family friend was far outweighed by Logger's desire for one of those birds. Like millions before him, he had well and truly broken the Tenth Commandment because he was so consumed with a craving for one – or two – of those birds. Two would be better, especially if one happened to be a cock and the other a hen. That way he could breed them and drop the original birds back to their rightful owner, no harm done. Simple!

As for me . . . Well, anything Logger wanted was OK by me. What's a sin or two between friends, or even a half a sin each? And, if God could take my mother, then there was nothing wrong with my helping to take a couple of pigeons – on loan, too – since I wouldn't get to see my mother again.

By the time Annie and Davey had kissed to seal their vows there were two pigeons missing from McGinley's loft and we had not even had to break the lock because someone had forgotten to click it shut.

'A doddle,' said Logger as he swooped in to pick up a Chequered cock and Blue hen, which he shoved down his shirt for safekeeping.

'Better than Joe Phillips' loft. At least there ain't no Alsatian to bite my arse!' Logger said, as he reminded me of the time when we were attacked by the big dogs in the backyard of Mr Phillips' home by Westminster Road Swimming Baths. That raid really came close to being disastrous because a couple of old Joe's sons were home, so, when the dogs were tearing at Logger's trousers, they came out and gave chase. Luckily, those lads were better fighters than they were runners, so the escape was executed without further problems. However, it didn't stop Logger's mother, May, from almost doing the job of old Joe's sons because the arse had been torn from his best greys.

The house was chock-a-block by the time Logger and I, his partner-in-crime, returned. Guests were flowing out onto the little yard with their booze, sandwiches and glasses of pop. Two girls of interest were in there. One of them caught Logger's eye. Her name was Maureen Cox from Boundary Street, Liverpool (there were two women of that name in the area and the other one ended up as Ringo Starr's wife). The other girl of interest was the sister of the groom. Her name was Joan and for me that was the beginning of a long and one-sided infatuation, but the only thing I ever admitted to was that I liked her, but always forgot to add, 'A lot'. As for Maureen Cox, when she wouldn't let Logger's hand above that suspended chuckling line where her nylons stopped, then he lost interest and sent me to nick a couple of bottles of beer from the storeroom in one of the bedrooms. We took them over to the pigeon shed to admire our latest trophies and applaud our success in acquiring such lovely flyers, which – we hoped – would breed and give us a good strain of bird before we let them go, knowing they'd return to their original loft. It was more of a loan than stealing.

Those were the days when invites to parties were always directed at people with talent: those who could sing, play an instrument (including the spoons) or had some kind of party piece. The stage for such acts was always the living room of the house in question. In our case, the kitchen served as the chatroom-cum-bar and the living room was the main hall, all 10 foot by 10 foot of it. In the case of this particular wedding (which went on for almost three weekends, by the way) we had the added luxury of a spare bedroom, thanks to the somewhat suspicious death of Granddad Riley and the unexpected wedding of our Johnny, where people could mingle and enjoy some extra entertainment without causing offence to any performance being aired in the living room.

Due to the job Davey held in a bonded warehouse, the stock of spirits was phenomenal, but it was all in lemonade bottles as unbranded Scotch, vodka, gin and other, rather mysterious, spirits. His father John had spent a fortune on crated beers, hence the length of time it took to finish it all off.

I loved it, especially the accordion music being played by Davey's father. For some reason, unknown to me, I had always wanted to play music but whenever I sat at a piano my hands seemed to knot up and my brain became a tangled mess as I tried to visualise the notes. All the same, it did not stop me from being mesmerised by the deftness of Mr Doran's fingers prancing about on that keyboard while the flat of his right hand pulled and pushed the squeezebox and those fingers vamped on the base keys to create the harmony of sound, which I loved to hear. Add all that to seeing Logger's mother, my beloved Aunty May, enjoying herself with Uncle Larry and the rest of the family just helped to make one of those happy times that settle in the memory, in order to be recalled to sweeten the more sour moments of life.

After that wedding, the friendly pull of the Doran family and the secret tugging of my heartstrings had me visiting Steel Street quite a lot. Davy's brother, Danny, took me down to the canal and showed me how he and his mates gathered coal from the muddy bed. Huge barges would be unloading into the gasworks after a long journey from the mining areas of Lancashire, causing a fair bit of the stuff to end up in the water, where it lay until the likes of Danny or other kids of the area dived in for it. No one bothered the lads as they dived for the stuff because the gasworks people knew if it was not cleared by the efforts of those youngsters then the build-up would eventually cause a problem for everyone using the canal, which in those days was a busy thoroughfare for horse-drawn boats and the newer prop-driven barges that plied the routes from the industrial sites along the length of the Leeds-to-Liverpool canal.

'I collect this stuff by walking along the railway lines down by the Seeky,' I told Danny, as we bobbed up from diving into the murky depths and feeling around the muddy bottom for the hard bits of coal.

'Ha, bet it's not as much fun as this, though, is it?' said Danny as he threw a few bits onto the gravel path next to our clothes for collecting when we got out.

'Fun? Bloody 'ell, Danny, I've got goose pimples on me goose pimples, me todger's disappeared an' I coulda sworn something swam up me arse while I was upside down, feeling in the mud!' I replied, as I threw my few chunks onto the path.

Danny laughed. 'Yer get used to it, Peter,' he told me before he dived down for another handful.

I watched as his feet kicked at the surface water in order to keep him facing the right way while he scanned the mud for more coal. It was then that I noticed a big rat sliding into the water on the other side. Suddenly my little penis seemed to be about a foot long as I thought of that furry creature making a snack of it. When

Danny surfaced after that dive, I was on the bank, putting my underpants on.

'Whatcha doin'?' he asked.

'I'm not taking any chances, I just seen a big rat slinking into the water over there,' I said.

Danny smiled. 'They don't come near yer. If you wear your undies, you'll have to go home with none on.'

'I'd sooner have no undies on than have no willy to put them over!' I replied as I slid back in the water. 'Besides,' I added, taking a deep breath, 'I just seen some girls going across Athol Street Bridge.'

Danny threw his chunks onto the bank then glanced over at Athol Street Bridge as my feet splashed the surface of the water. Except for a green Criddle's steam-driven wagon labouring across it, there wasn't any movement, but a slight splashing in the water caused him to look over at the other bank. There, stuck against a shallow up-post of an old wharf, was the carcass of a pig or light-haired dog, which had attracted a few rats. As I came to the surface, I looked over to where Danny was looking.

'See,' he said, 'they're having a good tuck-in over there, so your maggot is safe!'

'Yeah, and it's gonna stay that way,' I replied as I threw more lumps onto the growing pile before gazing over at the banquet being held on the other bank just as Danny once more disappeared into the depths. Such carcasses often floated in the waters, even in the part by Tillotsons' cigarette carton factory, where my friends and I often swam. It reminded me of when Robby Tully screamed for help when his hand had by pure chance become stuck down the open-mouthed throat of a dog floating just below the surface, being carried along by the flow as the current edged its way bit by bit towards the locks, docks and eventually the sea.

Lockfields was the place where the canal turned to go into the docks. Often there were dead carcasses, even human ones, fished out of there by the lockkeepers.

At the end of the diving we had a good sackful of coal, which we took turns in carrying, but the journey wasn't much of one. Soon I was soon gazing into the smiling face of my secret love, who, thanks to Danny, nonchalantly asked me for my wet undies so she could dry them on the iron door of the fire's oven. While quickly deciding whether or not I had skid marks on them, I froze somewhat and then I remembered that they were clean on that very morning so I handed them to her. Meanwhile old Mr Doran called for Danny to go to 'the Office' for yesterday's winning slips, so I went with him.

It turned out that the name of the fella they were going to see was Cabbage Jackson – he was the top rung of the bookmakers' ladder. After him you either went out the back door or into the canal, as Danny put it.

'He was at the wedding,' Danny reminded me, but so much had happened during that time that I couldn't recall anyone special until I saw him, then the memory of that ugly, fat fella returned with a bang.

The Boss Bookie had a booming 'kill-all' laugh, which attracted a few glances as it erupted like a jovially drunken king trying to goad his court into hysterics. But he wasn't loud that day, speaking from the top of three steps of his house and basking in the sunlight. You could scarcely hear his voice saying, 'Here, lad!' before handing Danny an elastic bound roll.

'Who's this?' he then asked as Danny pocketed the winning slips of who needed to be paid out. Upon learning I was the brother of Annie he smiled and then grinned even more after finding out that I was already a Dixie lad plus a 'basic' member of the family. He would need a trusty runner from the Buildings because he was in negotiation for the Melrose pitch of that two-patch conglomeration known as the Billogs, the second being Fonthill pitch (but that was not for sale, being run by a guy called Quigley, who was too set in his ways to change).

Although powerful, Cabbage had always gone by the teachings of his mother to 'live and let live'. If he couldn't have something fairly, he did not want it at all. But, if you crossed him, all principles went out the window. Through the Irish community, he had long tentacles and strong arms, but, like most such people, he was not immune to the ills of the world, such as being targeted due to his success.

Somebody had recently robbed him and taken his safe, but that was an ongoing situation, Danny told me.

'Wouldn't like to be in their shoes if he catches up with them,' he added, leaving me impressed by the aura and reputation of Cabbage Jackson.

Danny used his newfound knowledge to help Robby Jackson get a job as a runner for Cabbage, who laughed at the coincidence of their having the same surname, but due to Robby's disability he had second thoughts about allowing the lad to run so far and often with the betting slips. Instead he had him act as a holding dummy for the bookies so that, when the 'cops' came to nick the man, young Robby could just walk off and not even be suspected of minding the betting slips, especially wearing those leg irons.

CHAPTER 6

SOME PEOPLE, SOME ANIMALS AND SOME THINGS

Joe Mooney, God rest his soul! He was the man who hardly spoke to us, but taught us a lot just by being himself – quiet, diligent, respectful, reliable and extremely caring. I suppose you could say he was the concierge of those tenements because of the many jobs he did: changing bulbs on the stairs, swilling sick off the pavement, scraping shit from the back stairs and removing the odd carcass of a pigeon, cat or dog and even the occasional rat.

His black dog, Prince, was his constant companion and the muck cart he pushed around was his Rolls-Royce. He had a little cubbyhole on Melrose block; it was the garage for his pride and joy and the storage place for his brushes, shovels, spare bulbs and other bits and pieces used to keep our tenements clean and in good working order – or at least tidy and without dark corners. Often he would often reprimand us for throwing litter down or leaving a mess when chopping up wood for selling on, but we would never backchat him, because he commanded respect from most in those buildings, especially our mums.

A lot of the women liked Joe. He fixed the odd washing line, made sure that the landing lights kept shining, kept the bin chutes flowing if ever they were in danger of blocking up, and he was always the one they would call if hot ashes were tipped into the rubbish chute by mistake or as a result of pure laziness. We often saw him hurrying up onto the first landing with a hose draped over his shoulder, the fat end of which he would pass to the nearest householder and she would attach it to the mouth of the cold tap in her house so that a stream could be poured down the chute to extinguish the fire in the collection bin down on the ground floor.

Whenever we lads spotted Joe Mooney struggling with anything we would offer our help, which he sometimes accepted. He called most lads 'son' but, whenever he spoke to me, he always used my first name – it was as if he and I were friends. Often I used to help him when he turned up to clean the mess that the bin men had left after emptying the big main bins on the ground floor.

Those big, four-foot-high bins fitted into the wall between every second flat on the ground floor and were fed by a chute, which went right up to the top floor. Pullout openings to the chute were fitted into the wall between every second flat on each landing and sometimes, while lying in bed, I could hear people's rubbish landing heavily in the big bin at the bottom of the chute just outside my window. Often I arrived home to see a flood of dirty water running from the doors of the big bin, across the pavement and into the road, where it made its way towards the centre of the small roadway and ran along it until it disappeared down the nearest grid. My mum used to raise her eyes skyward for forgiveness after cursing whoever had put the hot ashes down our bin-chute; she couldn't reprimand anyone because it might have been any of the eight flats above who shared it.

The ground-floor wallahs, like us, had a separate bin fitted into the railings that formed our yard. It was the same type of bin as those fitted into the backyard walls of all the terraced houses in the surrounding areas. Metal lid flaps covered the bin, which lifted up for filling and dropped down again to prevent the rain, cats, rats or dogs from getting in.

Although dogs were not officially allowed in the tenements, a few people did have them and Joe Mooney wasn't one to report anyone for such an infringement because he was an ardent dog lover. His own dog, Prince, was a cross between some bitch and whoever's dog had caught her, but he loved him dearly. If you ever saw Prince then you knew that Joe was close by, and vice versa. Whenever he was working near to a house where a dog was kept, Joe would befriend it and Prince would appear to be its pal too. Joe would get on with the job in hand while the two dogs would have a sniff at one another and appear to have a little chat. Now and then, however, an occasional growl would be heard as if a disagreement was bubbling, but Joe wouldn't even look up from what he was doing. He would merely say, 'Behave, you two!' and that would be that. There was only one dog that Joe had problems with: Rex. He never failed to raise his hackles and bark like hell at Joe and Prince.

Rex was a kind of renegade; he didn't like anyone. Again, a cross of 'Bet you can't guess what type Mum or Dad is', he was a large black and brown dog, definitely mongrel or a new breed from the sky. He always showed his teeth and growled as you passed by the large set-back step of the doorway to the first flat of Owen block: 1a. A stranger coming into the square from Owens Road would be fearful because the growl, bared teeth and raised hackles certainly looked as though they spelled 'Attack!' However, Rex never bit anyone that we knew of, so the locals became a bit casual about passing by despite his threatening growls.

One day, however, we had to do a runner after calling a couple of policemen 'Dodge-the-army!' and we were being quickly overhauled by this bluebottle with long legs and a bloody great stride. Originally, we had been in Orwell Road when Joe 'Bullet-Head' suddenly got the urge to give out verbals to the two patrolling officers, but, when they quickly turned and gave chase, we flew. Up the entry, quick right, quick left, and we were soon out onto Owens Road.

I wasn't the worst runner but due to the narrow entry I could not overtake and was soon hearing those clodding boots gaining ground. By the time we drew level with Rex's house I was overtaking Robby but behind Joe, Mike, Mick and Billy, who had just taken to the safety of the stairs. Poor Rex must've been really mixed up due to the bodies that had gone flying by, so when I shouted, 'Fetch, Rex, fetch!' – hoping the bobby would think him to be our dog and slow down – I had no idea that the daft mutt would become even more confused and tear the arse out of Robby's kecks.

'Let that be a lesson to you!' the big bluebottle said as he brought his hand back and slapped Robby's protruding bare arse with all his might. He let out such a yelp that poor Rex wet himself and we all laughed as we watched from the safety of the second landing.

'Yer own fault for not having any undies on,' noted Mick Furlong as Robby showed off his bright red buttocks.

'Some commando you are!' Joe Keaney jibed.

Then we all laughed, but soon stopped as Robby scowled because he was angry and embarrassed and for us that was a dangerous concoction of feelings. Robby stormed off to get changed and we could hear him calling from the stairs, 'I'll be back, yer bandy, bullet-headed Tasker, Fishcake, fuckin' Nylon twats!' And not a word about 'rip-yer-kecks' Rex, who was sitting on his step and regarding us with a puzzled look.

This was the first time that we'd seen Rex look so docile and I pointed that out to the lads.

'Hey, this is a big change for Rex, he looks like he's laughing.'

Joe nodded. 'Yeah, look at its belly heaving. He's belly-laughing, ha!'

'I'm gonna get the bone off our leg of lamb on Sunday and give it to Rex, 'cos that's the best laugh I've had in a while!' said Billy with a giggle.

He did, and, after that first bone from Billy, Rex began to become a very quiet dog and soon a fat one, too, with regular titbits from us as we came to realise that all he ever needed was a little TLC..

One kid who was pleasantly surprised by the change in Rex's attitude was Robby Jackson, one of four polio sufferers during that fifties epidemic, who lived in those Billogs. Each time he passed the doorway where Rex sat, the dog really went wild. We thought it was due to Robby's leg irons and the clickety-clacking noise they produced as opposed to the ordinary walking sound of most people.

'Jacko' was the same age as our group and strove to run with us during our escapades, but those leg irons held him back from skipping leggers or climbing over the railway wall to go through the disused railway tunnel that we called 'the Seeky'. It was a popular shortcut through to the dockland area of Studholme Street or onto the footpath of the canal bank, which could take you anywhere in north Liverpool or a couple of miles the other way. South took you past Tillotsons' cigarette carton complex, where they made many different types of cigarette package – hundreds of local girls worked there.

The next big factory where hoards of girls also worked, the British American Tobacco Company, was even bigger. After that there were many small warehouses with barge wharfs attached and then the Athol Street Gasworks before the turn-off for Lockfields, which took the canal down to the docks via a system of locks, hence its name. Although the canal turned off for the docks, there was a 'cut', which carried on for a half-mile until it reached the gigantic Tate & Lyle complex, where the waters were used to cool some of the large machines within its massive compound. When the water came out of that factory it was hot, causing that part of the canal to be warm all the year round – it wasn't unusual to see kids swimming there in the middle of winter.

Lockfields was regularly used as a staging point for bare-knuckle fights at weekends. Grudge fighting was common there between bookies and other such men who were basically incapable or past fighting for themselves, but had enough money to hire a champion to fight for them. Logger's father, 'Big Lar', was often seen down there, especially when he was scraping the bottom of his pay-off packet after a trip to sea. The way Big Lar looked at it was this: I have to fight my workmates in order to keep them in line, so why not do it for money when I need it? His job at that time was chief stoker. Despite the many fights, it was rare for bad feelings to emerge from that bare-knuckle arena because most were believers in the Irish rules of such conflict, which emphasised fair fighting and the shaking of hands.

North along the canal took you out to the countryside of Litherland. You had to bypass many institutions such as the Co-op and Blackledges bakeries as well as many of the garaging yards of well-known local hauliers. Then began the winding flow through Bootle past tanneries and the Bootle Gasworks before reaching the open fields of Litherland on its way to far-off Leeds, hence the name: Liverpool-to-Leeds canal.

Litherland and the next little borough, Ford, was the furthest we ever went when travelling that canal. If we were to walk, it was a day's trek there and back. It was also full of danger, as you had to pass through the territory of the Bootle Bucks, who always seemed to want to fight, not that any of us were scared of those warmongers, but we couldn't see the sense in fighting without a bloody good reason so we usually stopped at their borders and, if we wished to go to the Ford part of the canal for fishing, got the bus out as far as Ford Cemetery and then walked.

None of those pursuits were open for Jacko due to his legs being in irons. It didn't stop him trying, though, especially after he had been talking to Joe Mooney, who told him, 'Lad, follow your heart. If you're hurting due to wanting to do something, do it and get rid of the pain!' And so he did. One time we were all coming back from a trip down to the docks and we found him struggling through the dark hole of that Seeky tunnel. He was as black as the ace of spades and as tattered as any ragman, but he was smiling as he said, 'Nearly there, am I?' We were amazed: he'd conquered the huge sandstone wall that bordered Commercial Road and the Tillotsons' stable yard, then clambered over another one, which kept you from getting onto the very steep, railway embankment. Then he had slipped, rolled and fallen most of the way down that slippery slope until he reached the entrance to the Seeky, one of four railway tunnels running under that impressive aqueduct-and-rail-bridge combination, which carried the Leeds and Liverpool canal as well as the mainline trains for Southport and Ormskirk.

Only three of those four tunnels were working carriers; they took you into the giant Sandon goods yard. The fourth, the Seeky, had been built more as an extension, to complete the span of the huge gap, but it mirrored the other tunnels down to the arched entrances, which allowed access between the tunnels while walking through. The Seeky tunnel was used mainly as a dumping ground for old cinders from the fireplates and anything else the engineers wished to offload as they cleaned their engines in the quiet of the other tunnels before being green-lighted to proceed into the vast expanse of that main Sandon goods yard. Sandon was the holding point for all of the railway goods wagons, which delivered to and took stuff from those north-end docklands.

Jacko amazed us all by having got as far as he did, especially through the 150-foot-long Seeky, with its many puddles fed by the constant seeping drips of canal water falling into the soot and grime of dumped cinders. Then there were the added dangers of old metal pieces sticking up out of the large soggy mounds like sharp spears. Even we, with our two good legs, had to be ultra-careful in the Seeky, and there was Jacko, doing it alone and for the first time – with leg irons on! He certainly earned the George Cross in our eyes for that effort, especially when he pointed out that he had fallen and rolled halfway down the very steep railway embankment and crashed onto the chunks of sleeper bedding, which consisted of sharp granite pieces. Out of sheer admiration for his guts we assisted him through the rest of the tunnel, then helped him to get up the other, equally steep embankment leading to the canal-side wall, which we helped him shimmy up onto.

Eventually he sat on that wall and faced the rear of Tillotsons' factory, which was on the other side of the canal he had just walked under. With his leg irons clinking as he dangled his limbs down that seven-foot wall, he sat, triumphant and smiling. In that moment he was the scruffiest kid this side of the washhouse – but also the happiest.

After that episode we did try to take Jacko to a few places, especially if we knew we would not be getting into trouble so there would be no running to do. When we took him to Formby, he found it hard to balance while waiting for the newts to surface for air, so he just stood down in the water, leg irons and all, and fished from that position. With his vitality, guts and determination he never ceased to amaze us. It made us wonder if, but for his polio, he would have been the cock of the gang.

Jacko's sister, Lilly, also had polio, as did two others in the Buildings. There seemed to be an epidemic of it in the UK at that time, which caused much fear due to the comparative lack of knowledge that doctors then had about paralytic poliomyelitis.

Another of those unfortunates was a nephew of one of our friends, Norsey Jones. The stricken lad was younger than our group and went by the name of Tommy Jones. His Uncle Norman (Norsey) blew us all down with a story that embedded young Tommy into the archives of our memories. It concerned a trip to Lourdes in the foothills of the Pyrenees. There had been a whipround to raise money to send young Tommy over to France so that he could visit the shrine of Our Lady of Lourdes. Anyway, when the little whippet got there, they readied him for a dip in the holy waters only for all and sundry to be doused in a lungful of resentment from the youngster as his five-year-old bellows felt the cold. He then belched out, 'Get me the fuck outta this, it's fuckin' freezing!' They tried to keep him immersed but he fought them off with the full strength of his little body, shouting, 'I'm fuckin' cured, I'm fuckin' cured! Look, I'll walk home!'

Most times Norsey was a terrible Tom-Pepper (a liar) but that story did match the type of kid that Tommy was and it got us laughing. We knew of little Tommy but hardly saw him for the first four years of his life. However, when he finally hit the streets and squares, with his crutches, he – like Jacko – made his presence known. There was something about those polio victims; it was as if their driving engines were bigger than most others'.

Little Tommy's father, also Tommy, was a fair and upstanding man. He was a fine boxer, who once stood up to the local bully known simply as 'K.O'. We once had the pleasure of seeing him fight to a standstill in a bare-knuckle battle at the top of Owens Road, just up towards Fonthill Road and beyond the Sassbar. The man he was fighting had recently become an in-law to that bully, so, when this became 'game on', the word spread like wildfire, because few would argue with anyone from that family due to K.O.'s influence. Tommy Jones, however, had no such compunction. When faced with climbing down to the bully or putting up his dukes, his fists went up. K.O. had nominated his new in-law to fight for him, making out it was the man's chance to show his mettle.

Punch for punch, that fight went on for ages. To us lads, all the toing and froing, coupled with the swapping of hard punches, seemed even and what had started as 'a bully taking advantage of a normal, nice guy' soon turned out to be two honourable men slogging it out over something they both felt to be right: honour. The young in-law showed himself to be both fair and hard after a half hour's praiseworthy pugilism during which both men gave it their all. Eventually they shook hands and departed on friendly and respectful terms. Even K.O. couldn't draw a biased note over the incident in order to declare his side as the winners. He could only stand by as everyone congratulated Tommy for having stood up to that family.

Even young Tommy got in on the act by balancing on his crutches with his armpits while cupping his hands to his lips and shouting after the opposing family as they walked off, 'An' I'll stick me crutch up yer arse if youse try it again!' It even drew a smile from his father's opponent, which to us showed the man to be decent.

For days afterwards old Joe Mooney bragged about having had a ringside view of the fight. He had never liked K.O., because he had once been knocked out by him when he was younger. It had been an un-called-for incident, which Joe felt had been orchestrated by ..KO merely to show people just how tough he was and how quickly he could demolish a man with a single punch. That punch had been delivered while Joe was ordering a drink from the bar after accidentally bumping into the bully.

'It's funny,' Joe used to say, 'but when a man sees no wrong in what he does, even though everyone else does, he tends to bring his kids up the same way. Sometimes those kids find a different route in life because of the better influences surrounding them, such as their mothers or aunts, but when the father's belligerent rule is instilled wholly, the kids have no chance but to follow in the same horrid ways.'

It was times like that, when Joe Mooney spoke, we could see that he was right, because one of ..KO's sons was a total prat and another was a semi-prat, but the eldest and middle ones were OK – tough lads, but approachable for negotiation whenever problems arose. All the same everyone was wary of them because of the tainted blood that ran through their veins; it kept them bonded and sometimes that bond helped them to ignore the rules of fairness and allow their liberty-taking brother to carry on without familial reprimand. Consequently, the lad continued to follow wholly in his father's footsteps.

I once had a taste of that bullying when I was seven, during one of those regular trips down to my grandmother's. The route from my house in Norris Green dropped me off at Stanley Park. I then had to walk from there down towards the docks via Walton Road and Westminster Road, and then down Orwell Road as far as the tannery at North Dingle. A block of very old flats stood on one side and Mick's butcher's shop was on the other corner of North Dingle. I would turn right, up North Dingle, then first left behind Mick's butcher's along a short entry, which led onto an olla, which had once been a bombed block of flats before demolition flattened it. That waste ground afforded me a full view of Fonthill Road and the Buildings beyond as a backdrop. The sight of it always made me smile after that journey: it meant I had arrived.

On a small square of this piece of flattened rubble sat three lads, all about the same age as myself; they were sitting in a circle. As I drew nearer I could see that they were playing marbles, so I paused for a moment to watch. A ginger-haired lad looked and then leaned forward and spoke to another, who had been engrossed but stopped and turned.

'Whatcha lookin' at?' he demanded,

'Just watching,' I replied with an innocent shrug.

'Well, fuck off!' said their leader. Then they begin to get to their feet as if the words 'fuck off!' were a challenge and their standing was an act of backing it up.

Still unperturbed and not even seeing that agreeing and going was the best side to common sense, I said: 'I've got as much right to be here as youse. I come by here almost every day on my way to my ninny's – she lives in them Buildings over there.' Then my innards began to boil, just like before you answer your mum or dad back when they have wrongly accused you of something, so I added, 'Don't wanna watch youse, anyway!' I then proceeded to walk off, only for my path to be blocked by their loudmouth, who just happened to be K.O.'s second-eldest lad, already known locally as 'a little prick', though not to me.

'Think you're hard, do yer? This is our olla!' he said in a threatening tone but not really looking at me; he was paying more attention to my rear.

Being a bit unsure as to what 'hard' meant, I paused to think about it when it happened: I received an almighty whack to the back of my head, and turned instantly to shout 'You bastard!' That unnerved them, especially the redhead who had bricked me, because he dropped the brick and turned to run as I shouted, 'I'm gonna fuck you now!'

Easier said than done, however, as that whippet lurched off from the olla, rounded the first corner onto Fonthill Road, took those first ten yards down toward Orwell Road with the speed of a startled rabbit, then turned left past the sweetshop and hit the cobbles of Orwell like a rocket heading for the skies on Bonfire Night. I was on his heels and gaining, with hope in my heart until I realised that he was heading for one of the terraced houses ahead and screaming, 'Mam! *Mam!*' as he went by.

In those days every door was always ajar and I was just about to grab him when he pushed the front door, slamming it back against the wall, and as he dashed in it rebounded fiercely onto me only for me to barge through for an uninvited entrance, and another slam.

The inhabitants of that house must have thought the war had started all over again, what with his yells and my curses vying for decibel supremacy to a peaceful life on this quiet Sunday morning.

He soon covered the short distance of that lobby, still shouting for his mam, who appeared at the top of the stairs as he got halfway up, with me halfway up the other half, but then I slowed as he disappeared behind her long skirt and she demanded to know what was going on, with him now whimpering that I was going to kill him.

Her puzzled, frantic enquiries were merely met with my shout of, 'I'm gonna fuck him, the bastard!' As I backed off a little down to the last step, the door to my right opened.

'What's all this blaspheming in my house on this holy day?' demanded an old lady, who looked a bit like my ninny with her pinny and sloppy, thick tights.

On seeing the blood flooding from the gash to my head, everything about my attitude was understood and the old lady began to soothe the situation.

'It's Claire Riley's lad,' she told her daughter as she put on her coat and scarf. 'I'll take him over to his grandmother's and sort things out.'

It was Joe Mooney and our Logger who took me to Stanley Road Hospital while the two women smoothed things over to avoid a breakup between the two families. It was then that I first found out about K.O. and his somewhat deranged second eldest, 'the Little Prick'. I got to learn about the bullying antics of the father and how his stupid second son idolised him. The first son was a bit of a tough, but much fairer than the father. Had it not been for the mother's influence, then he too would have been a bully like his father, but he did have a tendency to back his younger brother up whenever the lad was guilty of the sort of thing that he had done to me. However, I was too young to be a target for him, so I only had to worry about 'the Little Prick' fella who – I felt – was a gutless arsehole anyway, him and his brick swingers.

this voice drifting at me from out of the mist in my mind: 'Are you all right?' It was like a whisper, a very soft call. It went on: 'Little boy, little boy, are you all right?' I opened my eyes and focused. Ahead of me was a black shape: it was a car. The door was open from the front to the back and a lady's head adorned with a hat was popping from around the edge of that door, looking back at me. 'Are you all right?' she repeated, causing me to struggle to my feet in the hope of her offering me a lift. 'Yeah,' I replied, feeling a surge of energy as pride took over. 'Yeah, I'm all right, but . . .' I struggled to my feet and was just about to say that I felt sick and wanted to go to the station when she said, 'OK,' closed her door and then drove off, followed by the sound of my mumbling: 'Bastard, tight bastard!' I thought of what my ninny or any of those women from the Buildings would have done in her place: they would at least have come over to check because you just do not see kids lying on the side of the road without there being a reason.

After that it was all a blur – a hazy, horrible blur – as I struggled to put one foot in front of the other, lying down, picking myself up again, resting against something hard and then moving on and on, and ever so slowly on. Finally a man pointed at me, saying, 'There, son, that's it just there. Do you need help?'

'No, thank you,' says I before heading for the place he says is the train station even though it does not look like Town Green and Aughton.

The man in black coarse trousers with his little black waistcoat and hat looks at me strangely as I ask, 'Kirkdale station?' He nods and points at the train on his platform: it's a Dick Barton waiting to be boarded but I find it too hard to turn the handle. Suddenly a hand lunges out in front of me and opens the door. It's the station man, who says, 'This ticket says from Town Green, this is Ormskirk!'

Ormskirk, methinks, but that's miles the other away. How did I get here? Then I look blankly at the man and shrug, thinking, What difference the station, so long as this is the Kirkdale train?. I try to focus on him. My lips move in an attempt to speak but nothing comes out. Puzzled, he nods and smiles, then swings the door to and fro, saying, 'Get yourself in, son. Get yourself in!' I doggedly do so, then flop onto the long seat and basically drop off the world.

Enveloped in a cocoon of weirdness that one might call a floating, bumpy consciousness, I am semi-cautious of falling off my wobbly perch.

I travelled that whole journey oblivious of the stations as they came and went but aware of the jerky movements, stops and starts. Then, as if by enchantment, I raised my head and looked out: an 'Orrell Park' sign was just disappearing past my window. Next stop! I told myself, then manoeuvred my somewhat boneless body upright as we hit the dark tunnel from which I knew we would emerge very shortly onto Kirkdale station.

Being there meant I was close to home, the knowledge causing a surge of strength that helped me open the door of that Dick Barton train and almost flop out onto the station platform, where I stood swaying while I tried to focus on what direction to go in.

Opposite to that what the train has gone, I told myself, then turned and looked. Oh! I'd been in the first carriage, which made this a long, long walk. Then I've got to climb up *all* those stairs! I thought. It was a daunting prospect as I forced myself to move towards the far-off end of the platform, blearily eyeing the doorway where those stairs began and wishing I could cover the distance more quickly, even wondering if I could make it at all. I was moving so slowly that the station man left before I reached him, not that

I cared because I really was past caring about anything other than getting up those steep and many stairs.

Eventually, I emerged out into the bright light of the day, drained of almost all my energy after that gruelling climb up the stairs. Now all I had to do was follow the dark sandstone wall to my right and keep with it until I was home. So often my father had told me that this wall was the longest unbroken wall and pavement in Liverpool – all one mile of it. Hell! The mere thought of that mile, which I had so often travelled without a thought to its length, was so daunting. But I *had* to do it, I just *had* to.

I kept telling myself this as one struggling step turned into another and then a rest as I leaned upright against the huge blackened sandstone wall and looked across at the Kirkdale Homes. The words 'so near and yet so far' had never been more fitting. Then I began wishing I could wave to my mum, who worked there, and that she would come and take me home. But she was on the other side of that huge Victorian complex.

I am on my own and I have to do this alone, I thought. *Have* to!

Finally, the Billogs, there, facing me. The beginning of the service road, the olla beyond, the beginning of the washhouse at the end of that olla, and then, opposite that . . . my house!

The landings, the stairs, I can see it all now. Over there . . . *Got* to get there!

I rested my back against the big wall that had been the ensuring guide for this mile-long leg of my journey before summoning up every ounce of my strength and then . . . *push*! Oblivious of the screeching of brakes, a horn blowing and somebody shouting obscenities, I staggered across the road like a first-time drunk, knowing only the direction he has to go: straight onto the service road, which took me right to my door. Through the door, bear right, second doorway my and Ninny's room, then flop onto Ninny's bed – Ninny's big soft bed! Get between the sheets, rest head on those lovely sinking pillows – clothes, shoes and all.

The fact that I had now made it home released all of the holds that I had gripped onto in order to get me there. Letting go of that determination caused a fall into the oblivion of deep unconsciousness where dreams or thoughts just do not materialise.

In vain Ninny had tried to wake me.

The doctor was called for.

Ambulance sent for.

Hospital . . . Rheumatic fever.

Then Olive Mount specialist unit for months and months, the highlights of that time being the visits from my brother Johnny, our Logger and some of the lads and, much to my surprise, Mac the milkman and his boss, Johnny Parkes.

A fight with a boy who's been there longer than I have, who thinks, due to that fact, he's the Boss. Wrong, he ain't my boss. He gets a black eye; he is deemed to be sicker than I, so I'm kicked out. I now have to attend Alder Hey as an outpatient, where I must face a pep talk.

Me, all dressed up in my Sunday's; embarrassed Mum and sister Annie next to me; doctor in chair at his big desk; all of us facing him.

He starts: 'Listen, Peter, you are ill. You have a heart murmur, which means that a valve doesn't work properly in your heart. That other boy also has one but his murmur is much more severe than yours, which is why you could not stay in Olive Mount. We will give you medication that you must take every day. You cannot exert yourself *at all*! That means no running, swimming, riding your bike, climbing or exercising in any way, which means you cannot do the milk round, either!'

In that moment my world crashed; my mind seemed to become a kaleidoscope of the words 'no', 'none', 'swim' and 'run'. As someone handed me a large, circular container of pills, my hand barely fitted around it. I looked down through the orange Perspex at the contents, all tightly packed together. This was my life now – daily doses of pills, no running, cycling, swimming and no more milk round. I might as well be dead, I thought as we walked down that long, long corridor at Alder Hey. It was all bleary as tears formed in my eyes; I could hear my mum going on and on about what the doctor had said. Then I snapped as she said, 'Don't forget now, the doctor said—'

But, before she could repeat any more, I shouted, 'Fuck the doctor!' Then turned and threw those pills right back down the long lobby at Alder Hey Hospital and watched as the bottle turned and swirling in velvety slow motion, before crashing to the floor, where it burst open and released pills into a bouncing stampede of flibbertigibbets that seemed to jump, spring and fly in all directions to the tune of my poor mother's cries of surprise. All this on top of having been thrown out of Olive Mount Hospital, it was just too much for her. She screamed out my name and made the sign of the cross as if to say, 'Forgive me, Lord, while I kill the little bastard!' But I was off. I had really done it now, so off I ran, into oblivion.

I have often tried to remember what I did then but, try as I might, those few hours have always been a blank to me and their absence in my memory will, I feel, go with me to my grave.

It was late when I finally did arrive home, that I do know, but where I'd been I had no idea, so I could not tell anyone. After that it was a downhill slope for my feelings, especially when I turned up at

Wadham Road, only to be told by Mac to go home. He looked really sad but I still hated him for it. In fact I began to hate everything and everybody and even called the priest fit to burn.

I became Peter No Mates due to not being able to keep up with the antics of my friends. Even our Logger had to shrug when I asked him if I could go along with them to the canal. That, I think, was the moment when I lost it. As I turned to go, I felt so rejected. I had tears in my eyes and could see no future in being useless. I walked through the opener and smiled at Rex as I went, then stepped onto the little service road and stopped. To my right, 2a, Mrs Johnson's, and above that all of those landings: the top, No. 2e, where I used to live, next to Mick Kinsella. On the opposite side all the landings of Stanley Block and straight ahead the washhouse. There I was, all of thirteen years of age, choosing my place to die.

I began to run – well, trot, really – around and around that inner circle of road until the sweat began to trickle from me. The doctor had said that any exertion could kill me and, as there seemed nothing for me to live for, I decided to run myself into the grave. Around and around that arena I travelled, again and again until people began to come out and watch. I took off my coat and threw it against the wall of the washhouse as I went, then my shirt followed, and I ran on and on in my vest. More people appeared on the landings; some would go in and then reappear some time later as if to say, 'Is he still at it?'

I began to wonder just how long it would take for this illness to chop me down due to exhaustion or whatever it was that it did, as I completed yet another lap, but I wasn't even feeling peaky. However, I was feeling knackered after two hours of galumphing that concrete circle, and started to feel that those doctors had lied to me. Maybe they haven't lied, maybe they've just made a mistake, I told myself as night began to creep in. Then, just as I was near to feeling lost as to what more to do, our Logger came jogging beside me with, 'What the fuck you doin', Nylon?'

When I replied, 'Trying to kill myself!' he stopped and burst out laughing, which caused me to stop and demand to know why he was laughing, because I was being serious, but our Logger laughed like this only when people were being stupid or they had made daft mistakes. Sure enough, he came out with it: 'Yer daft cunt, yer can't kill yourself by running! Fuckin' hell, Nylon lad, where the fuck did yer get that idea?'

I'd have argued with him before I started that run, especially because my mam had been there when the doctor had said all those things, but now that I'd done all of that and was sweated down to my shoes it all seemed futile or, as Logger put it, 'fuckin' stupid'. However, at my very next doctor's appointment I was sent straight to Walton Hospital in an ambulance, where they admitted me just as soon as I got there: my heart had taken a hammering but they didn't know why. My doctor thought it had been a natural deterioration hence his emergency actions, but when they found out what I had done they really tried to get me to realise that I had forced my heart into such a bad state that it would be highly probable that I would end up in a wheelchair, even if I were to adhere to all of their demands and curb my rashness.

I agreed to do so and at the time felt that I would adhere to them, but began to behave rashly even while I was in that hospital. Because I could not go to the kids' hospital because of the fight I'd been in at Olive Mount, I was allowed to stay in the adult ward at Walton Hospital instead. I was not confined to bed as in Olive Mount, but I had to restrict my activities to slow movements. Most of the men in there were bedbound because of operations and I soon found myself helping out by being a general runaround for them. How

I wallowed in the courtesies of those grateful men as I ran their errands but, when one ornery fella began ordering me round is if I were the ward's skivvy, I took umbrage and told him where to go.

Mum shook her head and blessed herself as she took me home in disgrace for the second time. 'I can't believe you've been barred from another hospital,' she told me.

After that, I was allowed to go anywhere and do anything that I wanted, but Mac still refused to allow me to help him because he understood just how ill I was. The doctors had basically given up on me and my mum didn't have the time or the inclination to follow me around and correct my stupidity. By now our Johnny had gone into the army but our Logger acted like the big brother and tried to dissuade me from acting stupid. Even then, he gave up keeping me on that tight lead, which he knew to be – metaphorically – strangling me. So he had a word with the lads to try to take it easy whenever I was with them. That put me back in the saddle of roaming but not as much, because occasionally the lads began to meet up elsewhere when they knew they were heading for places that they might have to run from.

I could, and did, run, but in time became increasingly breathless. First, after a long chase and then after a hundred-yarder and finally after fifty, I was puffing and blowing as if I'd done a mile. To top that, I began feeling weak after exertion. It was then that the doctor's words really began to strike home. However, that was two years hence and in the meantime I remained a disbeliever as to my purported condition. Even the lads came to be thinking that maybe the doctors could be wrong, and so, after three months, things got back to normal with them. I still wasn't allowed to continue as Mac's helper though, and my family constantly worried.

Due to the lads bunking off from me now and then, I began

filling in my idle hours with one of Mare'O's brothers, Bow, and his constant companion, Tommy Connor. They were a pair of reckless, feckless and careless individuals, who took each day as it came and whatever was loose enough to carry.

Both Ninny's and my mum's eyes shot skyward as their right hands burned the sign of the cross on their bodies on seeing those lads call for me regularly. Unlike my other friends, Bow and co. didn't stop to weigh up the consequences of deeds that could be dangerous, dishonest or downright dippy – if it looked OK, it was. It soon became apparent that we had to have two ways of getting to a place but four for coming away, if we were to stay out of the vengeful clutches of those who didn't share the same points of view as ourselves.

'If it can move, it doesn't belong to anyone' was Bow's philosophy, and Tommy totally agreed, as they often carted off one trophy or another to be sold to the highest bidder or given away for a loosey, if no bidder could be quickly found. They were moochers – some thought of Viking descent – which Tommy could carry off due to his size, but Bow would have to pass for the Long Boat's Jack Russell. A deft dog he turned out to be, though for it was Bow who often sniffed out the booty with which Tommy was laden down for the trip home after a day's such mooching.

My previous trespasses on the docks had opened many doors and now I was learning how the offices opened and where the booty lay. Jumping from wood pile to wood pile and swinging from rafters was apparently for the mugs because no money could be made from playing around. Fun, to this pair, was the eventual escape after a hairy chase that could well have ended in their death or serious injury because the alternative was to be nabbed and locked up, which in itself meant an appearance before the magistrate and – this was the real bit they hated about such happenings – a public caning by our headmaster, Mr Taylor, for giving the school a bad name.

We began to venture into the city, which was dotted with busy islands – places that could have broken off and floated up from the docks such as the Fish Market almost facing Lime Street, Caszenou Street general vegetable market and the fruit market in Victoria Street. It was in those places that I first met up with the other kinds of Scallywags that my Ninny would call 'rogues', 'ruffians' or even 'little bastards' – those whose principles began with 'self' and ended with the same. Those townies would nick purses and brag about breaking into people's houses. It was then that I learned that there were a few types of stealing:

1. Stealing from those who just cannot afford to lose it, which cuts the victim almost to the bone.

2. Stealing from someone who misses it but doesn't pull his hair out in anguish. And finally . . .

3. Stealing from those who just don't know what is missing until a stock check is viewed and, even so, they merely shrug before writing it off as a loss.

The thin line of moral fortitude of those rogues made me realise that they didn't care who it was that they stole from and I found myself disliking them because they gave the impression that they would rob the eyes out of your head and then sneak back for the sockets one day. Their totally insensitive attitude towards people was an affront to all the principles that my family had tried to instil in me, so much so that I just did not like to be in their company.

Bow shrugged when I brought it up: 'Can't say I like them much myself, but they know the town better than we do and there's more to be made in town than from by our house or down by the docks.' His stance was understandable because he had long made up his mind to better himself, and the only way he could do so was to make money, for he knew that he stood no chance of climbing up any of the establishment's ladders to success.

Tommy agreed, and, although he and Bow had a thicker moral margin than those townies, they continued to mix with them because of the better opportunities that the city centre offered, and they couldn't operate without the cooperation of those rogues, and so the status quo continued. Not for long, however, because my first brush with the law came as a result of roaming the city, where the eyes of said law were everywhere and the vigilance of the people who worked there had been honed to cut silk due to seeing the daily misdeeds of those townies who plagued the city centre.

Those little prats who gave cheek would rob your most valuable possessions and leave a blind man without a stick – they were everywhere, just as we were. We dressed like they did, looked like they did, and now we were acting like they did as we sauntered into Wolstenholme Square that day in December 1957. It was not long until Christmas, when most people were thinking about what they could give, whereas all we were thinking about was what we could get, and those with anything that could be stolen were giving plenty of thought to how they could keep it. The bosses of those city distribution firms had well pep-talked their foremen about its being the season of 'grab-all' and the chargehands had instilled the need for sharp-eyed vigilance in those under them. Consequently, the wires were hot concerning our likes as we roamed around.

Being the know-it-alls that we were, we strolled into that square thinking we looked innocent, but the mere sight of us was an alarm in itself. So, when a case fell off a wagon at Dickson & Co. and then smashed open onto the cobbled floor, spilling out its contents of jars of pickles, we were already being eyed and I was spotted picking up a stray jar that had rolled towards us. Bow shot his hand out: 'Give us that, we'll have a laugh with it later.'

We got a laugh all right: we hadn't even cleared the square when one of the men from Dickson's came running after us just as two bobbies were coming the other way. Nicked! On 17 December 1957, we were accused of simple larceny at Liverpool Juvenile Magistrates Court. Result: a £2 fine each.

Mum and Dad were sickened. I felt so sorry for them, especially for letting them down. They blamed these new lads I'd been knocking around with – I knew that I was as much to blame, but I did get their point. I would have been better off with my usual mates – those Scallywags who never really crossed the line in such a way. It was that kind of talk that caused me to revert to my skittish friends with their apple pinching or 'finders-keepers' attitudes.

I don't know if God had any differentials when marking up the sins, nor did I ponder on it, because as far as I was concerned he was still the fella who took my mum and I was nowhere near to forgiving him for it. All the same the thought of a bolt of lightning sent as retribution for being too immoral preyed on my mind, so in a way my move back to the lads hedged that possibility.

When I was working for Mac I woke early every morning as if I had an alarm clock in my head, but, after being laid off, I found it hard to get out of bed. Consequently I was up at all different times ranging from early for school, just on time or 'Fuck it, I'm late!' I took advantage of the school not being able to cane me due to my bad heart by sauntering rather than rushing when the 'late' tag was out, and if I had an odd penny I would put it in a Beech-Nut vending machine on Stanley Road to purchase a packet of gum, then walk in chewing it just for the hell of it. The ensuing hundred lines didn't help with my English at all, because already I could spell such things as: *I, must, not, be* and *late*! As for those chewy machines, those oblong, metal-box vendors had a metal knob with an arrow engraved on it; when the arrow head was pointing towards you it gave out two packets, which was good to get because it meant that you could have one pack all to yourself and share the spare with the lads on the way to school or in the playground, whatever it turned out to be. Anyhow, wherever such a share-out occurred, you could guarantee that Joe Keaney's hand would always be first in the queue for a freebie. We were all used to Joe and his tight-fisted ways, so much so that it seemed unnatural if his hand was not there when anything was going free, even though we so often tongue-lashed him for it.

Soon after my court appearance poor Ninny took to her sick bed, causing our Annie to throw the blame my way as none of the family had ever before dragged our good name down. That made me feel so much worse and so to make amends I put myself at Ninny's every beck and call. I would check to see if she needed anything before I went to school and then do the same when I got home. At least that was until I got the feeling she was having me on.

One night I was heading into the house and just happened to look through her bedroom window to see if she was asleep but she was sitting up, reading. By the time I entered the house and shouted, 'I'm home, Nin! Do you want anything?' and pushed the bedroom door open for her reply, she was lying flat out, staring at the ceiling as if waiting for a beckoning hint from the Lord and not a sign of the magazine she'd been reading. 'Ding!' My bell rang, but I never let on, just began to back off. I would forget to go straight home or rush out in the morning without popping in to cater for any messages she might want. However, I did call in to say 'Goodnight' before going to bed. That was when I found them: those Bonamint chewies.

'Goodnight, Nin,' says I.

'Hey, lad,' she calls weakly.

'What, Nin?' I ask, thinking maybe she's thought of a new way to dupe me.

'Get my tablets out of that drawer,' she requests, indicating the top drawer of her tallboy with her index finger, which I go to. 'The blue ones,' she adds, as I begin to rummage – and that's how I come across those Bonamints.

'What's these, Nin?' I ask, noticing they look a lot like chewing gum on first glance.

'They're laxatives, son, very strong ones. I get bunged up now and then so the doctor recommended them to me.'

I give Ninny her blue tablets and then I get a bright idea about those Bonamints.

'Got a penny, Nin?' I ask, and soon I'm legging it along Stanley Road to the chewy vending machine on the corner of Woodbine Street.

Exactly the same size! I think, as I examine the two white pieces of gum in my hand. 'Good!' I conclude before swapping the contents of the pack that I've just bought for four of those from Ninny's Bonamints. With that done, I go to bed filled with excitement.

But I hardly slept that night and woke the following morning with a grin of approval for the dastardly deed I had cooked up. My recently lethargy had gone now that this plan had been born. I waited on the stairs facing Joe's house. When Joe appeared, I ran off and headed for Stanley Road, where I stood waiting on the corner of Woodbine Street until he could be seen before standing in front of the vending machine and feeding the slot, which I turned just as he came close.

'Bagsies!' he shouted just as I turned the handle and the packet slipped down into the takeaway cup. I made out that I was surprised, then brought up my hand with two packs in it.

'Here, I'll share this one with the lads, you can have that packet,' I told him.

'Great stuff, Nylon, me ol' mate!' said Joe as he greedily accepted the doctored packet, then hurried off before the other lads caught up and requested a share.

Job done!

Normally, when Joe's tummy had built up enough gas, it let him know via the usual channels that it was time for a release and he would smile and tap his friend on the shoulder. When I turned, Joe would wink and then nod and let it rip before looking down at his work as if nothing had happened. It was a general joke, which waited for its laughs until we were out in the playground, where we would laugh over Mr Murphy's latest attempts to try to figure out who had trumped without having the decency to excuse himself. That day seemed no different to Joe, who shortly tapped me on the shoulder.

I turned and looked; Joe winked and then smiled. I looked back down at my work, waiting for the rip that I knew would attract Mr Murphy's undivided attention, but it didn't come so I looked back over at Joe, who suddenly looked deathly serious and shocked. His face portrayed dismay like he had invented it.

'Joe!' I whispered. 'Joe?' I called again, only this time a bit louder for I guessed the reason, even though it seemed a little early for those things to have worked their disruption. He wouldn't even look my way; all he did was to stare down at his open, but untouched book. I'd never seen him so quiet and attentive.

Mr Murphy ('Muff') walked up the aisles, checking each boy's work as he went. When he got to Joe's desk, I watched closely. He looked over Joe's shoulder at his work and then he looked at Joe. Then he stood back a little and sniffed with his big conk as if to check his first registration of the smell that seemed to surround this pupil. One more sniff before he bent down and whispered something in Joe's ear. I felt like whooping out with laughter. Joe nodded slowly, his head still bowed. Muff then tapped him on the shoulder as if to say, 'Come on!' To which my poor pal stood up and my eyes darted to the grey material of his rump. Sure enough there was a telltale dark patch showing as he waddled off after the teacher, who walked straight to the door, which he kept open for poor old Joe.

The minute that door closed I broke the news to the class. Oh, there wouldn't be enough paper to print the things that were said and the jokes that flew around! Our friend, the classroom clown – Gilbertson – hurried to the door, where he spied through the keyhole for further news. As the giggles and funnies passed around, Gilbo kept at his station, raising himself to inform us that Joe and Muff had left the toilet and were heading outside the building. We all dived to the windows, standing on desks and chairs for a view of the unfortunate Joe, which soon gave us the best yet of this episode. Mr Murphy was first to come into sight, with Joe following, wearing Muff's old mac. He looked a right state, causing us all to burst out laughing. Tucked under his arm was a parcel wrapped in newspaper and that made us laugh even more as Gilbo said, 'They're his kecks, he must be bare-arsed under that mac!' Then Muff turned and looked our way, causing us to drop down out of sight but continue with the laughter and skits.

At lunchtime I could hardly wait; we laughed all the way to the dinner centre on the corner of Fonthill and Owens Road. For the first time in a long while I didn't bother asking for seconds, I just had to get up to Joe's house and find out what Muff had said.

I knocked on No. 6c.

What happened next sure scared the heck out of me.

The wild Irish father came to the door and glared down at me. Talk about anger, it just seemed to shine out of his eyes like Superman using his X-ray vision in the comics and I was the target.

Surely he can't know that I gave Joe those Bonamints, I wondered in a very troubled way. Can he?

'Is Joe in, Mr—' I stuttered.

With a deafening bellow he cut me short: 'Joseph you want, is it?' Then he reached out and grabbed me by the ear. With that tight grip on my appendage he dragged me into the house, shouting, 'Come in here! Come in and see what a shitty-arsed mate you've got!' Boy, was he mad, he nearly pulled the ear off me! Then he booted the toilet door open and pushed me forward towards the pan, which was shitted up to the rim, and there was a fair bit up the wall, too, as if Joe had tried to get to the toilet but fired off before he could get his arse in place. The toilet pipe, the wall and toilet seat, as well as the porcelain, were all peppered and my face was being pushed towards it all. 'See, *see* it! That's what kind of a mate you've got!' he growled as he shook me back and forth by the ear. 'Now you go back to that school and tell them kids what a shitty-arsed mate they've got! Do you hear?'

'Yeah, ow!' I replied, with a yelp that made him realise that my ear was still tightly in his clutches as he shook his hand. He let go so

I hurried off along the short lobby and out the open door before he could get another grip.

'Don't you forget now!' I heard him yell as I legged it away, relieved and laughing my socks off. If he thought for one moment that I would *not* tell my mates then he was off his trolley!

(Joe never got to know about the truth of the matter until we were eighteen, when we were drunk and I told him. I ended up with a black eye and was told to 'Laugh *that* off!')

That afternoon Mr Murphy gave his lessons as usual without any mention of Joe, but in the yard during the afternoon playtime he did ask Billy if his friend was all right, to which Billy shrugged.

'Dunno, sir, haven't seen him,' Billy replied truthfully enough, although of course he had heard all about Big Jack's annoyance from me.

Gilbo happened to overhear and approached Muff: 'Bad case of the wildies, what Joe had, sir, weren't it?'

'Don't know what you're talking about, Gilbertson,' the teacher replied as he tried to walk off towards where he saw smoke rising from behind the air-raid shelter at the bottom of the yard.

'Seen him walking off with your mac on, sir,' Gilbo added as he followed the somewhat irritated Muff and tried to engage him in order to stop him catching the lads having a sly whiff. 'What causes those wildies, sir?'

Mr Murphy turned around, looking angry. Gilbertson made him edgy – he knew that he had no control over the boy and hated his nonchalant attitude. 'Go away, Gilbertson!' Mr Murphy said before ramming his hands into his pockets, perhaps to stop himself from throttling this two-legged irritation. That was when he felt a Beech-Nut chewing-gum pack with two in it. He decided to chew on one, maybe thinking it would calm him down, so he put one in his mouth and began to chew on it as Gilbertson continued to follow him and talk.

'But, sir . . .' Gilbo' protested.

This time Mr Murphy turned angrily and popped the other piece of gum in his mouth instead of putting it in his pocket. 'Gilbertson, I will not tell you again! If you wish to speak to me about education I shall be more than happy to give you my time, effort and undivided attention, but I have no wish to talk small talk with you because you have no proper sense of respect, nor do you have the intellect which could hold my attention satisfactorily, especially outside of class time. Now, please, please go away!'

'All right, sir, whatever you say,' said Gilbo before he walked off, grinning like a gambler who had just fiddled a win.

Mr Murphy glanced over at the shelter but the smoke had stopped rising.

That evening, as Mr Murphy drove home on his scooter he said his usual prayer to the Holy Mother to help give him safe passage and was happily riding home when an invalid cart tottered on the edge of Sandhills Lane as if letting people know that he was about to cross the road. Muff told himself to be careful in case the crippled pedaller decided to go too soon. Suddenly he must have felt that he wanted to break wind and, able to do so without worry or etiquette of silence, took a big deep breath and forced it out just to see if he could hear the noise above that of his scooter's engine. Much to his horror he felt his pants fill. He closed his eyes in embarrassment and ran straight into Crippled Johnny, who had decided to take a chance, especially as there was only a little put-put scooter coming.

When Joe learned of Mr Murphy's accident, he laughed. 'Serves him right. That bastard took half a packet of Beech-Nut off me when I shat my kecks!' But deep down he did feel sorry for the man, who had suffered a broken arm and leg as well as soiled pants, because at least he had shown some compassion for the mucky-trousers episode, which was more than his own father had done.

Crippled Johnny, however, never remembered a thing. He had lots of scratches and bruises and a whopping great lump on the back of his head. His cart would have to be replaced but that would come from the teacher's insurance and so he eventually ended up much better off.

Meanwhile, I ended up back as Ninny's servant, but this time I knew she was not acting, because her new ailment was directly attributed to her being blocked up: her Bonamints had not worked as they usually did, causing an internal backup. But it wasn't long before she was back on her feet and things got back to normal with the lads. They were soon going out at night and, although Mum, Dad and Ninny were not happy with so much activity, they felt more at ease now that I was back with the Scallywags.

Above left: My Uncle Larry fought on the cobbles, and kept hard men in line for a living, but was no match for the acid tongue of his wife, my Aunty May.

Above right: Uncle John, pictured above working at sea and below with my Ninny. In order to adopt me he was forced to give up his work. I often felt guilty when I let him down by getting into trouble.

My Ninny was a pillar of
strength for the whole family,
and a truly remarkable
woman. This photo of her
holding me is very precious.

Left: I always thought my adopted brother Johnny looked dead rakish in his army fatigues – even if he was only posted locally!

Middle: One of my favourite shots of Logger (bottom right), taken at nursery: he has just pinched the toy gun from the lad behind him, who is in the process of turning to wail in protest to his teacher. Logger looks as though butter wouldn't melt. Some things never change.

Below: A very precious shot of me with my real mum, Claire, and a baby Diane.

Above: That rare thing, a snap showing not just one but *two* Scallywags (from left): Joe Keaney and Billy Vaughan. We didn't carry cameras and there certainly wasn't a lot of money to spend on film.

Below: And—finally—another of your very own Peter Stockley, smiling for all I am worth alongside beautiful Diane.

CHAPTER 7

RIP VAN'S TRAPPED LITTLE MAN

Although the seasons, customs of the area and quirks of life ruled what the lads did, they were very spontaneous, too. If something promised to brighten their day more than what they were presently doing, they would drop everything and follow that instead. The rewards of such a move were mainly monetary or the promise of love. Billy Vaughan ('Rip Van') had the hots for Betty, but had no wish to let anyone know of his desire to taste the fruits of her teachings. One night at the Hop dance hall down on Great Howard Street he got the nod and the wink from Betty and planned a little 'offman' (in other words, a leg-over or leg-it situation) with her, so he told the lads that he was not feeling too good, which, on the face of it sounded all right, because he had been a bit miserable; but, when they realised that Betty had also gone missing, they put that proverbial two and two together and the hunt was on!

Betty was a petite, laugh-a-lot girl who knew all of the lads,

161

ranging from those in line for call-ups down to the under-teens with the pimples, snotty noses and in-ground dirty knees, who had just realised she had something magical to teach them. With a mother who loved the daily juice and a father who preferred not to be around to face up to his responsibilities, she was left a lot to her own devices, which meant learning for herself and learning it fast. Once she discovered that she could make the boys eat out of her hand, she set about doing just that with her black waspy belt bordering a shortish skirt, which was topped by a very low-cut blouse.

Billy was just as hooked as the rest of the lads when it came to wanting the honey from that particular pot, but the 'not wanting to be seen wanting' syndrome that surrounded her had to be overcome via subterfuge. Betty had become highly adept at recognising the signs: the beckoning head nod, the finger to the mouth or the quick 'See you over Joe Dodds's in half an hour!' So, when Billy had whispered, 'Can I take you home later, but don't let them know,' she widened her eyes, smiled and said, 'Sooner rather than later!' For Billy, that was truly a eureka moment. After indicating ten minutes and outside, he then spent six of those minutes complaining to his friends of an upset tummy before scurrying off to meet his carnal instructor.

Now the fox was loose with the vixen, and, with the pack having scented their disappearance, the hunt was on. Armed with the knowledge of all the available dens, those hounds began their hunt. Their first deliberation concluded that Billy, being a creature who liked comfort, would want to be snug on Betty's couch, so that was where they headed for first by hurrying to cover the mile and a half before the amorous happenings could begin.

Betty lived on the first landing of Fonthill block. From the front, but at the rear (on Fonthill Road), her flat was at ground level and eyes focusing, then someone would feel their mental connections begin to join up, bringing with it recollections of the previous night's deeds, and the day's verbal sparring would begin. Someone would ask an impertinent question, then the denials would flow and soon the skitting would begin as those with the slower biologicals began to properly awaken.

By the time we reached Kirkdale station most avenues from the previous night's doings had been bombed almost out of existence, leaving the debris of those skitting dissections laughed over or as burning embers of retaliation to be furthered during the day. Normally, we would pay for this journey because it was not worth taking the chance of 'bunking' – losing a day's opportunity to earn some money merely for the sake of the train fare did not equate. So pay we did, then made our way down the long steep stairwell leading to the main platform, which must have been in the region of eighty steps eased only by a slight pausing place about halfway down. Easy going down but a bit of a slog when returning after a hard day's graft.

Of course the main topic of the conversation while waiting for the train would be 'Dick Barton' or 'Open Sesame'. The difference between the two types of train was private or open carriage. The Dick Barton trains were those carriages with single compartments, whose doors you had to open manually, and they had leather pull-straps with which to open or close the windows. We liked those carriages the best because we had the privacy to say and almost do as we wished. They were the scenes of some hilarious and sometimes daring antics that would have got us reported had they been witnessed. When I first enquired as to the names given to those trains, I was told by our Logger, 'Yer never see Dick Barton in a train where he has to wait for the door to open, do not been as my mother always said: thick as pigshit. All the same, Mac's little talk did niggle at me, enough for me to want a break because I couldn't get my head around that 'take it easy on the knobheads' attitude that he had tried to sell me.

Ha, it was like divine intervention! The pea-picking season had arrived. I asked Mac if I could go out with the lads and he reluctantly agreed, which made me feel a bit bad but, then again, I had missed out on the previous year, so I felt that the change would be OK.

Pea and bean picking were in fact a break from the confinement of the dockland, a chance to earn some decent money and breathe in the uncontaminated air of the countryside –not that we noticed that particular aspect as the smell of horse- or cowshit wafted up our snouts. We looked on each day as a trip out – those days were virtually our only holidays, as no others were ever on offer because the majority of families just could not afford it.

Such a day would begin the previous night as we slopped stuff onto two pieces of bread and then slapped them together like bricks being bonded by mortar. We would then straighten out a bread wrapper and fold it around those briquette butties until they resembled a neat pile. Just to ensure that the greaseproof didn't unroll, we would wrap a page of the *Echo* around it and then shove it in our bag, along with a bottle of dandelion-and-burdock pop or cream soda, which we had to be careful not to break because there was threepence deposit on those bottles.

The following morning up and out of the bed for 5.30, dress, ablutions, cup of tea and a piece of toast, then answer to the 'Neeows!' by leaving the house and heading for the noise, or, if you were the first up and ready, get out and make the noises yourself. Then the march up Melrose Road – it was always the same, that mile-long walk. It would begin with the feet dragging and the bleary throat but I fought it off and carried on going out to the fields. The morning it hit me proper, I woke feeling a lot better and joined the others for that lengthy walk, train ride and trek that got us to the fields. Due to the early mornings, the air had a chill, which I countered by wearing a largish, loose jumper that Mare'O referred to as 'a smock'. She used to call, 'Hey, Stock, where did you get that smock?' It brought a laugh at my expense but she didn't dwell on any one person and continued right through the day with chat, innuendo and funny quips, which helped kill the boredom that could arise from bending, plucking and picking all day long. Like her mother, Mare'O was a good worker and kept up front, with the leaders dragging us along with her, as we stooped and plucked our way upfield. By the time the early-morning chill had dissipated I was the only one not to discard any clothing. I felt sickly; everything felt weird.

At bagging time all I could do was sit and stare. I didn't touch a sandwich, nor drink my lemonade, and I certainly couldn't join in with the banter that everyone else was enjoying. It was as if they were there and I were somewhere else, even though I could see and hear and touch them. I didn't even have the strength to get up and resume work after bagging. Mare'O and a couple of the lads came over but I merely shook my head: I couldn't do it. I had to go home. I remember telling them all they could have my sarnies and lemonade and telling Mare'O she could have my half-hamper of picked peas, then I stumbled off the field and out onto the country lane.

Being on the move was a mixture of nausea, extreme effort and light-headedness. I would stumble along for a few paces and then lie down and rest within a spinning world of weirdness. Then I would struggle up and do it all over again. During one such stop I heard heavily or was out of work came to depend on that little godsend and could ill afford to give much of it back to her darling benefactor.

Consequently, the likes of Mike Kinsella, Mick Furlong, Robby and me had it easier than the other two because they came from big families, especially Billy Vaughan, who was the eldest of his clan and therefore, at times like this, one of the breadwinners. However, we fully understood the situation and never rubbed the facts of their hardship or our good fortune in their faces. Mind you, even though Joe Keaney had to fork more out than we did, it didn't stop him adding daily to his little stash for which he was renowned. It's a wonder he wasn't nicknamed 'Crab's Arse'!

Although Robby Tully came from a large family, he didn't have to fork out because he was second from youngest in a long line of working young men. However, his father made him hand over some money merely to teach him that 'You have to pay your way in life or end up thinking that life owes you.'.

The tediousness of a day's pickings was always soft-blanketed by the comradeship. It wasn't just us lads, but many times during that season there would be girls too: Joe's sister, Marie, Vera Marsh, Nan and Mary O'Rourke (known locally as Mare'O). They were but a few of the female characters to cheer up our days. Most of those girls were older, quick-witted, good-looking and extremely funny. – more like big sisters or pals to us lot than just girls. Often, their humour came from the fact that they had many brothers and felt so much at ease when bantering with the lads that they often left us blushing and without any snap-back quips because they knew more about the male side of reactions than we did about the female ones.

It was towards the back end of the season that I was struck down with a disease that, basically, threw me down and kicked the heck out of me: rheumatic fever. For a few days I'd had a sore thick clump of green dangly growth, 'is a vine. See all the pods on it, see!' he would say, pointing to the little green bulges that were obviously not leaves. 'These are what have to be picked.'

Then he would move his hands down the vine, stripping each pod as he went and throwing the pods into the hamper by his feet before raising the empty vine for his pupils to see clearly that it had been stripped of pods. 'This is most important! *Very* important! So important that you can be chased off home and not be paid for the work you've done up to that point. Make certain you check that *all*, I repeat *all*, of the pods are in your basket and none are left on the vine because that means the harvest is being wasted, and *that* is what we will not stand for. Remember, you shall be chased home if I find a lot of waste behind you. The rules are: stick to your drill until the field ends, don't leave any waste and no messing about!

'You work till dinner and then stop for an hour for your baggin'. Then till four o'clock. We have a tea break between those times but, if you decide not to have one, that's up to you,' he would add, with a shrug of his shoulders. Then he would leave you to it, and woe betide anyone who did not adhere to what he had said. We all knew – we had seen him chase a whole family home for leaving swathes of vines with lots of pea pods still attached, and not a penny for the few hampers they had already picked.

The average number of hampers filled per person in a day was three, giving you seven shillings and sixpence to go home with. Multiply that by five and you had one pound, seventeen shillings and sixpence – or £1.87 – at the end of the week. Less the daily one shilling and sixpence it cost for your food and travel, you showed a profit of six shillings a day, which you handed over to your mother and prayed she would be generous. Depending on the family situation, she mainly was, but a woman whose husband drank yer?' Logical, I suppose, but, then again, I had never given it any thought up until then.

As for the Open Sesame trains, well, those carriages were the ones we had to behave in because they were open-plan, which in those days meant lots of eyes and people to report you should you offend them. Not that we ever wanted to upset anyone, but, when you are engrossed in frivolity, you tend to forget the onlookers. As for the description of the train being Open Sesame, they were the words we used to say just as we pulled into our stop, where the automation of those electric doors caused our command to be obeyed.

A half-hour journey brought us to Town Green and Aughton station, where the rush to the finishing line of the farmer's yard began. Ticket 'clicked' by the disgruntled stationmaster, then off we hurried, especially if there seemed to be more people to be considered for the jobs than were on offer. Those toffs whose lovely houses dotted the long country lane must have cursed us at that early hour as we ran, shouted and joked our way past their homes in our quest to become pickers for that day.

It wasn't until the farmer gave you permission to collect a hamper that you felt at ease after the long trek from the train. That hamper was yours for the day. You picked your peas or beans into it and, when it was full, you took it over to the scales and weighed it. When it reached the magic hundredweight mark, the farmer tipped the peas or beans into a sack, issued you with a 'tally' and then gave you your hamper back to go and start over again.

Often you would hear the farmer explaining to the uninitiated: 'Each field is lined with "drills". This,' he would say, as he kicked back the vines to show a mound of earth from which the thick vine was protruding, 'is a drill, and it runs from here right to the other end of the field, and this,' he would add as he pulled up the first

It was all the same to me and the lesson I planned could still be administered.

How wonderful the coordination of the body is! Without any practice my eyes and brain had collaborated to work out the distance and weight the bottle needed to travel, as well as just how much power the muscles should generate in order to send those missiles into the air and crash-land almost on target to give the little raiders the shock of their lives.

The first exploding bottle stopped them in their tracks; the second put them to flight. Job done! With a satisfied smile on my face, I picked up the crate and hurried off to complete my deliveries. At least – if I was a target – they now knew that I was no pushover, which is a good shield against any group of bullies.

Mac asked me to go borrow a shovel and brush. He was a stickler for doing things right when it came to stuff like glass on the floor or my dropping rubbish because I was too lazy to put it in a bin. He didn't exactly tell me off but he did point out that it would have been better for me to have merely stayed by the cart but keep staring at them until he arrived back.

'That way they would have gotten the message that they were as subtle as woodworm in a cripple's crutch and pissed off. No need for the mess and no chance of hurting them, even though you only meant to scare them,' he ended up saying, which made sense to me but I had learned from bobbies who walloped you for being wrong, then booted you on the way. It was better than a trip to the police station or being taken to your home.

Mac nodded at this. 'All well and good, Peter, but a clipped ear or a kick up the arse can't cripple you, can it?' I reluctantly let the matter drop there, but would do the same again because of that brick-over-the-head incident, which could have damaged me had I

SOME PEOPLE, SOME ANIMALS AND SOME THINGS

Time is a great healer, my ninny used to say, but in this case it was not merely time but the many happenings after my mother's death that caused me to put that incident to the back of my mind, where it was buried by the deeds of Hilda and the hidings from my father, along with the fact of my mother's photo being smashed. They all covered that bricking memory, which was then patted down by my stay in the Woolton Vale remand home and the subsequent battle for me to be adopted.

It was Joe Mooney who caused the dust to be blown away after seeing K.O.'s lad hanging around the Buildings with a few of his cronies. I'd heard about him because his growing, harrying antics demanded to be told, but by this time the memory of our encounter had been dulled almost to oblivion. Old Joe reminded me of that incident one day when I was minding Mac's cart and noticed the heads of that little gang, run by K.O.'s lad, popping out of the entry that led to Orwell Road.

'I thought you didn't remember, that's why I've told you,' said Joe and then winked at me. 'Just in case he does try anything and you'll know exactly who you're tangling with. Not saying he will but, well, it's better to be safe than sorry, innit?'

Safe I chose to be – *my* way – as I loaded up my carry-crates with the next delivery plus a couple of empty bottles, then left the cart before Mac got back and hurried up the stairs to the second landing, where I put down my crate, picked up the two empty bottles and waited. Sure enough, those little heads that I had seen popping out from the entry suddenly had bodies with legs and were hurrying over to the unattended cart, but the one I wanted to be there was not: just like most 'leaders' of his ilk, he led from the safety of the rear and wanted no part of being caught. I shrugged.

you could see through the living-room window. Joe shook his head and then looked over at Joe Dodds's yard opposite Betty's bedroom window. Having scoured the horseboxes, the secluded yard of the dinner centre, the entry behind Logger's house and even Logger's pigeon shed before all the other nooky haunts of the locality, they'd more or less given up any hope of finding them. Nonetheless, they had continued to roam, just to kill that odd hour so as not to be in too early and have Mam or Dad say, 'You can come in early tonight so start making it a habit for other nights!' So they decided to backtrack a little as far as the Seeky tunnel, with its dark, dank, dripping atmosphere and sooty puddles.

It really was a wild guess for them to look for Billy and Betty there, but – as previously stated – it helped to kill the odd hour before going home. Although there was no sign of them in that stinking conglomerate of tunnels, Robby got everyone to sniff up like hunting dogs. He felt that he could almost taste the alien aroma of a lady's scent lingering in the air of staleness, and Betty was renowned for the stuff, which she used freely, borrowing the squirt bottle from her mother's room every single day. We then knew they had been there or had at least passed through. So where would they be now? It really did get intriguing.

Like five detectives, Robby, Mike, Mick Furlong, Joe and I held a moonlit discussion at the home end of the Seeky, near to the bottom of that very steep embankment, which led up to Tillotsons' wall. Tillotsons was a massive printing factory where they manufactured cigarette packages for such brands as Bar One, Woodbine, Senior Service, Three Nuns, Robin, Black Cat, Craven 'A' and Gold Flake, to name just a few. All packed and tied by females. Thousands of young girls and women worked there, packing the various products before they were loaded onto wagons or the big barges that used the Liverpool-to-Leeds canal to transport goods to the hinterlands and docks.

Although wagons were fast becoming the main haulage vehicles of that time Tillotsons still had a few horses and carts, which they parked in the stables situated just on the other side of the big wall at the bottom end of the steep embankment where the boys were discussing Billy and Betty's possible whereabouts. They knew that Betty's house was in darkness (Joe had already ear-checked Betty's dark bedroom for noises) and Mike Kinsella had checked the horse-boxes over Joe Dodds's haulage yard, but all to no avail.

They had to be somewhere – but where? Then, as if in unison, Robby and Mick Furlong both said, 'Tillo's stables!' and off they hurried. Now trying to race up that very steep embankment in order to be first to catch their friend with the sexy Betty, a few of them took a tumble on the slippery grass and slid back down, causing the others to stop, look and finally laugh as the ungainly managed to stop their sliding and once more began their clamber.

Joe was first up and astride the wall, where he leaned down to give the others a helping hand as they attempted their climb. Mick Furlong nearly pulled poor Joe off the wall as he attempted to scale that final barrier.

'Yer stupid Fishcake!' slagged Joe as he fought to regain his hold. 'This is a fuckin' arm, not a bleedin' rope!'

'Sorry, not used to this. And less of the Fishcake, yer bullet-headed twit!'

'One more mouthful like that an' you can climb it yourself, fatty!' hissed Joe.

'Sorry, come on, pass your arm down!'

Joe returned the helpful hand and drew Mick up onto the wall next to him then they all dropped to the other side into a kind of mini-alley next to the stable block. Robby pushed past me in order to try to be the first to collar randy Billy and – hopefully – get an eyeful of Betty's flesh, but the only couple in there were an old stallion and a even older mare, and one of them had just had a crap.

'Shit!' said Robby without intending a pun. 'Even Betty wouldn't put up with this smell. Let's go!'

When we got back to the Buildings our Logger and Joe's brother, Tommy, were standing in the opener, chatting and having a fag.

'Where you Scallywags been?' Tommy asked.

Joe recounted the night's events, causing the older lads to laugh as their own amorous attempts to dodge away from the crowd came to mind.

'We've just seen the little German sneaking up the Fonny stairs with Betty as we walked by, about five minutes ago,' Tommy told us, and then laughed as we all scooted off up the street towards Fonthill block.

Logger watched as we disappeared around onto Fonthill Road. 'Ha, they're like whippets heading for a greasy drainpipe, Tommy!'

'Doubt if the little German could grease that particular pipe, Logger. Besides' – Tommy pointed to the entry facing as an old man came stumbling out of it – 'there's old Black-Bob, they must be shouting up in the Orwell. He always leaves when they shout last orders.'

'Yeah, he doesn't like getting caught in the rush. Betty's ma won't be far behind. She gets one at last orders, then pisses off unless she's latched on to someone who's paying for her ale.'

'Hey, what say we go and sort of hurry her up?'

'Why not? Should be a laugh,' Logger replied with a mischievous glow.

The light was on in Betty's living room and shone onto the faces of the lads as they sneaked up and peeped through. Sure enough, Billy was there and although they could not hear what was being said, the lads knew he was doing a bit of bragging about how he had successfully evaded all of his mates and got her home without ridicule. However, for all his boldness he showed complete surprise and a lot of coyness as Betty threw him down onto the couch and then set about snuggling herself atop of him before proceeding to kiss him passionately.

Maybe she was aware that her mother would be due home soon or perhaps she was just keen as she grabbed Billy's hand and shoved it up her blouse. None of the lads could stand too close to the wall as they ogled the uncomfortable Billy and slagged him for his embarrassed caution. Then, as if that were not enough to have their thermometers boiling, she slid her hand down and undid Billy's belt and then pulled down his zip with the expertise of an escape artist. Poor Billy, he didn't know whether to let go of her tit and save his sausage or enjoy the moment and savour both. By that time we intrepid voyeurs were in the red and rising fast, but wanting Billy to make the moves that we were visualising ourselves.

It was bedlam all round, especially in Billy's mind as Betty soon had her hand around the throat of his pride and joy.

It was about this time that Logger and Tommy planted the idea in Betty's mother's head that she should hurry home. Then they decided to join the younger ones in order to get a grandstand view of the devilry.

Suddenly, Betty jerked herself up, but it wasn't to make any contact with Billy: her acute hearing had picked up the sound of her mother's key sliding into the lock.

'Get dressed!' she hissed, then fixed her clothing as she hurried out to meet her mother coming in and delay her a little as Billy shot behind the open living-room door, where he proceeded to fix himself by ramming up his zip and then – to the surprise of all – he winced. His face was a mask of pure pain: he had trapped his pride and joy between the slides of that fastener! Logger was first to realise what had happened. For him it brought back painful memories, but they didn't last long as he gleefully told us what was happening. Everyone else laughed while Billy fought hard to control the pain and still stay hidden behind the door, with Betty's mother peering into the apparently empty room.

The sound of all the laughter outside her window made her pause, but she decided it was nothing to do with her, and turned to go into the kitchen. But the devil in Robby caused him to knock on the window and shout out, 'Behind the door, Dirty Billy is behind the door!' Although she did not hear the words, Betty's mother did hear the knock on the window and walked back into the doorway, causing Billy to curse all and sundry.

Meanwhile, the group outside of the window were all shouting to Betty's mother for her to look behind the door, but, being a bit the worse for wear with drink, she could not hear well enough to decipher the combined shouts. She walked towards the window, which she proceeded to lift up, and shouted at the now-departing sleuths.

'What youse all hangin' outside of my house for, eh? Piss off, the lot of you, otherwise I'll be round to see your mothers tomorrow!'

While she was busy doing that, Billy was ushered out by Betty, who looked down and giggled when she recognised what he had done.

'Ah,' she murmured as she pecked him on the cheek, 'you poor thing! Come back when it's better.'

By now there was a steady, slow stream of people coming out of the entry, which led from Owens Road and Orwell Road, where the Orwell pub was letting out. The lads ran up to Billy, who was painfully trying to make his way home without bumping into them. Joe Keaney was now torn between getting home before his father and getting a few words of skit in at Billy, so he just ran up, calling back as he went, 'You were shit, Joe Mooney's dog Prince could've done better!'

'If you pricks hadn't been there, I would've!' Billy winced. 'An' what's the idea, tryin' to get me caught?'

'Get you caught? You was already caught! If it hadn't been for our quick thinking and knocking on that window, she would've caught you good-style. Bloody ungrateful git!' Joe shouted over the landing, with a twinkle of congratulations to himself for having thought that up so quickly.

'Piss off!' said Billy as the others began to bombard him with criticism and skits. By this time Joe was hurrying along his landing as he thought more and more about his dad being home before him. It was one of those cast-iron rules that the big Irishman had for his under-sixteen-year-olds, like a commandment: thou shalt not be late. And his deadline for them was closing time, which was then ten o'clock.

That night was one of the longest nights of Billy's young life, as he later told it. His home, 8e Stanley House, was a three-bedroom, top-floor dwelling with a coal-hole, larder, bathroom, kitchen and living room just like the others in those Buildings. Although not very nice for the mums and dads due to the long trek up ten flights of stairs, the young 'uns could bounce up and down them. However, soon after being left alone by the baying mob, Billy basically crawled up and felt every single step of those ten flights for his poor trapped foreskin seemed to object to every movement. Each stretch of his leg caused a painful tug on his John Thomas. He had so many tears in his eyes that he looked down at the ground when his mother opened the door. Thankfully, she was making up a bottle for one of the younger ones so didn't take too much notice of him as he walked in and then headed straight for the bathroom.

Try as he might, he could not free that poor bird's necktie from between those tightly knitted bars and gave up when his mother knocked on the door, saying, 'Have you fell down there, Billy?'

'No, Mam,' he replied, then picked up a towel and let it hang down in front so as to hide the skinny protrusion from his zip.

'That's a first, lad,' his mother said as he walked out past her.

'What's that, Mam?' he asked, thinking maybe she knew something.

'You, getting a wash without being told!' she said before hurrying in herself due to having been kept waiting.

By the time she came out of the bathroom Billy had gone to bed. This struck her as odd, but, with nine sets of clothes to put out for her children and the house to tidy before she made her husband's carry-out, the weary Rose simply shrugged and got on with her chores.

In the dead of night, with the bed full of his five younger brothers soundly asleep, Billy first tried to ease the zip down to release himself from that predicament, but his efforts only succeeded in bringing tears to his eyes. In all of his fifteen years he had never known such painful anguish. Many times he tried; by now he was cursing Betty for having pulled the zip down in the first place and feeling totally sorry for himself for having wanted to sample that sex thing anyway; but his main worry and feeling of creeping embarrassment was that his mother would find out the following morning, especially when his siblings would rise and see that he still had his clothes on – in bed! What a commotion that would start, and then she would ask that all-intrusive 'Why?'

What would he tell her?

That time came. But it was not any of his brothers who said anything, nor was it any of his young sisters, who all got up at the same time and ambled about getting dressed, queuing for the bathroom or nibbling away at the toast-and-jam breakfast that their mother had been up making for the nine of them. Dad had long left for his day's graft on a building site and was thankful to do so, knowing the chaos of that preschool hour. Billy thought he would avoid the bedlam by staying in bed, for he had a day off thanks to the huts of those in their final year being reroofed. But the simplest things are often the ones that end up sinking our attempts at subterfuge, and this was the case here: he needed to pee.

As everyone knows, when you have to go (especially in the morning) you have to go, otherwise life is just not worth living. Concentration is out, mobility almost ceases and urgent calls must wait until you have been. And for men, just so you are in no doubt as to severity of the situation, it reminds you by pumping up the pressure and presenting you with a stiffy that would make you feel proud at any other time. However, when one doesn't have mobility of all moving parts at one's disposal, this can become a problem, as poor Billy began to discover.

When the kids had all gone to school, Rose called in to check on her eldest, thinking it strange that he had not made an appearance. Seeing the agony he was in, she pulled the blankets back and, when she realised what was wrong, she helped him out of the bed and into the toilet, where they were joined by her mother, old Mrs Parle, who had come over to look after baby Brian while her daughter went to the washhouse. Poor Billy could only squirm with embarrassment as both women examined the trapped little monster (which wasn't *that* small at the present time), and then, in despair and fully aware of her son's situation, Rose helped him into the bath and told him to let it go.

Anyone would think that Billy had a shower-head fitted in his fly as the urine spurted everywhere: up, down, to both sides and all points in between. Then, it all met by the plughole for a final dash down into the drain, he felt the relief as the culprit of his pain shrank, taking away the strain. He was so relieved that he could not feel the pain of the piece that was still firmly trapped in the jaws of his zip.

The two mothers looked at one another and sighed their 'ahs' at his plight, then giggled openly at the funny side of it before taking their red-faced darling to Stanley Hospital, where he was set free by a buxom nurse who tickled his chin and made him look skyward as she said: 'You *are* a big boy, aren't you?' But, before he could answer, she yanked the zip down as fast and hard as she could. By the time Billy stopped yelling his dainty dicky was being painted with purple iodine and the nurse gave it a little pat before pushing it back into his Y-fronts.

'There,' she said kindly. 'If you always make sure it's safely tucked away like that, you'll never have another accident!'

We all fell about laughing when Billy recounted these events and were very, very glad it hadn't happened to us.

CHAPTER 8

WHEN GOD MADE WOMEN

September . . . Time to gather in the potatoes. Spud picking. This was really a time that a lot of the people from those Buildings loved, especially the women. It was bloody hard, backbreaking work, but the change of scenery, country air and the freshness of everything just enveloped them with a pleasantness after almost a year of drudgery. It gave them a break from it all (as well as big bags of free spuds) and most of all, a good few shillings in their coffers, which in many cases was sorely needed.

Those whose youngsters were not at nursery or school took them out to the fields, where they would play as if they belonged there, adhering to the country rules as if bred by them. Of course there were the occasional misgivings when a youngster got too inquisitive about a tractor or some other machinery, but a quick word from Mum about not coming ever again seemed to work a treat in the minds of most curious children. Playing about in the honest dirt and discarded, rustic potato stems seemed to satisfy those kids, especially when there was a field mouse to chase, a pheasant to throw things at or a rabbit hole to poke a stick down.

My aunt Mary had been married for a while and had two lovely children, both boys. The first had been christened Tommy after his dad. However, fate had been a little unkind to her because her second child, Paul, became a victim of those times when tight lips and closed ranks were a part of 'the System'.

Just after his birth Paul was dropped on his head by a nurse and the resulting injury became classed as cerebral palsy by those 'cover-up' people who ran their departments with vicelike grips of silence on all happenings and showed no conscience concerning the victims of such malpractice. In those days the words of doctors and other such officials were taken as gospel, so Mary accepted her lot with the fortitude of the women of that time and got on with taking care of Paul as 'her life's achievement'. Her husband, Tommy, a military policeman, was a loving father to their first child, but did not like the idea of having a badly disabled son. He kept nagging at Mary to have the child put into care but she was steadfast in her resolve to keep little Paul as close as humanly possible for as long as she was able.

She took him everywhere, even to the fields during harvest time. The strong arms of those 'hamper lads' lifted that pram onto the wagon and off at the other end. As the tractor ate into the field, they moved young Paul each time they moved the hampers. It was a good arrangement and Mary often tried to give the lads a couple of shillings for their constant help, but they would not hear of it.

The farmer's hand, Tommy Threlfall, threw in his help by ensuring that hot water was available for all Mary's needs, whenever she wanted it. All those little kindnesses helped her cope with the gigantic task of looking after Paul personally, each minute of every day, no matter what she had to do besides.

At the beginning of the year the field was ploughed from end to end with furrows, into which the seed potatoes were planted. Then at harvest time those long drills were split up into lengths of approximately twelve farmer-type strides, with one length being allocated to each picker. Spaced along each length were a number of hampers for the picker to throw the potatoes into once the tractor had churned them up. A horse then trundled down the whole of those lengths, dragging behind it a giant rake contraption called an 'arrower'. This churned up the remaining potatoes to be picked and thrown into the hampers. The hamper lads moved those hampers to keep in line with the ever-decreasing drills and that process was repeated until the whole field was harvested.

During the spud-picking season the ladies did the work day in and day out for five days, resting on the sixth (Saturday) in order to go to the washhouse with their enormous weekly wash and do some much-needed shopping. On Sundays they rested again by doing the Sunday roast, along with the week's ironing and the washing-up, as well as the carry-outs for their men for the next day. Finally, they would lay their children's clothes out for school the following day and then retire for a well-earned sleep.

Monday morning, they would happily wait for the wagon to collect them so they could begin their backbreaking chores for another five days. Hard work it was, but seeing them gave much credence to that saying, 'A change is as good as a rest'. Often the women looked revitalised each Monday morning as they waited to board the wagon outside my house; it was their laughter and jocular attitude that constantly surprised people such as Tommy Threlfall, the farmer's driver, and me, who often witnessed them in their chirpy moods. I knew from my own mother, who held down a nine-to-four job, just how hard they all worked, and most had large families to look after, too.

Many a time the women would get pregnant – outside of working hours, of course – but they would keep on working during that gestation until the last minute, or near enough to be back within a week, but some would leave it as long as possible and be back picking as soon as they could.

One such person known for working to the absolute limit was Mrs O'Rourke. That particular year she was nearing the end of a pregnancy term but braving it out. Her son, Bow, was in my class and we used to hang about together. She was a large woman, as was her friend, Mrs Connor, and they both had big families. From the size of them one would think it impossible for them to stoop and pick and stoop all day long, as was required to achieve a day's work, but somehow those ladies fulfilled their duties and more, even when they were expecting. In fact they were among the best pickers to get on that wagon.

It was funny to watch them board each morning, their big rumps being helped up by the driver as he would a cow up a slippery ramp, his leathery hands pushing on their buttocks.

'Oh Jay-sus! Give another push there, Tommy, will yer?' Mrs O'Rourke would shout, much to the glee of Mrs Connor. 'Don't know what you're laughing at, Mary Connor . . .' And then, as she finally mounted the wagon, she would call back to her friend, 'It's your turn to get your arse tampered with next!'

'Maybe, Rourky girl, but you're there to pull me up and get me outta his evil clutches quicker!' Mrs Connor would call back and everyone else would enjoy the banter.

My mother would often be out watching before she left for work because she gave Tommy Threlfall a cup of tea each morning and in return she would get a half-sack of potatoes every week. It seemed a fair exchange to both parties, although neither was asked for.

The big red wagon would arrive and park up on the olla facing Ninny's house then Annie would come out with a piping-hot cuppa for Tommy, who often had to wait twenty-five minutes or so for all of his pickers to arrive and get aboard. Another bonus for Annie was that Tommy would look favourably on taking Logger and me out on a Saturday when it was basically for the sons of those who had worked all week. It gave the youngsters a chance to see how hard their mothers worked and put money in their pockets that they would otherwise not have had. Nine shillings for a half day's picking seemed like a fortune to those lads who would be home by one thirty and ready for the football or any other thing to capture their interest and become involved in.

The rear of that wagon had a small hut placed on it, back to back with the cab. This had a few seats inside and was their only protection if it rained while in transit. It was a high-sided wagon, approximately five foot, the sides being made of slats, as was the back, which dropped down and formed a type of ladder once it was disconnected and rested properly. The pickers rarely saw it in its proper flat-back form without the sides, when it carried large loads to market or it was seen but not recognised as the same wagon due to those three sides being missing.

Snake Eyes was a son of Mrs O'Rourke, and through his mother had become a hamper lad – they were the ones who went around the fields accompanied by a tractor and open-sided cart used for tipping the hampers of picked potatoes into. Then they went to the farmer's yard, where they would weigh, clean and bag them.

Snake Eyes was a bit older than Logger but a lot less principled and had no compunction about using people to his own ends. He tried to model himself on the spivs of the war days but lacked the suit, shiny shoes and greased-back hair. Every other thing about him spelled shiftiness: his slanty, ever-blinking eyes (more an affliction than habit), his quick talk, slippery chatter and ever-probing questions such as, 'Where did you get them?'; 'How much are they?'; and 'Wanna buy this or sell that?' Those were his favourites. He certainly wasn't the norm among the young men emerging from that age group, who had not been involved directly in the war but had seen a lot of the misery caused by it, mainly the harsh poverty. Consequently, work was not his forte, although survival was. For some reason he had digested life from the happenings around him and looked on the fiddlers, not the workers, as the providers. As a means to that end work sometimes provided the avenue into fiddles, hence his appearance on the potato picking line. Snake Eyes looked on the daily freebie bagful of potatoes that the pickers were allowed more as a right than the concession that it was.

Of course I already knew Snake Eyes to be a manipulator with a fiery reputation and a large mouth to advertise it. Often he had taken charge of selling firewood and gave us only a ha'penny per bundle, whereas the usual rate was a penny per bundle for those hiring the carriers, whose arms used to ache with the work. He also had a harsh attitude towards people: snappy, belligerent and demanding. Sometimes he came across as OK and he could joke as well as the rest of the older lads – that was how he sucked the younger ones into doing his dastardly bidding.

Although heavily pregnant, Mrs O'Rourke kept turning up for her job on the fields and picking her length as usual but struggled a little to keep up with the others. However, unbeknown to her and with the collusion of her coworkers, the farmer strode her length to ten instead of the usual twelve. The tractor came and churned as the women picked and threw to fill those baskets, then the arrower uncovered the remaining spuds that were hidden just beneath the surface of the churned soil. The pickers would then walk behind the arrower and gather up those remains to join the others in the hamper. It was hard, laborious work, but the women found it fulfilling and therapeutic as they laughed and joked and discussed the troubles of their world, men and shortages during those tasks.

When the hampers were full or near to, the hamper lads would drive down the field, picking up the hampers and tipping them into the back of the short, high-sided trailer, then head for the farmyard, where they would be emptied and sorted before being bagged. Then the process would begin all over again, with one difference: the topic of conversation would be different. One time it would be football; another it would be a local but important happening; girls were a frequent topic; and so was gambling – the football pools, dice and cards, along with who had won or lost and how many times the 'scuffers' (police) had raided those little gambling schools. No matter what they discussed, they did so with a jocular twist and peels of laughter could often be heard amid the grunts and strains of the job.

Snake Eyes soon set about charming the younger lads on the Saturday run by cracking jokes and letting them think he was on their side by telling them about the pitfalls of the job before adding, 'If youse get into any difficulties then let me know and I'll see what I can do to help youse.' Not even realising that they would not need any help, nor could they get into any difficulties just by picking spuds, the younger lads nodded their appreciation, but by nodding they had put themselves into a kind of IOU situation of accepting a favour even though no real favour had actually been given. So, when

Snake Eyes came around with a sack and asked the lads to half-fill it with spuds and take them onto the wagon when they were going home they felt obliged to do so, even though they already had bags of their own, which were destined for their mothers.

That first Saturday Tommy Threlfall noticed all the lads with their extra half-sacks full but said nothing. On the second Saturday, however, he felt that someone was taking the piss. By the third Saturday he mentioned it to my mother as she gave him his cup of tea and asked her if she could find out what was going on.

I saw nothing wrong in explaining to Mum that Snake Eyes was behind the extra spud taking, which – unbeknown to me – was sold on to Arthur in the fruit-and-veg shop. To Snake Eyes it was making a living out of what was available, but to me it was being used. Meanwhile, Tommy Threlfall saw it as 'taking the piss' but not stealing, as no fixed amount for the freebies had ever been put to the pickers. However, he knew that his boss would certainly come down heavily on him if this free-for-all were to become the norm.

Mum smiled when she saw the notice 'ONLY A HALF-BAG PER PERSON!' on a large bit of card pinned up on the back of the wagon so that it was in your face as you climbed aboard.

Mrs O'Rourke was the first to speak out. 'Aye, aye, Tommy, what's this?' she asked as his hand butted up to her big cheeky bottom in order to give her that final help onto the wagon. She often took two bags home because her crowd had to live on potatoes, as did her friend, Mrs Connor, who had an equally large family.

'Sorry, girls, someone's been abusing the quota,' he informed them.

'Who?' she demanded as she stood, and then turned to help her friend across the final threshold.

'Ask your lad!'

'Who, our Snake Eyes?' she questioned curiously as her hand went out to Big Mary Connor.

Now the two biggest were aboard, the others clambered up that railed tailboard to take their places for the day. Snake Eyes, Tommy Keaney and Logger were the hamper lads for that day and were the last to board before the 'ganger' threw up the tailgate and locked it. Then, as he climbed into the cab, he heard Mrs O'Rourke shouting at her lad, '*You*, yer fucking, greedy nuisance! They've put the blockers on our spud ration because of you!' Meanwhile Tommy smiled and turned the key in the ignition causing the big engine to roar into life – at least his notice was having the desired effect.

Mrs O'Rourke began flagging towards the end of that day. It was just not like her to fall behind, so the ganger told Snake Eyes to make it look as if he was worrying about her and to jump in and help with the picking for the final hour. The sweat was pouring off her by the time they all boarded the wagon for going home, so Tommy took the unprecedented step of putting her up into the cab, thinking he might have to make a hospital detour. But the gallant lady made no such request and was soon cracking a joke outside our house as she clambered down from the wagon.

'Some woman, that!' Tommy told Mum as they watched Mrs O'Rourke waddle off on the arm of Snake Eyes, heading for those side stairs. 'She's got to climb all of those stairs now.'

'And then do the tea for them all when she gets up there,' added Mum as Tommy shook his head in amazement. 'We all do it, lad,' she told him as she turned to go in. 'The trouble is, you men don't recognise a half of what we do. Granted you work harder for eight hours and five days, but we work longer – eighteen hours for seven days!'

Tommy watched as Mum entered her home. She was right and he knew it. He waved as she closed the door, then walked over to his wagon, which he would have to drive all the way home, but then he would park the vehicle up and forget it, along with his work. He would have his evening meal put in front of him before going for a pint or settling into his armchair for the remainder of the evening before he went to bed. His wife, however, would clean all the pots and pans, do the dishes, get ready the clean clothes for him and the kids, make his bagging for the potatoes, tidy around and clean the mucky bathroom before turning in next to him, where she might just have to put up with his amorous antics due to his feeling refreshed after those few hours in the chair.

He shook his head as he turned the key to bring life to his wagon. One day he had heard me arguing in the barn during bagging time. I was sticking up for my mum against Snake Eyes, who had stated that men work harder than women. Where I'd got it from he had no idea, but I had stated adamantly, 'When God made woman he took the hardest working bone from Adam and began to carve it. The bits that fell to the earth became beasts of burden.'

At least the kids have noticed how hard their mums work and appreciate it too, Tommy said as he slipped the vehicle into gear and drove off.

Tommy Threlfall's head must have had barely touched the pillow that night when Mrs O'Rourke's baby was delivered at eight and a half pounds. The next morning she was ever so slightly thinner and looking somewhat worse for wear, but she winked at Mary Connor as Tommy put his hand up to her butt in order to get her up onto the wagon.

'Watch your hand, Tommy lad, there's a big space there today!' she chided. Apart from that and telling everyone that the girl child was healthy, she did not mention her ordeal, nor that her day was arduous as she bent and picked her way through it.

When God made woman . . . Tommy repeated to himself as he remembered my words and he could hear Mrs O'Rourke's laughter coming through into the cab while driving them all back home that evening

That weekend they had 'jars out' in the O'Rourkes' to welcome the new member of the family.

During a school week the women had the 'luxury' of working on the farm without the added worry of where their kids were. Mrs O'Rourke would alternate keeping her kids off school to look after her newborn until the youngster was stable enough to be brought out in a pram. There were enough of them to ensure only one day off a week per child. Occasionally, another hand was needed, but enough women made themselves available to step in and help out without Mrs O'Rourke having to take a day off from earning. In return, she would have to ensure that a bag of spuds would be on offer. That 'I'll scratch your back if you scratch mine' attitude was highly prevalent in those days.

At weekends I was always happy to go out in the fields just to be with Logger, who was so often out gallivanting with the older lads. Although we didn't go out as much as we used to, it made no real difference to our relationship because our bonding had been solid from birth. That feeling of being related and being a part of one another was always there even though often we now took different routes, Logger being with his mates, I likewise. Being tall and therefore accepted more by the older lads, Logger had matured more quickly than I had, but he still seemed to enjoy my company. However, the older lads refused to accept any short-arsed younger ones because we could not keep up. Besides, we looked like what we were: snotty-nosed kids.

Occasionally the opportunity arose for me to accompany my cousin when others were thin on the ground or when Logger had something to do that required a helping hand and he could please himself whom he chose. He liked showing me things; the feeling of being the chief was good to experience and helped hone his teaching and leadership skills, just as the older lads had sharpened their skills on him.

Often we would sneak our way onto the docks during the hallowed lunch hour and learn to drive the bogies and cranes by messing about on them and copying what we had seen the men do to lift and carry the various cargo. It was dangerous, some might say foolish, but it was highly educational and each time we messed about it lit the fuse for more knowledge about the manipulation of those machines. In an empty shed we could enjoy lots of fun and learning, and we spent many hours doing just that, which made us quite proficient at driving those machines. Few of the kids from those Buildings headed into the world of work without a fair idea of what they were getting into and how things worked. Logger was determined to learn as well as to pass on his knowledge, which meant that I was getting a first-rate hands-on education.

The various age groups in those tenements meant that it was like being in a queue where you could see over the shoulder of the next person and plan to do the same or better once you reached that stage.

Along our routes of trespass Logger showed me many things; we played on everything that was open to us and used any unattended vehicles to learn how to drive and operate them. With Logger even the warehouses fell into the bracket of schooling. I soon learned how to use the hoist and understood the workings of those dangling ropes, which took loads up three or four floors and lowered them to waiting wagons as necessary. It took a while to understand how hard to pull on the control rope for the hoist to work, but, once we mastered it, we really had fun, taking one another up and then lowering one another down. What we had to remember then was to keep a tight hold.

One lad didn't: Wil-Wil Brown, a friend of Logger's. He helped Logger to have a ride up and down with the hoist but, when it was his turn to be raised up to that top floor, he failed to keep a tight hold on the rope and slid down, burning his fingers and getting the hook stuck up between his jacksie and his ball bag. The screams were relentless. First, we tried to help by lifting him up off the hook but then we had to drop him back onto it as the men came rushing out from the warehouse innards. Poor Wil-Wil damaged his manhood that day and was told that it would make it harder for him to become a father. That shook us all up but it didn't stop us from doing it all again – happily without incident. We lost touch with Wil-Wil after that as, understandably, he didn't fancy playing out so much!

As much as we were adventurers and opportunists, we were not out-and-out thieves. Logger saw to that. He wouldn't let me break open a case to steal the contents but he did condone picking from the contents of a case if it was already open, which was usually a choice of tinned salmon, tuna, fruit or other such edibles. Those snacks became our only form of sustenance during daily jaunts, which kept us roaming due to our yearning to be there and to learn as well as enjoy. Every day was basically the same but vastly different as we conquered one thing or another during the school holidays or mini breaks.

I felt myself lucky to be asked by my cousin to go for some dry ice after we had finished our second Saturday of the spud-picking season. That morning Tommy Threlfall, the farmer's ganger, had prompted Logger's thoughts about the Lecky-ice when he mentioned, during their bagging time, that he had a party coming up for his young daughter, then went on to say how much of a nuisance the warm weather was when they were trying to keep the ice cream solid and the salad stuffs cold. Logger jumped at the chance to supply the solution. Even at that young age it paid to know how to influence people into looking favourably on you when you wanted work.

Lecky-ice is frozen carbon dioxide and has a magic allure of underwater bubbling; our favourite was to throw a piece into the canal and watch as bubbles came to the surface, then burst and let out a puff of smoke, which was actually gas that would then mix with the air and evaporate completely. Another attraction was to put a penny on it; the reaction would make you think that you were getting an electric shock as the penny vibrated. It could burn the skin off you or cause frostbite if you were to hold it in your bare hands, and it never melted, merely evaporated by returning to its original form – gas – which seemed heavier than air as its white cloud form snaked off the block and headed downwards.

The ice-cream men were the first to introduce the boys to it. If you were a good enough customer they would give you a bit of the stuff when you purchased an ice cream. How close the man was to finishing his day would determine how big a chunk of the dry ice he would give you. However, those ice-cream men could not always oblige when asked, which caused a few of the more determined boys to backtrack them in order to find out where they got it from, then they began to go there direct to scrounge their meagre wants or to steal a bit. That knowledge came in useful whenever there was a party because the dry ice brought the temperature of the larder down considerably and kept the beer very cold in the bath.

'How much do you think we'll need, Logger?' I asked as we trekked through the Seeky tunnel, carrying the half-sack of spuds that Tommy had just given us.

'We'll see if we can get a couple of cobs. *Ow!* Logger yelled as he stood on the rim of a metal hoop, causing it to fly upright as if by magic and smack into his knee. It was one of the main traps when walking through that dark and dank tunnel, which we knew to be a kind of booby-trapped place.

'Bastard!' Logger said, as he rubbed his knee.

'Glad it wasn't me. I hate hurting my knee like that,' I said.

'It wouldn't have hit you in the knee, short-arse!' Logger jibed.

At this I nodded in agreement as I thought of the size difference then touched my nether regions and felt even more thankful that it had not hit me.

'Sometimes bein' smaller can be downright dangerous!' I muttered to myself as I thought about such an accident, causing Logger to look over and almost certainly to wonder what his cousin was going on about.

Eventually, we arrived at the little factory on Bankhall Lane. Saturday afternoon, it looked deserted, but Logger knew they worked 24/7 and found a side door open that the men used for smoke breaks or nipping out to the pub. Meanwhile, I thankfully rested my bag of spuds on the ground while my cousin went through the door. However, my rest was soon disturbed as my illustrious cousin came almost flying through the door, his ejection assisted by an irate bonehead.

'An' *stay* out! Had enough of you little fuckers snoopin' in here, trying to steal things!' As Logger landed on the floor, the man looked over towards me. 'And *you* can fuck off, too!' he added, then clanked the door shut. We could hear the sound of a lock being forced across.

'What did you do?' I asked, bursting to know.

'Nothing!' Logger replied sharply, implying the truth because of the sharpness of his retort. 'I was just looking for Ross, the big woolly-headed fella who normally gives us the bits. That's who the spuds are for.'

'How come that one threw yer out then?' I said, my screwed-up face asking the same question.

'Think he just got a shock seein' me. It's like a spaceship in there, like those Flash Gordon films, only there's no music, just weird noises an' pipes banging with hissin' and steam and stuff.'

'Did you just appear outta nowhere, like in them movies?' I asked, my eyes now lit up with expectancy.

'No, I just stood behind him and waited for him to finish doing what he was doing . . .' Logger began to laugh as he realised the direction my thoughts were heading in. 'Ha, yeah . . .' He nodded, then laughed some more. 'He did shit – when he turned around his eyes near-popped and he shouted, "*Argh!*" Ha, then he turfed me out!'

Now we were both laughing, but we still had no Lecky-ice.

'What we gonna do now?' I wanted to know, thinking I would have to lump the spuds all the way back through the Seeky and up that very steep embankment.

But the beauty about being a 'sniffer' was that you got to know a few things. Logger had begun sniffing around this place a few years ago with 'Onk', Tony Owens (who was eighteen months older than he was, the same age difference as that between my cousin and me). In those days they really had to sneak around because the very sight of us trespassing, even though we had the honourable intention of asking, got us a clipped ear. Consequently, the lads really had to sneak up and steal any bits they wanted. That was how he and Onk ended up on that roof some six years previously – they used the skylight as a way in because it was always open to release excess gases and keep the walkways clear. Anyway, this particular day followed a few days' rain, which left the asbestos roof slippery as wet fish. Onk slipped and Logger tried to save him but the movement and weight caused his precarious hold to lose its gripping power; both slid down the roof, gaining momentum as they went and eventually, with a yell and a yelp, they fell off and down to the ground, where Logger sprained both ankles. Tony had to carry Logger, piggyback-style, all the way up Sandhills then along Commercial Road and across Stanley Road until they reached Owens Road, where one of his friends hurried to give a hand.

Apart from learning that you do not try to cross a wet asbestos roof, during those travels Logger found out that the men often dodged out to the local for a drink throughout the course of their shift, leaving the side door open. He deduced that the door was used for nipping out for a smoke, but no one was smoking and so someone must've gone for a drink and left it open.

Sure enough, standing by the bar and downing the dregs of a pint was Ross, his woolly hair looking wilder than ever. Seeing our Logger's face pop round the door, he smiled.

'What you after, yer little fart?' he asked.

I was sitting outside on my half-bag of spuds when I heard Ross's loud laughter booming out as the door of the pub opened and he came out, still chuckling away at the story of his workmate getting the fright of his life.

The exchange was soon done, which left me still carrying as we made our way back through the Seeky tunnel – Ross had given us a large block of ice wrapped in the farmer's sack after pouring our spuds into a big drum. Logger lent a hand to navigate the puddles and trip objects of the Seeky while I struggled with the weight; he also helped me up the steep embankment leading to the big wall prior to the large sandstone wall of Commercial Road, where we had to pass that big lump of dry ice over each seven to eight foot of it.

Getting that big block home was a testimony to our tenaciousness, while acquiring it was a demonstration of a learning process that would take us through life as well as ensuring a long and fruitful relationship with Tommy Threlfall.

Logger had to curb such forays whenever his father came home because Big Lar (Larry) knew such wanderings could lead to trouble, and that was not allowed. Each homecoming was an event that changed my cousin's life for a few weeks. Every payoff was a happy occasion after a three-month (and sometimes longer) trip. My own dad was always happy when Lar came home because they used to sail together until he was forced to give up the sea because of the stipulation that the authorities put on him over adopting me. Now, the only thing he could enjoy with his once-constant pal and brother-in-law was the homecomings.

When a crew first join a ship they have to 'sign the articles' or 'sign on'. The signing is a contract, which puts them under the lawful control of the captain for the duration of the voyage. Once the trip is completed, they 'sign off' and are paid their money, less any fines incurred during the trip or subs they have taken out. Mainly those subs related to going ashore at the various ports of call and the money paid to their wives for the upkeep of their homes and children. Consequently, the payoff day usually saw those men disembarking down the gangplank with a fair bit of cash in their pockets and wearing a snazzy suit and tie. Hence the first lines of the song 'Maggie May':

I was paid off at the pool at the port of Liverpool,
Three-pounds-ten a week, that was my pay . . .

Fair to say, Logger was always happy when his father came home because the whole atmosphere in the house changed from the same old day-to-day feeling to one of light airiness. Sweets and lemonade became abundant, his mum looked brighter and his younger siblings cried less. That sort of thing was not confined to 44 Owens Road: it was the type of ambiance experienced by all returning seamen who had paid off after a few months on the high seas, especially the whalers, when nine or more months was the norm, so those payoffs were much larger.

On his first days home Lar would check on the kids' progress and hobbies with interest and he would even spend some time in Logger's loft; but, as the days flew by, he would become more interested in the Orwell, Roundhouse or Melrose pubs, just like most such men, who had become accustomed to their families being mainly on paper via a photo or letters. The people who held their attention most were those they worked with or those with similar interests. It was no use trying to get the kids to understand the hardships of a boiler room where the sweat was dragged out of you by the heat of those furnaces or the fact that you not only had to tell someone what to do as their chargehand, you had to make them do it if they were ornery about their work. Although big and strong, Lar had his work cut out when a man was being awkward because they were always as fit and strong themselves thanks to that hard labour.

Although the chance to escape from it all after a voyage was at hand, via his wife and lovely children, Big Lar also felt the need to talk about the pressures of life at sea and the only ones who really understood such chat were his fellow workers. Consequently, his time became split between the only places where he could meet those men and the company of his family, which led to his wife criticising him, and the longer he was home the more arguments they had. Those quarrels led to Logger wishing his father back at sea, so it became a cruel merry-go-round – or, in Logger's case, 'the norm'.

With the money in his pocket fast disappearing, Big Lar spent less time steeped in inebriation so he had more time to be critical of things, especially the antics of his son, Logger, and his daughter, Ann, who were the oldest of his growing clan (Pauline and John were just in the juniors and Stephen had yet to come out of his pram). He began to question what Logger wanted the fare for each Thursday, having seen four of them go by (his son would have to look smart to go and see the probation officer). However, backed by his mother, Logger would say he was in a choir down at the cathedral and Thursday was practice night.

The sweets had stopped being plenty and the cups now held water instead of lemonade; the dingdong of the occasional ice cream man's bell caused a shrug and in their place was the constant utterance of 'No money!' Logger knew what was next: a visit to the 'two to one'.

'Two to one, you don't get your gear back' was so often said as you stood beneath the three golden balls that hung up outside those pawnshop doorways. The local one had an entrance in Orwell Road, with its shopfront on Stanley Road. It was that window where Logger had seen their Sunday clothes hanging after the ticket had run out. Now it was looking as if their Sunday best would end up there again and that would lead to more arguments, really ferocious ones, as his mother bit at the fact of the careless drunk spending after the high of a whoopee payoff, followed by the 'not-so-slow' slide into the offices of the NAB (National Assistance Board) and their demands that you rid yourself of your valuables before daring to ask them for subsistence – hence the pawnshop.

May's rightful argument was, 'Oh, going back to sea, are yer? Going to leave us with no Sunday best to wear while you bob about on those fuckin' waves! Well, I'm not having it, not this time. I work myself to the bone for our kids and this house, this cockroach-infested house, which we could be out of if you would spend a bit of your payoff to grease the palm of one of those estate agents . . . But no, you *drink* it, don't yer? *Don't yer?*'

Big Lar could only bow his head in shame during such onslaughts. All that brawn, that mighty physique with its steel muscles, the mean machine of the engine room who would whip any revolt back into subservience, cowed by the might and right of a wife and mother's lashing tongue – all nine stone of her.

That day, he stormed out to avoid the tempest, then walked the streets because he had no money, even though he had spent his on those who had none, but now did. However, they dodge meeting him when they know he has no more cash and quickly fail to notice him and shift pubs, should he walk into where they are. He is lonely now and it shows with drooped shoulders and a glum face. His family would give – especially his brother-in-law, Johnny Boylan, my adoptive dad – but Lar's pride is such that he dodges them, not knowing where to go on this Saturday morning, but going anyway in search of solace.

He heads for the docks, where the type of home that he has known, worked and lived in for all of those years lies – the homes of those who ran the gauntlet of the U-boats to cross the

Atlantic, the Mediterranean and Bering Seas and survived. The sight of the big cranes and various coloured funnels gives him a kind of peace; thoughts of his many trips help soothe the wounds that his wife's words have left. But they lie open, smarting, and he knows they cannot be fully healed while those Sunday clothes are still in that pawnshop.

The sight of a barge pulling alongside a boat, then heaving its hatch boards back for sacks of kernels to be ripped and tipped into its open holds, makes him give thought to coming ashore. His brother-in-law, Johnny Boylan, has already done so – admittedly because the authorities demanded it, if they were to place Peter in his charge – but he has done it all the same and is surviving the wrench, albeit with regret as the ebbing pain has been replaced with an incoming tide of sorrow due to Peter's rather rebellious stupidity.

Big Lar watched as the dockers aboard a Jala boat ripped and tipped those sacks. Could he do it? he wondered as a cloud of dust would separate from the falling husks and be taken by the breeze towards the rear of the ship, where it would disappear into nothingness before being followed by another. The contents of bag after bag after bag tumbled into that barge, reminding him of the shovels of coal that he would throw into the fiery furnaces of the ships, but instead of dust being blown away, you would get a sudden upheaval of flame as the bits and dust on the shovel were ignited by the immense, radiating heat. The sight of another barge edging its way into the basin made him think of the locks through which they came, four huge steps from the level of the docks up to canal level at Lockfields.

Lockfields. A chance to make money by basically doing what he already did for a living: being tough and keeping the troublesome toughs in their place. Though more of a bruiser than a fighter,

Larry's toughness, strength and stamina helped cancel the skill he needed to show good as someone's champion.

Cabbage Jackson was not so much a belligerent man, but he did like to see a good fight, so feigned much of his belligerent attitude in order to get into an argument so that he could become involved in a challenge. He used a lot of string to tie that knot but it was a knot worth watching unravel as he stood in the Wine Lodge on a Saturday night and snapped at the other bookies of his calibre, calling their system fit to burn or throwing a hint that they were lousy organisers when it came to their men being nicked for taking bets.

'On the day you know it's going to happen, youse should do what I do – let a stand-in take the bets so when they come to take your usual man, who only has false bets on him, you don't get claims for bets that weren't put on!'

Cabbage was, of course, referring to the new covert arrangements he had organised with the police whereby they would not have to stake a place out and waste time with all that surveillance, which was often thwarted by the 'Dixie' lads. Instead, by prearrangement, they would walk up and arrest the bookie, then take him off to be charged. Once that formality was over, the arrested man was allowed to return to his patch and resume as if nothing had happened. In itself that used to bring tribulations because the bets already collected by the bookie were taken from him as evidence, but those missing slips caused problems, especially if the punter stated his bet to be worth more than it originally was.

The first attempt to sort that situation out resulted in the detectives taking only a few of the slips, but they still had that flaw, which allowed large, unsubstantiated claims. One officer tried to put that right by copying the few betting slips that were taken as evidence and then Cabbage came up with the idea of a stand-in to take and hold the bets of the day when the regular bookie was due to be taken, together with false betting slips already made but tailored to look as if all bets were minuscule. That system appeared to work well, but Cabbage had not informed his peers about it beforehand, because he only liked successes. Now that he knew it to be so he decided to rub it in, hoping to annoy them and tempt them into a challenge.

In the meantime, those who really ran those Lockfields fights, the gypos, were organising their big event for that month: one of the Dorans against one of the Doyles. Both families were from over the Boundary Street Bridge and both men had fought and won in the Love Lane gypsy camps. Now those travellers wanted to see which of the two men was the tougher.

As for Big Lar, all he wanted was to earn enough to get all his stuff back from the pawnshop and leave his wife with some money before setting off to sea again. He had spent a few hours watching and thinking as the dockers split bags on the deck of that Jala boat and emptied their contents over the side to spill into the tethered barge below. He then decided that he needed money, just enough to buy his entrance into the Wine Lodge.

A quick word with the chargehand on the dock got him someone who would give him the price of a pint to take his place and fill in the remainder of the day tipping those bags over the side into the barge. It was dusty work, but would earn him his entrance for the Wine Lodge.

Moorfields Wine Lodge was one of the places where the bare-knuckle men used to meet in order to get their fights. People such as Cabbage Jackson and Quigley, the local bookmakers, would meet there socially and, if they needed a fighter, they would pick one from those already there. Larry had decided to give it a go and see if his skills were needed because the money that he would receive to champion for someone – win or lose – would be enough to get him out of his current dilemma and leave enough over for him to finish off his leave without having to pawn anything else.

The men needing champions would pay for someone on a hire, win or lose basis, often with a bonus if the man won and especially so if it were an out-and-out grudge fight. Once a fight had been organised anyone could bet on the result. Often the bookies recuperated any layout that they made by taking bets on the men they had chosen. During the past few years Larry had fought a few fights and had earned a solid name for it. Consequently, when men were looking for a good fighter, Larry – if present – was always considered.

By the time he arrived at Moorfields Wine Lodge, Cabbage Jackson was arguing loudly with two other bookies, Lance and Quigley. They'd had enough of his taunts and insinuations, now they were wild-eyed enough to throw out a challenge, which was accepted by the twinkly-eyed Cabbage.

Unbeknown to Quigley, Cabbage had noticed Big Lar come in and had sent his chief bookmaker over to the pool of fighters to buy him a drink and drop him a fiver to ensure that the big man would lay himself on only for Quigley. He wanted his own fighter, Keaton, to be solidly beaten and knew that Big Lar was the man to do the job.

As would be the norm, they would meet at Lockfields on the Sunday afternoon, just after the 11.30–2 opening times, followed by a crack and a joke outside their local before heading for Lockfields via whatever route was handy. Then all would be ready: the fighters, the bookies and the travellers who had organised it all, with their waistcoats and bowler hats on snugly, gold watch chains dangling.

It certainly was a spectacle, with – sometimes – two or three fights going on at the same time; but, in general, it was the one gathering that made or formed a ring where all of the fights were fought. That day it was a one-ringer. As requested, Big Lar had secured the place of Quigley's champion with an added bonus for a rout because the bookie not only wanted to come out on top, he wished to rub Cabbage's nose in it.

Cabbage, however, had no intention of winning. He had purposely hired a bully from his own area by the name of Keating because the man was getting too big for his boots and needed pegging down a bit – a big bit, due to having given information to thieves. The reason Cabbage had done it this way was, first, for the pleasure of watching a wrong 'un being beaten and, second, to get all his money back by having a stand-in bookie offer very good odds against Keaton, who he knew was going to lose because he had ensured that Quigley's champion was better. On top of that, those bullies were – as all bullies are – good fighters against lesser men.

Keaton had never put himself up before because, like most bullies, he didn't have the guts to stand and slog it out with a good 'un who knew how to. However, on this occasion, Cabbage had lured him into fighting for him with the promise of cancelling a heavy debt. Knowing full well the man couldn't refuse, Cabbage was set to see his plan completed. Afterwards he could really top his day by watching the Doran vs. Doyle fight and maybe win money on that too. He knew that Quigley would add a bonus to ensure a good defeat of his man, thereby adding to the punishment meted out on Keaton. Afterwards, Cabbage would take great pleasure in letting his pals Quigley and Lance know that he had organised it all from start to finish.

There's more than one way to skin cats! Cabbage thought as the grin of satisfaction spread across his chubby cheeks. His day was well and truly blessed.

Although the swapping of those punches was real and bone-crunching, Big Lar's advances were choreographed via nods and the shaking head of Cabbage. A nod meant good hard punches while the headshake meant easy on the power, and finally, when the big man rubbed his chin, Larry was to go for the ribs.

Over a period of twenty minutes Keaton had been pummelled: he lay unconscious, oblivious of the fact that his mouth and ears were bleeding. A couple of sidemen carried his limp form over to a grassy patch, where a quack was waiting to administer first aid or to order a drop at the steps of the Northern Hospital.

Quigley smiled as he paid Larry his money plus the promised bonus, but the inflated tyre of his smugness was deflated when Cabbage came over and dropped a handful into Big Lar's hat himself.

'All will be revealed,' said Cabbage as he touched his nose and then let out one of his enormous laughs at the sight of Quigley's face. But the beating Keaton had received was not in any way a put-up: Quigley's man had won and he had the right to rub it in, but somehow felt duped. As always, Cabbage was showing the way, but where this was heading, Quigley had no idea.

May Riley had fed and bathed the younger kids by the time Big Lar came home smiling, if a little bruised, pressing the money that would release the pawnshop pledges into her hand. The Rock and the Piece of Silk stood facing one another in that tiny living room – in his eyes 'the wannabe good father and husband', in hers, the 'wish you were'. But the reality was the tin bath on the stone floor, still with its grimy water of three washes, the glowing embers of that small coal fire with its constant companion – the Big Kettle – standing on the hot metal plate. Then young Ann washing dishes in the 'cold-fed only' Belfast sink in their small kitchen. As if in an attempt to cover up their situation by socialising, the Rock asked Silk to join him in the Roundhouse pub, and she accepted just to escape, for a short while, from her facts of life.

Down at Lockfields Quigley was totally subdued after the elation of his win and the exciting battle between Doran and Doyle, in which Chris Doran had won in the fifth after the fiercest fistfight ever seen by those spectators. Doran had been carried off shoulder-high by those exuberant gypsies to their Love Lane encampment, where they intended to whoop the rest of the night away, celebrating 'The Year's Champion Fistfighter'.

Young Danny Doran had been watching the events of that day with a few of his mates. They had made a day of it with lemonade and a few sarnies. His friends had gone now but curiosity caused him to stay: he wanted to see what was happening with Keaton. From his perch up on the lock-keeper's roof he saw Cabbage murmuring into Keaton's ear. He could only barely hear what was being said but could read the body language of fear as clear as day.

'You, you fuck! You think because of your size you're a big man. Well, let me tell you, it's not the size that counts. It's your heart what makes you. Now look . . . ' Cabbage pointed over to a gap in the fence, where a tinker's van had pulled up. They opened the back doors and dragged out the limp form of a man whom Keaton must have recognised, because he began to squirm as they tied a small safe to the man's back with the aid of a net and rope.

'I'm going now. I'll leave you to ponder your own fate for giving that louse the information about my house and that safe on his back!'

Cabbage then beckoned to the now-enlightened Quigley, and

Danny watched as they walked off along the canal towards Boundary Street rather than be witness to what was about to happen.

Poor Danny was trapped there as he watched. He stooped really low, almost below the parapet of that little sandstone hut, as the tinkers helped the loaded man to his feet after reviving him with something they stuck under his nose. Then they walked him over to the side of the canal and – to Keaton's, and Danny's, horror – let him fall in.

It was a happening that Danny would keep to himself for many years before relating it to someone during his fiftieth-wedding-anniversary celebrations at his home in Elane Street, Dingle. One of the things that Danny often said during those years was, 'Always keep on the decent side of people because you never know how bad their ugly side really is!'

As for Big Lar, he began to go down to the Wine Lodge a lot during the remainder of his leave. They were mainly afternoon sessions that finished at 3 p.m., and then he would visit one of the local afternoon drinking clubs until five. On his way home one evening he saw his son, Logger, all spruced up and heading for what Lar believed to be choir practice. He decided to follow the lad and surprise him by watching the action, but got the shock of his life upon reaching Great Crosshall Street and seeing his son enter the huge, ornamented offices of the Probation Services.

There was hell to pay. May Riley was accused of hiding the facts of their son's many minor convictions, while Logger was given the tanning of his life. The clothes ended up back in the pawnshop and Big Lar was waved farewell for his next trip by two fingers.

An irreparable crack had finally appeared in the hull of their marriage.

CHAPTER 9

PENNIES
FROM HEAVEN

Johnny Butler had moved into his new home, courtesy of the council and Josie. The lads had helped him to move in and there had been a few donations of various bits of furniture from well-wishers. Although it was all second hand, it helped make the home that he had always wanted; he even had his old mates from those homes call on him. For a few months the place became a real hive of coming and goings before the old guy got his twisted form out and about due to missing his usual haunts and the accompanying banter, as well as the many ciggies.

He had heard of the Lockfields fight between Big Lar and Keaton, so, when he saw Logger by the Sassbar, he was keen to congratulate him on his dad's win; but young Logger was still smarting from the bruises he'd received. Besides, his father was a firm believer in keeping his business to himself so he knew nothing of that fight, nor of any of the others for that matter.

Not much chance of a ciggie there! Johnny thought to himself as Logger merely shrugged off his congratulations and announced that his father had gone back to sea. So J.B. tried another tack: 'Believe you've joined the Tanks, haven't you?'

Now that clicked, Johnny thought, as Logger smiled and nodded his head.

'Nearly never, down to you,' he replied, as he pulled out a packet of cigarettes and pushed one Johnny's way.

'Why me, like?' asked Johnny as he snatched the fag from the offering hand.

''Cos of all what you said about the army and the way it treats people like dogs instead of human beings.'

'That was my time, that was war.' He waved the cigarette at Logger: 'Giz a light.'

Logger pushed his arm out towards Johnny, offering the lit end of his fag first. The transfer was soon made, causing a puff of smoke to expel with Johnny's next words.

'Suppose they've got more time to be human, now it's all over. Who else joined? Or did yer join alone?'

'No, Tasker and our Nylon joined as well.'

As they chatted, Logger added that most of the younger lads had given the Army Cadets a miss in favour of the Sea Cadets in Bootle, courtesy of Joe's father knowing the man who ran it. He had just finished telling Johnny that when Joe's brother, Tommy, came along, wanting Logger to go to the pictures with him. Logger agreed, but not before Johnny had also bummed a cigarette off Tommy, leaving the lads laughing at the fact that Old Johnny had not changed even though he had got his wish of a home of his own. He still felt the world owed him, they thought, for which they could not criticise him considering the state he was in due to National Service.

When Joe and the other lads began to parade themselves around in their Navy Cadet uniforms, Johnny used to skit them, but, when Mike Kinsella and I appeared in our Army Cadet uniforms, Johnny showed his bias and praised us, although that soon changed once he realised that his cigarette rations had been cut. Suddenly, he grew a liking for those sweat-shirted wallahs and found good things to say about them. The lads, however, were not that bothered; in fact, Joe Keaney hated it all. Had it not been for a chance meeting between his father and Reg, the man who ran the Cadets (apparently they had been chums in the Old Country), Joe would never have joined at all, and told Old Johnny so.

'Well, if you want out, all you have to do is . . .' Johnny advised with a twinkle in his eye and the thought of five ciggies going through his mind.

'What?' Joe hopefully interrupted.

Suddenly those five ciggies in Johnny's mind jumped to ten. 'Tell yer dad how much you like the place and hound him with shows of how you can salute and stand to attention and all stuff like that, but do the opposite in the Cadets. Be shite, they'll soon throw you out, and your dad won't mind because he'll be pissed off with you bothering him with it all anyway.'

So Joe began to bombard his father with his 'Look at me doing this, Dad' and 'Come out on the landing while I show you how good I can march.'. The first few times were OK and Johnny's advice seemed to be working as the feeling of being harassed began to get to Big Jack, especially after a hard day's graft when all he wanted was to relax or go to the pub. Instead of feeling proud of his son, he began to wish that he had never suggested he join the damned sea thing to begin with.

As for the other end of that plan, Reg had put up with Joe's sloppiness, thinking the lad to be a touch backward, but he didn't wish to let on to Big Jack for fear of hurting his feelings. When Joe's negligence lost them their much-prized lifeboat, it was the last straw, however.

In the evenings the lads would all get together and dissect their day, repeating the funnies or relaying the things that had been of most interest. The antics of their first trip in the Cadets' lifeboat made the headlines of any other day seem minuscule, though. For quite a few weeks they had been bombarded with pictures of the lifeboat and the names of the various parts, from the keel to the rowlocks and from the lifting eyes to the rudder; they had completed papers on them and even had memory tests appertaining to the different types of sail that could be attached once a mast had been stepped. At first they had been enthusiastic but the talk without the walk became boring: 'Show a dog a bone and it will want to chew it!' Those lads had seen the picture, written and mouthed their theory and now they wanted to sail, or at least go on the water, which, in the case of the Bootle Sea Cadets, was the Cut – the Liverpool-to-Leeds canal at Bankhall, where they had private access via the Slate Works.

First laugh was Mick Furlong (Fishcake), who was so eager to untie the boat from its moorings that he tripped and went in headfirst, causing the coxswain, Reg, to stop everything and kill a half-hour giving another lesson on safety while Mick dried off a little in the sunshine. Then he split the group into two sixes, the first of whom would row the boat downstream in the direction of the city, but only as far as Tillotsons, a distance of about a mile and a half. Meanwhile the other group would accompany him by marching down the footpath beside them, watching and listening as they went, then swap places for the row back. Each trip would include rowing, giving and taking orders and a variety of exercises such as 'Stand by', 'Oars', 'Give way' and 'Toss oars'. Tossing oars meant taking out the oars from their rowlocks and standing them upright so that it looked as though each man had a mast in front of him. The finished action looked smart, like a salute – it greatly impressed Joe.

They planned two trips each, a distance of two and a half miles per group. During this journey there were two bridges: the Bankhall Bridge, fifty yards from the beginning, and the railway bridge. They would emerge from that some forty yards before the place where they turned, by Tillotsons factory. Although almost a football pitch in length, the bridge by Tillotsons was not in any way an obstacle because it was very high and spanned the canal completely; it could easily allow a barge from each direction to travel through at the same time. The first bridge, however, allowed only single traffic due to its narrow width and its height also left a lot to be desired, especially if a barge had a small chimney.

The first trip had those marching wishing themselves in the boat while the lot in the boat were getting pissed off with the constant changing of orders, such as 'Oars', 'Stand by', 'Give way' and 'Toss oars'. It was more like a weightlifting session as they heaved those oars out of their rowlocks and stood them upright for the 'Toss oars' command, which made the end product of the exercise look awesome as they held those oars upright as if they were going into battle with another boat by clouting the heads off the occupants.

Instead of merely rowing as one did on a boating lake Reg kept doing it by the book with 'Prepare to give way' – meaning for the lads to lean forward while holding their oars ready for the first pull. Once he was satisfied that they were all ready, he would say, 'Give way together,' encouraging them to pull on their oars together and propel themselves through the water. However, instead of that being the first of many strokes and a speedy journey along the canal, Reg shouted 'Oars', which meant that they merely held their oars horizontally above the water until given the order to 'Give way' again or some other order. It felt so monotonous as they stopped and started, then lifted up those heavy oars into their vertical positions of 'tossed oars', only to lower them again and start all over once more. The half of Joe that wanted to be in the boat soon began to give way to his 'pissed-off' half, which added to his lousy side, making him feel bad.

By the time they reached Tillotsons, even showing off his strength by doing 'Toss oars' effortlessly had become a bore, leaving him happy to swap with the marchers.

'Piss on this,' Joe told Billy Vaughan as they walked slowly along the bank.

'It's not that bad, Joe! We can have a laugh by doing things wrong later.'

'I can't – that Reg will tell me da and you know what me da's like,' Joe replied sullenly.

Just then one of the lads on the boat let slip his oar from his hand as he tried to lift it straight for tossing his oar. It went crashing down onto the head of one of the lads at the front of the boat, splitting his head open.

'Wow! Did you see that?' shouted Joe, as if he had suddenly woken up.

The injured lad was stunned as Reg panicked a bit and tried to get the boat to shore, but no one was rowing. Meanwhile, the ensuing panic aboard that boat caused Joe's mind to go into overdrive because he was thinking beyond the injured lad. He remembered that a rope was stowed in one of the lockers and shouted to Fishcake to get it out and throw it to him, which he did. It didn't take long then for those on the towpath to pull the vessel to shore, where they helped get the lad off the boat.

Joe's quick thinking had impressed Reg so much that in the confusion he nominated him for being in charge while he took the injured lad to hospital and sent the lad's friends to inform and fetch the parents.

On the evening of that day the back stairs by Joe's house rattled with laughter as Billy the bandy German took the chair by standing on the stage of the middle crosswell and addressing them all as they used those stairs leading down from the second landing for theatre seats.

'Anyway, poor Thomo, that's the lad who got his head cut open, gets took to the ozzy [hospital] by Reg and a few of his friends, leaving . . .' At this he stopped and pointed at Joe, '*Captain* Keaney in charge.'

Mike Kinsella, Logger and the others and I all laughed as Joe got up and took a bow.

Bandy carried on: 'Do we take the boat and tie it up at its dock in the slate works, like blustery old Reg would expect us to?'

Billy pulled a face and placed his right hand on his left chest, then shot it out and up towards the roof of the stairs, saying sharply as he did so, '*No!*' Then he pointed his outstretched arm towards his friend: 'Tell them what you did, Captain!'

Joe stood up from where he was sitting, but did not step down to the stage of the middle crosswell, where Billy was standing. Instead he defended himself from where he was.

'We were there to row the boat, I thought . . . Well, when you take command you just carry on, dontcha? Just carry on, like where the other fella left off, yeah?'

Everyone nodded.

'Yeah, so that's what I did!' he insisted, then sat down.

'That's what he did all right, made us row the boat all the way from Bankhall to Tillo's at full pelt, slave drivin' bastard!'

'Yer liar!' Joe called out. 'You said youse liked it.'

'Yeah, the one way was OK, weren't it, Mick?' said Billy, bringing Fishcake into it.

'I didn't mind the rowing bit, it was that rope he used to lash us with when we slowed down. Near knocked my eye out with it.'

'Couldn't have youse slackin', could I?' Joe defended.

'Yeah, but if you had to whip anyone you coulda just done it to them other two, them brothers from the top of Melly Road,' said Mick.

'Fuck that, 'ave you seen the size of their brother?'

'Shithouse!' Mick added.

'No, get it right: wise person,' Joe replied, causing laughter all round.

'OK,' Billy butted in, 'we'll go with that – wise shithouse, Captain Wise Shithouse! Now, what about the coming back bit?'

'I wanted to see if youse could get back quicker than what it took to get to Tillo's.'

'*Not* that bit, *Captain* – *not* that bit! The bit where you got us to toss our bloody oars,' Billy insisted.

Joe held out his two hands, face up. 'Mistake! Takes a man to admit one, Billy, me lad.'

'And a fuckin' dummy to make such a one!' Robby Tully announced his late arrival as he came down from the third landing.

'How was I to know?' said Joe, hands palms up as he shrugged.

''Cos you were the coxswain, knobrot!' Robby replied. 'You were facing that way and you could see what was coming.'

'Yeah, what do you say to that, *Captain*?' Billy asked sarcastically.

'Just have to say, sorry, lads. That's all I can do, innit? Ha, it was funny, though! Got to admit that, haven't youse?'

'Funny' to Joe was that he had put them all through the drills of stopping and starting on their way back, then persuaded them to row hard and get their speed up before ordering 'Toss oars!' just as they were about to go under that low and narrow bridge at Bankhall., the result of which was a steaming head-on collision between the upright oars and the bridge, but the sad part was that the angle of one oar was such that it held fast as it hit the bridge, causing the up-end to go ploughing through the deck of the boat, holing it in such a way that the water simply roared in and those who could not step out got a good soaking as it rose as high as the seating.

'Poor Reg!' Billy said, as he thought of their leader with tears in his eyes. 'I've never seed a grow'd man cry like that before.'

'He told me to fuck off,' said Joe indignantly, but no one was listening now as laughter became the king on those stairs. Even Joe himself ended up laughing until he had as many tears in his eyes as Reg had had streaming down his face on seeing his beloved pride and joy in such a state.

Logger, Mike and I ended up rolling about much more than the others because it was totally new to us and therefore funnier, but the others had lived it – and got soaked – so there was an element of laughing at oneself. Meanwhile, Joe was just glad to be out of those bloody Cadets altogether, without incurring the wrath of his father.

With Joe out, it didn't take long for the others to follow, but none of them wished to join the 40th/41st Royal Tank Regiment. Mike Kinsella, however, loved being in those Cadets but I didn't share his enthusiasm. Like Joe, I felt that I'd been more or less pressed into it all and the discipline reminded me too much of the life led with my father and stepmother before I ran away. All the same, I kept at it because my brother Johnny and my cousin Logger loved it, just as Mike did.

Meanwhile Logger was developing a crush on guns. It was beginning to overtake his love of pigeons, but the only place he could get his hands on them properly was at the Altcar rifle range. Therefore, whenever a notice went up on the board for a trip to the range, or a field exercise, Logger put his name down for it. It was one such field trip that got me into the bad books of one of the NCOs, a corporal by the name of North, who had kept on having a go at me for being lazy when the truth of the matter was that it was my worsening heart condition due to that rheumatic fever, which I had not told them about for fear of their not accepting me.

'It's only a day, Peter,' Logger told me. 'They split you up into two groups and one group hunts the other – it's fun!'

And so I agreed to this but only if there was no running involved.

'It's more like huntin' than racin', Nylon, lad,' Logger assured me.

We ended up at Altcar, which is a large area of the coastline between Hightown and Formby, covering hundreds of acres, with marshland, fields and woodland. There, we were all given rifles, issued with a clip of blanks and then split into two groups. At first this worried me, thinking I would not be with Logger or Mike Kinsella, but, as luck would have it, we all ended up in the same group. As usual, Logger took charge after it was explained that our twelve-man group would be split into four threes and then we would toss to see who would be the hunters and the hunted.

For me it suddenly became fun after it was explained that we had a big area to go and hide in before the other side came looking for us. Logger led the way and took us to a small copse, where he wanted to set up a trap for those who were coming to try to capture or kill them. Meanwhile I spotted a largish den made from branches; it had been made but abandoned by a previous unit from a different day. As we looked inside I had an idea.

'Hey, Logger, I could lay down there, right in the edges, and you could cover me with these dead leaves. Then once they come in and look, then go, I could come out behind them and you could be waiting, and we could trap them.'

Logger looked, thought it out and then nodded, perhaps thinking, Peter's no good for running around, but he could be used as bait.

It didn't take long for me to curl into the round edges of the base of that hut and be covered in leaves by Mike and Logger.

'Hope they won't prod any sticks into me!' I called out.

'They won't!' Logger stated firmly, and then he hissed, 'Shush! I think someone's coming!' Then he whispered, 'You dive over there, Mike, by that bush, then, if it's them, we'll get them in our crossfire. You stay there, Peter. If we get caught, you can sneak out and rescue us.'

'OK,' I replied. Then all went quiet. I heard a fart, then a rustle of the leaves as I presumed Logger and Mike to be hiding due to the enemy's approach. Then I heard some more rustling and finally, a voice: it was Mike Kinsella.

'Come on, Logger, it's not them! We can hide over here and have them in a trap once Peter comes out behind them.'

'Peter's worried in case they come in and prod him with a stick or something,' Logger told him.

Mike laughed before saying, 'Can't see it, can't see *anyone* going in there!'

'That's what I told him, didn't I, Peewack?' Logger whispered.

'Yeah,' I replied from beneath my thick blanket of leaves.

'See yer soon, Peewack.'

'OK, Logger, see yer.'

After the noise of their footprints died away it all went silent, deathly silent. It was kind of pleasant, except for a smell. I guessed it was the fart I had heard. From experience I knew that those smells tend to linger for ages, especially in the picture houses, when you want them to go away quickly, or even on the bus or tram, when you have to let one go and hope to hell nobody knows it's yours. I smiled as it reminded me of Joe Keaney and that Bonamint moment, but then frowned as I remembered Big Jack and how I felt the man was going to rub my face in Joe's splattered mess.

Ugh, horrible! I thought as the reality of that possibility ran through my mind.

But the smell continued to linger. Farts don't last that long, surely, I thought to myself.

I began to get suspicious and moved a few leaves. Peek-a-boo! There it was, like a living nightmare, as if smiling at me not a yard away, and still steaming: Logger's upright turd, like a little steaming mountain.

No wonder he said they wouldn't touch me with a stick. You bastard, Logger! I thought. You shitty-arsed bast—'.

Suddenly there was a noise; not a loud noise but a creeping one. Then a few noises, like leaves being crunched down slowly; it had to be them. At this I froze, hardly daring to breathe, and all the while hoping nothing of me was visible. Suddenly, someone had spotted my 'companion'.

'Eugh! Look, Corp, some dirty bastard's had a shit in here, look!'

'Argh, stinks! Whoever done that should go see a fuckin' doctor,' a second voice said.

'Must be a bloody queer: look at the size of it!' said a third voice.

'Ah, come on, let's go!' one of them demanded.

'We haven't searched, they gotta be close – it's still steaming.'

'If anyone's in there, they're dead already!'

By this time I had no idea whether it was the first, second or third voice speaking, but what they said was true: the smell had almost killed me. My lungs were bursting for fresh air and, thankfully, I heard them dismiss the den and walk off. For a short while, I waited and listened and then began to emerge, but I took great care not to disturb the watchdog that Logger had left, for it would certainly leave a mark, that was for sure.

The few seconds it took to manoeuvre myself round that watchdog seemed much longer as I held my breath for the whole time. Getting to the open was like escaping from somewhere truly horrible (and it was). I took a couple of long gasps of uncontaminated air. Finally, I was completely free and looking for the enemy.

They had gone around the hut and were heading away from my position. I pulled back the bolt of my rifle and watched as the first round went in. Now I was ready, but was I to shoot them in the back or merely shout, 'I got youse!' and let them surrender? By this time they had reached a small clearing so they had nowhere to hide.

Surely this is the best place to shoot them, I thought to myself as I aimed the rifle. Then the horrid thought of hearing them say 'You missed!' snaked through my brain. Got it! I thought. Shout first, then shoot. Yeah, it sounded about right. There I was, less than eight yards from them, gun loaded and ready to fire. Where the fuck are Logger and Mike? I wondered. Surely they can see me – and them.

Suddenly, a shot rang out from beyond the clearing and Logger's voice shouted, 'I gotcha, Corporal North! You other two are bagged.'

Corporal North, however, shouted in defence, 'You missed!' He then fired off a shot as they retreated back towards me. Once safely behind a tree, the trio began to fire back at Logger and Mick. Now they were only five feet away from me as they lay on the ground and concentrated on Logger and Mike. As all of my questions about how to go about it had been answered, I decided to shoot them in the back – well, sort of.

Each shot that was fired off hid the sound of my approach until a leaf-bound turd splattered against the tree that Corporal North had snuck behind. When the dismayed corporal turned around, he was looking down the barrel of my gun.

'That didn't miss, did it?' I said gleefully. 'Hands hoch!' I added with an upward movement of my rifle.

Back at the camp an argument ensued, first due to the corporal not having surrendered, then my use of Logger's watchdog, the latter having received most condemnation. The corporal gave an excuse for his noncompliance, which, due to his long service and experience of the army's mentality, sounded correct and was upheld. Meanwhile, I was mildly rebuked for my actions because the adjudicator took into account my lack of experience and that this was my first foray.

On his way back from Altcar, Corporal North gave me the dirtiest of looks, but Logger butted in with, 'You know you cheated, Corporal. The least you can do is be a man about it, but, if you don't want to be one, just let it drop.'

Things came to a head when, during one of the drills in the hall of the barracks at Park Street, I wasn't paying as much attention as I should have been during a lesson in self-defence. Corporal North, who was unaware of my condition and thought me lazy because I always failed to keep up in PE, was particularly peeved on seeing me being jocular with Mike during the lesson. With typical army severity, he approached me, almost snarling into my face as he snapped, 'Stockley, I am trying to show you how to defend yourself!'

'I *was* listening, Corporal. Honest,' I said.

'Were you?'

'Yes.'

'Well, then,' he said, as he slammed a rifle smack into my chest, perhaps thinking this was his chance to take me down a peg or two. 'Hit me with that!'

'Don't want to,' I said truthfully, as I took hold of the rifle just to stop it being used to push me backwards.

'Listen, you useless piece of shit, I'm not *asking* you to: I'm *telling* you to!'

Being called a piece of shit really peeved me, so much so that I swore while replying.

'I don't fuckin' want to!' I said angrily.

'Hit me, that's a fuckin' order!' the corporal boomed.

Major Elsworth spoke to the policemen after having interviewed those who had witnessed the corporal's head being split open by my sideswipe with the rifle butt. The law had been notified by the call for an ambulance, but, once the major had clarified everything, no charges were laid. But I left, anyway, with a mind to join the Merchant Navy for a future and never ever to go near the army again.

Because his relationship to me was a known fact among those NCOs, Logger also thought it wise to move on. However, he liked the Cadets, so he went to Shaw Street, where he joined the 8th Irish, with their red and blue plumes adorning their berets. For Logger there was an added bonus: that particular regiment had its own rifle range in a massive hall beneath the Shaw Street barracks, which they got to use frequently instead of having to wait for the occasional weekend at Altcar. During the storytelling on the back stairs, the lads all had a laugh about the incident, but exonerated me from any blame, which made me feel better.

NINETEEN FIFTY-SIX: the year Doris Day brought out a song whose title entered the lexicon of popular culture. When trying to judge how things would turn out in a job, after leaving school, or when anyone had to go to hospital for tests, the answer would always be 'wait and see' or 'God works in mysterious ways'; but once that song – 'Que Sera, Sera (Whatever Will Be, Will Be)' – came out, it became the *de facto* answer for most forward-looking questions. Our mums took it up, dads were heard to say it, and even the teachers began to mutter it. There was a version in Yiddish, Hindu, Tamil and French; even our ninnies began to mouth it whenever our futures were discussed. 'Que sera, sera' was so often followed by a shaking of the head and the sign of the cross due to their hopes for our wellbeing. At least it gave us a break because, once those words had been uttered, it meant that we were in the hands of the gods and it was up to them to guide and protect us or let the wolves have a meal.

'What you gonna do when you leave school, Logger?' Joe Keaney asked one day as we all played 'Pull Out' in the square.

Pull Out consisted of having a long length of rope tied up onto one of the higher landings and left dangling down to the ground, but with plenty of slack left. One of the lads would grab the rope as high up on the down piece as he could while the others all took hold of the slack end and ran backwards, pulling away at the rope and causing the one holding on to be raised up as we ran backwards. The real aim was to get the rope as straight as possible from where it was tied to wherever you could, backing up across the square in an effort to pull it straight. This usually ended up with the lad holding on being raised some twenty or twenty-five feet in the air. It was a trial, but we liked it.

'Dunno,' Logger replied, as he took hold of the rope with Joe and Robby. 'Whose go is it?' he added.

'*Mine!*' Robby Jackson shouted from the sidelines and then hobbled over in his leg irons and grabbed the rope as high up as he could. On this occasion it was attached to the clothes-line hanger outside Tully's house on the third landing.

'Thought you woulda gone for the Merch [Merchant Navy] like your ol' fella,' Robby Tully said as they all backed up and pulled on the rope, causing Jacko to rise up and up, like a parachutist.

It was one of those games that we played when there was nothing else to do. Sometimes we would attach the end of the line to the top landing, but that would really take you up high when it was pulled – you daren't let go because the ground was solid concrete or equally solid tarmac. It was the one game that we all played straight because fooling around could really hurt someone.

'Don't fancy that, couldn't do all them months at sea – it makes yer a stranger to yer kids. I wanna be home with mine, if I have any,' Logger added, then shouted up to Jacko as he hung there, 'Shout when you wanna come down!'

'*Now!*' Jacko demanded, as he felt his arms beginning to ache and also spotted his mother glaring her disapproval.

As they lowered him, Logger shot Robby's question back at him: 'What about you? You gonna join the Merch, like your brothers?'

'Some days I feel like I'd like to, but others make me feel not to. You know what I mean, like?'

'Yeah, like you can't make up your mind! "*Que sera, sera*", eh? Reckon we all live by "what will be, will be".'

Just then my brother Johnny came round the corner in his Army uniform. He stood watching as the lads hoisted me to a height before lowering me. It brought back memories of when he had done the same thing with his friends; everything was just as it used to be except for the people. That lot had been but babes when he himself was hoisted up. However, the game also held bad memories for him: he was the reason why we all stuck rigidly to the proper rules.

Johnny had been raised to the height of the third landing and was being lowered when someone started messing about and yanked on the rope again, causing it to twang and jolt, which in turn ripped the rope from out of his hand. He fell a good thirty feet to the ground, where the impact smashed his knee and damaged his hip. Seven years later he was still suffering. The doctors said they could find nothing wrong that would cause this constant pain, so he had to live with it. He let on to the lads as they played, then passed on the fact to Logger, that Major Elsworth wanted him back in the 40th/41st, if he would care to go. But Logger had told him that he was settled where he was. When I asked about myself, Johnny merely smiled and then gently patted my head.

'You don't fit into holes, Peewee, you fuckin' make them!' he said, then walked off, laughing.

That evening, Logger and Joe's brother, Tommy, had gone to the pictures with Datty Phillips's daughter and her mate, prompting the lads to also vote movie – but without girls, or money. They would have to 'bunk in'. But first they needed a bunking wire, so they ended up rummaging through Arthur's backyard, which was full of boxes of stinking faded fruit, sprouting discarded potatoes and browning leaves from trimmed cabbages, cauliflower and soft nasty-smelling lettuce, as well as . . . a bunking wire.

'Fuckin' 'ell, the old doorman will soon be able to smell us out if we get in there!' said Mike as he wiped his shoe in order to remove a squashed orange from the sole.

'Yeah, it does reek, dunnit? Remember when we had to clean it out after last year's Bommy [Bonfire] Night?' Joe reminded us.

'Yeah.' Robby nodded. 'I was bloody sick for a week. Couldn't do that regular, like they do at the fruit market – me guts couldn't stand it.'

'Your guts go bonkers at the drop of a hat,' Billy reminded him. 'Remember when we wuz looking through the window of Micemeat Mick's in Orwell Road?'

'Oh, yeah.' Robby nodded again. 'When we saw those mice running all over the block, which he cuts the meat on. Didn't 'arf turn me, that did – I won't eat anything if I think it's from there now.'

Walton Road had three picture houses all within a one-mile stretch: the Astoria, the Victoria and the Queens. The Astoria was noted by locals as being the best (especially for courting men who wanted to impress their dates), while the Vic was ill placed, so did not do very well unless it managed to get the most popular films first. Then there was the Queens, situated next to the Co-op garage, used for their bakery vans, but easy to bunk into due to only having one doorman who doubled as an usher and if need be the ice cream seller during intervals. The poor guy was also disabled and walked with a limp. His forearm was constantly raised to waist level, his wrist hung limp. We never knew if the man was a wounded war veteran or a had a palsy.

There was nothing wrong with Duncan's intuition, however, so, when he saw the group saunter past trying to look inconspicuous, he knew what we were up to and went round to the other side of the emergency door, which he knew we used whenever we bunked in.

Then he waited by the dark curtain for us to enter. He must have loved getting these little revenges for the names we all called him.

Billy had the bunking wire, which he drew lightly across his shin, back and forth, to give it the banana shape needed in order to work properly. Then, under the watchful gaze of his friends, he slid in the readied wire, pushing slowly so as not to distort the shape. The aim was to keep pushing until the wire hit the long bar, where it would land and start to straighten out. Once he felt it touch and begin to push back as the bend began to straighten, he stopped and gently reeled it in until it caught that all-important knuckle where the down-bar crossed the emergency push. He would then pull gently but firmly until the wire tightened and the pressure of that catch would grow until it was ready to click open.

Click.

The door moved slightly, bringing smiles to our faces, but Joe held back, knowing it was just as dangerous to be the first one to go in as it was the last, so he positioned himself in the middle. The draught went in first as the door opened wider, causing the big black curtain covering the door to billow like a swaying skirt, and the lady opposite, wearing a turban-style hat, to turn and look. But the hidden Duncan put a finger to his lips, so she turned her attention back to the film and the antics of a canoodling pirate.

Billy stepped back; he had done his job and now the honour of checking the all-clear was left to chubby Mick 'Fishcake'. He reached out and began to push aside the black curtain, glimpsing the swooning lady with the turban as she ogled the pirate seducing his wench. Then he looked to his right. Nothing! But before he could look to his left Duncan's torch came crashing down and thumped the unfortunate Mick on the head with a resounding bash and an echoing 'Ouch!', which became muffled by the closing curtain as Mick quickly retracted his poor head. Duncan sprang into the doorway and grabbed the swinging door as he grinned at the retreating lads.

'Serves youse right!' he quietly hissed as he pulled the door closed.

'Ya spaccy git!' Mick shouted, clutching his forehead in pain.

However, we were used to such hiccups during our adventures and regrouped after a short pause to discuss Plan B, which was one of the other cinemas. The Astoria was quickly chosen but, as we walked past the foyer of the Queens, Duncan changed our minds for us. He came out onto the wide front steps, by the centrally placed kiosk, where you would give the lady your money, then enter to either side. His jibes got us so annoyed that they stopped and cooked up a plan to wipe the smile off his face. As we all walked back towards him, that smile faded.

'We're coming in,' stated Joe and then began to walk up the steps to his right.

'You're bloody well *not*!' insisted Duncan, then moved over to block him just as I ran up the steps to his left and hurried in.

The lady in the kiosk smiled as this game of cat-and-mouse played out, with Duncan running from side to side like a well-worked sheepdog. One by one the boys slipped in until they were all gone, leaving Duncan absolutely livid.

'Leave it out, Duncan,' the teller called, with tears in her eyes. 'You've got to admit they deserve to get in after that.'

'Get in they may have done, but now I've got them – or at least one of them. You see if I haven't!'

'Leave it till Mr Timms gets back,' she suggested. 'He shouldn't be long now, he's only gone to fetch tomorrow's newsreel.'

'I don't need the boss to do my job,' Duncan stated before he went inside to begin his search.

When you have a picture house full of people of all ages and it's fairly dark, it is hard to pick out any one person, let alone five or six of them. Slowly Duncan tramped the walkways, trying hard to recognise one of those monsters who had eluded him. But, without the brightness of that entrance light, the features of the youngsters in there staring intently at the screen as the reflections of light soon played across their faces were impossible to identify. Then he noticed that the lady with the turban had company: I was sitting next to her.

Ha! he thought, remembering earlier that she was alone. That's one of the little bleeders.

He pretended to have missed me as he walked past, and then got to the top of the aisle. His ruse had worked: I had settled without turning to look back. With each step back towards me Duncan's heart beat faster as he slowly made his way along the row behind until he was almost level with me, then he reached across and grabbed my collar.

'*Gotcha!*' he triumphantly exclaimed before leading his captive back out to the foyer.

'Told yer, Kelly. Told yer I'd get them,' he proudly announced as he paraded me in front of the pay desk, hooked up by the collar.

'Them? That *one*, you mean,' Kelly corrected him.

'I'll soon put that right,' he told her. 'Give us the office keys!'

'But Mr Timms isn't back yet.'

'No, but by the time he comes back, I'll have a few more of these locked up,' he replied, with a shake of his hand, causing my head to nod. 'See, even he agrees. *Give!*' he ordered, putting his funny hand out towards the pay-point of the glass frontage. Kelly placed them in the change dipper for him to scoop out.

As the door slammed shut and locked, I felt bad: this would be the first time that I'd been in trouble with the police since that pickle incident in the city (see Chapter 6), but, more importantly, I'd let my parents down again. Although I had given no thought to that during the run-up to this particular adventure, the idea of letting them down greatly saddened me.

The office was no more than twelve foot by ten, with a desk to my right and a steel cupboard with a double door hard up against the wall to my left. A filing cabinet was positioned against the wall further up, facing the desk, and a wastepaper basket stood in front of that, with lots of pieces of paper scattered around it as if someone with a bad aim had been using it as a target.

I rather hoped one of my friends would be caught because I didn't relish the idea of going to the police station alone. As I stood against the side of the steel cupboard with my back to the wall, I thought how I would tell my mother and began to worry. I knew my brother Johnny would understand, for I'd often heard him boast of such things in the past; Logger would laugh, even though he wouldn't like it himself, but, then, he always laughed. I smiled as I visualised Logger laughing – he seemed to laugh at everything except the one time when he'd been seized by a groundsman during a hunt for wood pigeons in the cemetery at Long Lane, close to where I used to live. He had cried then, 'Let me go! *Please* let me go!'

It was the only time I'd seen him short of a smile.

Try as he might, Duncan just could not distinguish between the legal and illegal viewers in that auditorium, but what made him give up the search was that he had tried to collar a totally innocent lad whose mother nearly killed him with a wild glare. He shrank off – at least he had one of them.

In the meantime I was still wallowing in my misery of bad thoughts and lousy hopes that one, just one, of my mates might join me. I leaned my head back against the wall, then felt it: a draught.

A draught meant a window or door, or what? I *had* to see. I craned my neck to try to get a line up the back of the large cupboard but couldn't quite see, so I put my fingers to the cupboard and my foot to the wall and then pulled as hard as I could. Thanks to all the hard work down at the milk depot, my limbs were still strong despite my bad heart, and the big obstacle moved slightly. Once more I looked and, much to my joy, I spotted a little window. Now I had to put all of my efforts into moving the big cupboard because I could not get up to the window as it was.

Mr Timms came whistling along the pavement with the next day's newsreel under his arm, then turned into the opening of his picture house just as Joe came flying out of the place as if it were on fire, crashing into the unfortunate manager, sending his newsreel spinning off into the street. Luckily, there was very little traffic on the road, so it lay there while Joe scarpered, ever so quickly, across the same road and down one of the facing side streets. Mr Timms got up just as Duncan came out, breathless.

'Where is he? Mr Timms, sir . . . '

By this time I had all but managed to pull out the huge cupboard barring my way and was climbing up to the window with the help of an office chair. For a few seconds I fiddled with the catch, then had to bang the window for it to open, which it finally did. With a sigh of relief, I hauled myself up and sat on the ledge looking down at the darkness far below, which gave access to only a very high-walled bin yard. Further along were more accessible yards with lower walls, but I would have to get up onto the roof first.

Behind me was a drainpipe going past the window, which rose a foot or so above the roof. If I were to take that route it would give me the height I needed to get a footing on the steep tiles, but it was dark, so I would have to be careful – *really* careful. However, I would have to turn myself in order to get to it safely, so I popped my head back into the office in order to turn, and that was when I saw that little green moneybag. I'd seen them before, those bags: Micemeat Mick had one in which he kept change; Arthur from the fruit-and-veg shop often had one when he was taking the till money out to go home with; and now here was one, atop this cupboard, just lying there.

I reached out and grabbed it, then opened the neck to peer in. The sight of all that money inside shocked me into a kind of numbness. I looked straight ahead, then back down into the bag. Yep, money, lots of it. Then down my jumper went the bag, just like a pigeon I'd caught among the warehouse rafters.

It was an extremely precarious climb up onto the roof, then a gingerly executed slide along the tiles until I'd travelled two more drains along, where once again I used all my clambering skills to lower myself out and down across the gutter, then onto the straight of the drain before I felt safe enough to begin the slide down. Even for a youngster who believed he was indestructible, it was lovely to make it to the drain with my hands and feet and to know that from here on in it was plain sailing as I gently slid my way down the pipe.

A lit window slowed me as curiosity prompted a look inside. The sight that met me, a large middle-aged lady standing naked in her bath, soaping herself and raking her creases with lather, almost caused me to slip. Then she looked up and screamed as she saw my ogling eyes and gaping mouth, ghostly through the misted glass. My speedy descent caused me to miss my grip as I misjudged a joint from a sink connection to my right, and I fell the last ten feet into the yard, stumbling into a bin and knocking it over. The noise was deafening – at least to me – so I quickly unlocked the back door and fled.

'You've put him *where?*' Mr Timms growled as Duncan explained what he had done.

'In your office, sir.'

'Bloody hell!' ranted Timms at the thought of an urchin roaming free in his office. He ran up the stairs but then realised he had no keys and was about to run back down when an out-of-breath Duncan arrived with them.

The sight of the empty office with its swung-out cupboard prompted Mr Timms to climb up onto the chair and look for the moneybag. Poor Duncan spotted the open window and his heart sank. As Mr Timms got down from the chair, Duncan looked down at the floor, awaiting the backlash, but it didn't come. Mr Timms seemed preoccupied with something and whatever it was certainly seemed to be saving Duncan from an ear bashing as that preoccupation turned into a twitch of a smile. But when the manager eventually spoke it was not with anger in any shape or form. He put his hand on the stuttering Duncan's shoulder, telling him, 'Don't worry, Duncan, you meant well. I'll call the police and you can tell them how it happened. Go and get yourself a cup of tea.'

'Yes, Sir, Mr Timms. Thank you,' he replied, almost in shock due to the leniency he'd been shown. Then, as he began the walk back down the stairs, Mr Timms's face lit up and he walked back into the office, where he whooped with uncontrollable joy as he punched the air. Only that morning he'd borrowed £150 from the takings to pay for his terraced house his mother-in-law had offered him but due to a mix-up with his army backpay, he couldn't get the money out of the bank on that day, the timing of which had been part of the deal. Now, he felt, he didn't have to pay it back.

Happy days, thanks to Duncan!

As I walked down Orwell Road my head was really buzzing. I'd checked the bag but stopped counting at £130 in tenners, over £75 in ten-bob notes. More than twenty weeks' wages for Dad, and I didn't know how much Mum brought home but I knew it was less. I could give it to them and they would be rich. It made me feel so good, but then I felt guilty because I also knew that they would not accept it. They would receive the odd leg of lamb from the dock with thanks and a smile and they would welcome a few tins of salmon from the same source because that was a fiddle and as such was acceptable, but not, definitely not, stolen money.

All through the war they had survived with the occasional fiddle but never had they stolen from anyone. Indeed, Ninny was so holy that she would have had a heart attack at the thought, even though this money would get her relief from the bunions that she accepted as some kind of penance. The potential answer to all that was in my bag, but, sadly, it was an answer to nothing. Nothing at all. Then I smiled as I thought of Johnny and Logger – they'd think of a way to distribute it.

Had it been up to Logger the money would have gone in his pigeon shed, where it would have been slowly milked for a long, long time, with some passed to his mother, who was no prude in such matters and viewed magical appearances as manna from heaven. She had lost her purse a few times and never had any of them returned, and so, when she once found one herself, she looked on it as part of that merry-go-round of fortunes and kept it. However, she would give her last penny if she thought the other person needed it more than she did, so the Almighty would surely have no real reason to frown on those principles.

Johnny was a through-and-through realist. He'd seen the results of the war and what it had done to people, and fully understood what had happened in Europe. He had been closer to the deaths and horrendous injuries than our Scallywags or those of Logger's age and he had a real admiration for those unfortunates whom everyone called 'the Kirky-Homers'. As a child during the war he had looked out of the window of his house and watched the ships coming and going on the not-so-distant River Mersey and worried where his father was and prayed ever so much for his safe return. He was young and innocent enough then to believe in prayer and often said a few for his father, uncle and everyone else who he knew sailed the seas; those times worried him greatly. Now he was married and about to become a father, he had no preference towards the sex – all he wanted was a healthy child, whom he could love and care for.

When Logger accompanied me to Johnny's house that night they sat in the parlour on their own and discussed the episode to date. First, Johnny had to know everything. Had anyone been caught and detained? No! Good. Was there any chance that I might have been recognised by anyone? No! Good again. Was there any chance that this would hit the *Echo*? It wouldn't do for any of the other lads to read about it and then come and start asking.

'Let's wait and see,' Johnny said after that long discussion, and he took the money for safekeeping. 'We'll put all this to bed for three days and, if nothing appears in the newspaper, we'll make plans. Now get yourselves off home!'

As they walked to school the following morning Joe laughed when he thought about himself almost being nabbed by Duncan and described his subsequent offman as rocket-fuelled. Billy had walked out as if he were with a couple who were leaving – that was just as everything heated up with the arrival of a bobby, who stationed himself at the top of the aisle with Duncan, who was acting like a feral cat looking for mice. Robby and Mike had shot off when I got nabbed; they saw it as a warning. But Mick was settled because he had met his aunt and uncle and they had bought him an ice cream, so he watched the films with impunity.

'What happened to you?' asked Joe, thinking of the police side of things.

'Nothing. I scarpered as we got to the doorway. He let go of me to get the keys off the woman on the desk, so I legged it. Did he get any of youse?' I replied.

'No, but the police came. We thought it was for you.'

'Naw, must've got someone else or something else happened.'

As the rest of the lads arrived to join the conversation, the facts became wilder until there was little room for further exaggeration beyond someone having found a dead body sitting next to them. Then we came upon the chewing-gum machine.

'Whose turn is it to put the penny in?' Joe called out, knowing he had put one in a few days earlier and forgetting we had passed there ten times since. After a bit of banter I offered to do so. Billy and Mick were left with the half-piece of chewing gum at the bottom of the pack for which Joe received an ear lashing since he never seemed to end up with it. The incident of the previous night at the Queens picture house suddenly seemed buried already.

Gilbo, the class clown, more or less filled the morning and helped me forget the money problem by coming in late. Francis Gilbertson was Muff's daily nightmare. He had the most crooked mouthful of teeth that anyone could have without having been hit by a truck, but was always smiling as if to prove that he didn't care about the state of his ivories. An insomniac would be proud of the bags under his eyes, too. He also had a lot of grandmothers: almost every time he was late he used the excuse that his grandmother had died. We all cottoned on to that and so did Mr Murphy – eventually.

'Wait a minute, Gilbertson. You said your grandmother died a few weeks ago.'

'I know, sir. She did, sir – fell down the stairs, sir, she did.'

'Well, what about this one then?' he asked, as he reached out and gripped Gilbo's sideburn and lifted. 'This is the third grandmother who has died according to you.' He yanked upwards on the hair. 'People only have two, son. Now, what's your excuse?'

'Ah, ow! Widowed, sir. Me mam was widowed, sir – me dad died in the war, sir.'

Muff let go. 'What's that got to do with it?' he asked, thinking maybe he had guessed wrong, one way or another.

'Well, me mam got married again, sir, so that gave me another grandmother, sir.'

Now that the picture was within the realms of possibility Muff eased off a bit. 'You're a very lucky lad, then, with three grand-mothers, Gilbertson.'

'*Four*, sir.'

'*What?*' Muff looked puzzled.

'Me mam didn't like that fella, so she got rid of him and married again.'

This time Muff shook his head. 'Go and sit down, Gilbertson. *Now!*' he said, fearing a verbal conflict in which he might get lost, with this buck-toothed gremlin who seemed set to become his destroyer.

Gilbo walked over to his seat, wearing his natural toothy grin and causing every single one of his peers to smile. Muff shook his head. Having this lad to contend with was worse, much worse, than having his beloved motorcycle vandalised. As always, a quick silent prayer settled him so he could get on with the lessons.

But for me the day went rather slowly as thoughts of the money crept back into my mind, ending with Muff slapping my legs for not paying attention during an algebra lesson. I felt that I deserved that but later became really annoyed when I saw Gilbertson asleep in the corner seat and Muff ignoring him.

'Hey, sir!' I said to my teacher later on during playtime in the yard.

'Yes, Stockley?' Mr Murphy acknowledged.

'How come you gave me a slapping for not paying attention when you said nowt to Gilbo and he was bloody well asleep?'

'For starters you will stay behind and write fifty lines out of, "I shall not use foul language in front of my teacher."'

'But, sir!'

'No buts, just do it. Number two, you are worth giving some time to. Gilbertson is what one would call "a lost cause" so no manner of punishment will correct that.'

'So he gets off with it, like?' I questioned curiously.

'Gets off with *what*, Stockley? Not learning? He wouldn't learn if he were awake, so nothing changed by him being asleep, did it?'

I quickly examined that reply and found myself agreeing by nodding, but it was plain that I was still looking for a different answer while doing so. Muff smiled as I walked off, shaking my head, but clearly trying to make sense of it all.

Gilbo was enjoying a cigarette with Mike Kinsella when I walked round the back of the shelter in the playground. He offered me a whiff.

'Wanna go?'

I took the half-cigarette and dragged on it before handing it back, saying, 'You're a lucky bastard, you!' Then I walked off, blowing the smoke out of my mouth as I left.

Gilbo tried to decipher what had been said, then shrugged and took another drag of his cancer stick before offering Mike a whiff.

'What's with him?' he asked as he handed over the fag.

Mike shrugged and then remembered something Betty had told him recently: 'Might be due on,' he said. They both laughed just as Joe entered the smoke zone.

'Quick, boys, give us a whiff,' he said, his hand outstretched. He took a quick drag and then did an offman, saying, 'Muff's on his way down.'

That caused a panic as they extinguished the fag and hurried out into the open, where Muff was sauntering towards them only to realise that he had been a little slow when he saw Gilbertson emerging with his toothy grin, saying, 'Too late.'

At the same time Mr Timms was glad to see the fingerprint men finally leave. He had done his utmost to contaminate the scene by moving the cabinet more and smothering the window with Duncan's fingerprints under the guise of getting him to climb up to the little window to see if he could spot the culprit, who might – according to Mr Timms – still be out there somewhere. In his statement he had also said that he often had boys in that office, where he would give them a strict telling-off instead of involving the police. This was backed up by the staff, who regularly witnessed it. Now, as far as Mr Timms was concerned, it was down to the lucky little thief to stay clear of dropping himself in the mire by overspending or getting caught with his loot.

Meanwhile Johnny had gone to see his sister's father-in-law, Mr Doran, and was laughing at the tales of how he was relentlessly pursued by the police – so much so that one would think him to be Public Enemy No. 1 instead of a man willing to stand a bet. He listened to his tale of how he had become a bookie instead of a runner.

'I realised that the bad days for bookies never outshone the good days,' he said, 'so I began to take a chance and stand my own bets by choosing the ones from my daily take, which were less likely to win, and standing those myself. It was a form of cheating but I knew that my boss had done the same because he had actually told me so.' He shrugged. 'I did it myself, just like he did.'

Which made much sense to Johnny. However, during his earlier days he had managed to give the local police the runaround and they had never forgotten it, especially now that some of them had climbed the ladder and were in a position to harass him during quieter periods.

'Now, what can I do you for, Johnny?' he asked after finishing his story.

Without giving a full explanation of the origins of the cash, Johnny wanted to know if he could say that he had won £190 on the horses. At this Mr Doran whistled and smiled almost at the same time. It was obvious he was going to say yes and just as obvious that he did not wish to know where the money had come from because he knew Johnny would not be up to anything that would harm anyone.

And so the deal was set up: Johnny wanted me to get the credit, so it was proclaimed that I had – while messing about – picked out three horses for the following day. Johnny pretended to be enthusiastic and called for a little syndicate of threepence each from his mum and dad, his aunt May, himself, and with a penny cut for Logger, who had helped, supposedly, by cutting out all of the horses for that day and making a type of bingo with them. Mr Doran had said he would pick the winning horses and arrange them in such a bet that it would return the required money for Johnny to make his windfall public. To add to the reality, Johnny took the money down to Doran's and left it with him. The stage was set.

After that Johnny stayed away from his mother's house for fear of having to reveal the names of the horses that he didn't have, but as soon as he was told the horses' names he rushed there and told his mother the good news. He then went to the Roundhouse pub and broke the good news to his father. After a few drinks he decided to go to Mr Doran's house and pick up his winnings, elated with a job well done.

It wasn't that far to the bookie's home and I was already there, having lingered most of the day just to fill my eyeballs with the image of my longstanding crush Joan under the guise of hanging out with young Christie. As far as I was concerned, the business of the money was over and done with once Johnny took charge, so, when my jubilant brother appeared, walking down the street, I merely gave him the thumbs-up and carried on playing with Christie around the huge gas storage tank overlooking the area, but particularly Mr Doran's street because it was directly facing their little two-up, two-down terrace.

That old cobbled road never got much traffic because it didn't really lead to anywhere other than the other side streets, which made up that little conglomeration of tucked-away houses. The lads and I were halfway up the steps of that gasometer when they noticed some suspicious-looking men. To me the men meant little because I was a stranger to the movements of the area, but Christie had been warned to be wary of men sneaking around (his dad had never hidden the fact that he was a target for the police due to his bookmaking activities).

'Coppers! Have to warn me da,' Christie said as he clambered back down the steps of the slippery holding tank.

'Me too!' his twin Brian said as he followed in his wake.

However, I decided to watch from my somewhat elevated position. I saw the lads heading for the entry, which would take them to the back door of their house, but then I spotted Johnny coming out of the front door, smiling and carrying the cloth bag with the money inside. Although I had no idea that he could be a target, I felt it wise to run down and at least inform my brother of the presence of the two dicks who seemed to be stalking the street. When I got to the bottom of the steps and squeezed through the railings, I saw the detectives walk briskly towards my brother. Then they nabbed him, one to each arm.

'You just come outta the bookie's house,' said one as he snatched the bag from Johnny's grip.

'What bookie, that's me sister's father-in-law's house,' Johnny told them.

'Yeah, and this isn't paying-out money neither, is it?' the copper with the moustache said, as he waved the bag in Johnny's face.

'That's money for me sister. It's . . . it's for furniture and stuff for their new house.'

'Oh, yeah! What does she live in? A bloody mansion?' his clean-shaven colleague asked, as the other one showed how much money was in the bag.

'It *is*! Go ask Mr Doran, then.'

'Oh, we intend to, boyo!' the one with the moustache said, then turned Johnny back towards No. 13 Steel Street, where he'd not long come from and where Mr Doran and his boys were now standing on the top step of the door, watching.

All three walked towards the very disappointed Mr Doran as I watched from the gateway of the gasometer. Then I got a bright idea. The copper with the moustache had a hold of the bag with the money and was holding onto Johnny with his other hand, so I ran after them, then built up speed as I drew near. Focusing on the bag, I hoped with all my heart to be strong enough to snatch it from the bobby's grasp. The nearer I got, the bigger the man's hand seemed to be as it clutched the cloth moneybag. Plimsolls near to melting, I reached out to snatch the bag and almost at the same time I tripped, which sent me flying into the back of the detective, my head acting like a battering ram as I struck the big man's kidney. The collision kept me upright, so my hand grabbed the bag just as the surprised bobby let go with a yell of severe pain. Grimacing, he dropped to the floor on one knee. His surprised colleague could only look on as I carried on running, like an athlete fit for a gold medal, the moneybag swinging from my hand like a cloth baton.

'Get after him!' roared the downed detective.

'But what about—' The clean-shaven fella was about to say 'our prisoner' when the grimacing moustache cut him short.

'He's no bloody good without the evidence. Get the kid!'

Mr Doran and the family laughed as I disappeared round the corner at the end of the street with the detective trying to get up speed in his clumpy leather shoes..

It wasn't until I was on the canal bank that I realised my mistake: I was good and fast when twisting and turning, but on the straight of the towpath the big man started to overhaul me. I glanced behind – I was half a football pitch to the good, though losing ground fast.

The Seeky! I thought to myself as breathlessness began to kick in. Bit to go, shit, gotta climb the wall! Can I do it quick enough?

One more look behind. I could almost feel the cogs turning as they calculated the speed of the giant man against the distance to reach the access wall of the Seeky, then my climbing time with no slip-ups.

Yeah, only just, I told myself as I readied myself for the change in pace and that all-important, no-slip climb up eight feet of sheer wall. The bag, the bloody money bag! was my next thought. Once again my brain twirled into action. No can do, boy. Throw it over and then follow! I told myself.

The gravelled path seemed to fly past, as did the clumps of grass stuck to the cracks of the coping-stone edges of the canal as I strove to outrun my pursuer. At last the wall! My lungs were close to bursting as I flung the bag over, then clambered upwards, my little fingers clawing their way into the wider brick spaces and pulling while my feet jammed hard into the wall in order to make the ascent as fast as possible.

'Stop, yer little bastard!' the bobby shouted as he realised what I was doing, all the while knowing he was powerless to stop the little urchin except by way of causing the kid to panic and, hopefully, slip. 'Stop! Otherwise I'll throw this brick!' he yelled loudly.

I could hear the crunching of the gravel getting closer but carried on. One valiant effort sent my arm flying upwards, allowing my fingertips to reach the edge of the last brick.

Got it! I told myself. Now pull! I added, as my other hand grasped the same edge by the barest of grips, but it was enough to raise myself high enough to release and pull again. It was so very hard but equally rewarding to feel my belly touch the flat side of that top brick, where I let out a cry of relief, and then, as I felt a touch on my heel, I lifted up my legs and landed on the top with my middle and rolled over.

Looking down at the red-faced cop, I smiled. Suddenly I felt full of beans and raring to go as the big man jumped up to grabbed at the top of the wall. I dropped down and looked around for the bag. It was halfway down the steep embankment but not the way I wanted to go: I needed to go to my right, where the little narrow path led into a secret tunnel. Gingerly, I edged my way down that steep embankment, which had a long drop onto the railway lines. If I were to fall, it could result in my hurting myself or at least disabling myself long enough for that bobby to catch up. As I grabbed the bag, some of the money fell out onto the grass; it seemed a lot but when I looked inside there was still a lot left, and so I decided to leave it, especially as I spotted the arm of the big policeman struggling over the wall. Just as I gained the path to take me down to the Seeky, I heard the angry man's voice again: 'You little bastard!' I turned; the bobby was about to turn onto his belly and drop, so I gave myself wings and fled into the darkness of the Seeky tunnel.

Whenever my pals and I had gone through the Seeky it always made us feel apprehensive, even scared, but this time I felt the dark, damp and echoing hollowness to be my friend: if I could stay on my feet, I knew that, at the end of it, I would be free.

Take it easy, I told himself. Just trot, don't dash and you won't fall.

And so I made my way across the mounds of soot and brick or metal debris that I couldn't see but knew were there from past trespasses.

With the silhouette of the boy in front of him the policeman tried to follow quickly but soon realised that the puddles had deeper hearts than one would think and the hidden but upright obstacles of metal, wood or brick were solidly entrenched in the grime of the dumped soot and cinders. As he'd attempted to hurry, he had twice tripped, so slowed down. After deciding to take long quick strides instead of running, he fell foul of a metal hoop, which pinged up and struck his leg.

'Bastard!' he mumbled and then realised that the next tunnel ran parallel, so he stepped down a little into it via a joining arch. Now he could run.

Emerging out into the bright evening light, I glanced at the steep embankment I still had to clamber up and wondered if my legs would take me and would my battered heart hold out, too. Yes, I told myself before I began the slog upwards through the clay-sodden soil and grass sods, using them to haul myself up while using each step to push. It was hard, much harder than it used to be, due to my bad heart, but I was determined to get away.

The grass sods were not so kind to the officer due to his weight, so he used two hands to ease the load that he was putting on those roots; it helped but was not good enough to make a gain on the lighter youngster he was chasing.

I soon found myself at the wall, the final wall before Commercial Road, where I would drop down and hightail it for Melrose Road and the Buildings, my home, where I just knew this chase would end, for no one could catch me within its confines.

Not so far away, on the other side of that wall, Crippled Johnny was effin' and blindin' because he would have to hand-pedal his carriage all the way down to Sandhills in order to pick up a little contraband that he could make some money on. Going down was not so bad but having to pedal the bloody thing all the way back up that incline would be tough on his arms and there were no able-bodied kids about whom he could con into helping him. He took one last look up Owens Road before setting off, but there was no one to be seen. Begrudgingly, he gripped the pedals of his carriage and made a start.

I was just about to gain the top of the wall, the moneybag tight between my teeth. One more grab and I could haul myself up onto the copping stone and be atop the wall. I flung myself up hard, but my hand slipped and I tumbled back down, twisting my ankle as I landed. Clasping my skinny little bone, I winced and then spied the exhausted copper puffing his way onto the little path that led to me.

Fuck the pain! I told myself as I jumped to my feet and then started to climb again.

With the moneybag once more firmly gripped in my teeth, my hand reached that top brick, but this time I clung on. I was about to haul myself up when I felt a firm grip on my ankle. The copper didn't know that I'd hurt myself so his squeeze was not intentionally painful but it sent tremors through me.

'Let go!' I shouted through clenched teeth.

'Oh no, sonny! You lower yourself down here or I'll drag you!' he threatened. 'But first pass me that bag, there's a good boy,' he added with a smug smile. Then he gave an extra tug just to prove his point.

'Argh! OK.' I grimaced, then brought my free hand to the neck of the bag. 'Here!' I called loudly, with a now-free mouth, but I threw the bag over the wall instead of dropping it down to the gloating and highly expectant officer.

'Fetch that!' I added, as the cop let go of my leg. He scrambled past me up the wall to retrieve the all-important evidence while I dropped back down and hobbled away.

All the bobby was concerned about was retrieving the bag, but, when he got to the top of that wall, all he saw was a invalid carriage whizzing off towards Sandhills at a great speed to the accompaniment of the song 'Pennies from Heaven'. It resonated clearly in the air but faded fast.

That night, there were 'jars out' at Ninny's after the ninety-five quid that I had re-covered from the embankment was shared out to those with a stake. Johnny had always had intentions of giving me a fiver from the takings, but, even though half had been lost during the chase with the bobby, he still gave me a fiver, his reason being, 'If he hadn't done what he did, we would have had nothing!' He smiled as everyone thought he meant stopping the bobbies (which was true), but truer still was the fact of our little secret: that he had taken it in the first place. To a hard-headed God, stealing is always bad, but to a considerate man it is a circle with one hundred and eighty degrees of blame.

As for Johnny Butler, he smiled at people when they asked how he came about the new furniture in his home *and* a new TV. He said it came from the army by way of his solicitor, who had been fighting his case for years for backpay. For that information people paid 'one cigarette'. From then on, Johnny Butler felt the world owed him less, even though he never ceased to hold his hand out for more.

CHAPTER 10

MY INITIATIVE

Woodwork and metalwork were often a lovely break from the comparative 'norm' of schoolwork. The huts accommodating those classes were in a different place from either of our schools: Chancel Street, just off Orwell Road, and by pure coincidence overlooked by the back bedrooms of the house, where earlier that lad ran inside, having split my head open with a brick.

That centre was a prefabricated, single building with an entrance in the middle of two classes, one on either side of the doorway. The whole building was surrounded by a playground, laid with tarmac but fenced off with six-foot-high metal railings. Chancel Street was shared with a large storage depot for Irvings grocers' suppliers, while the other side of the centre was the back doors of the houses in Fonthill Road, which was the south continuation of the Fonthill Road, which ran past the Billogs.

To the left as you went in was the woodwork class; to the right, metalwork. Mr Davis was the woodwork teacher, a small but very amiable fella, who got on well with most of the lads and tried his best to teach us the basics of his trade in the hope that some of us would become joiners. For those who had no wish to be in that trade he hoped to furnish them with skills enough to tackle the small jobs about the house that often need doing, but for that they had to want to learn.

Our very first job was to make a boat from a piece of wood about nine inches long and three inches wide, with a depth of two inches. It taught us how to measure up, plane the wood, chamfer the edges, saw and chisel and . . . be bloody careful in case you cut yourself, which so many of us did! At first I didn't think that making such a boat was a challenge, but it turned out to be so and taught us a lot during the process. I remember taking it home; it had taken some six weeks to make but that was only six lessons, which in turn was about twelve hours; but when you are all listening to instructions and having to wait before starting, due to people having to be told more than once, it worked out at a mere eight hours or slightly less. Dad looked at it and said, 'Nice one!' then got on with what he was doing. But I wasn't put off because it did look so ordinary, which is what I thought to begin with until I had to tot up all of the different techniques needed to complete it. I grew to like that woodworking class.

As for the metalworking class, well, it just did not appeal to me. I think it was the touch of the metals that put me off and the dirt seemed to bury itself in your skin. I was used to dirt and grime from my dockland delvings but that mucky metal mess sort of touched the nerve ends with me, causing a dislike I never conquered.

Consequently, I got on better with Mr Davis than I did with Mr Wright, or the other metalwork teacher before him. Anyway, what I am really getting to here is that I helped them out due to a shortage of materials. It all began when I wanted to make something big that I could impress my family with; to date we had progressed from that little wooden boat, gone past the stage of making camping stools and were now merely walking in that class and getting on with our work almost without the usual pep talk and safety aspect, which had preceded all lessons. I wanted to do something really good, like you see in the shops, then – somehow – homed in on a coffee table. However, there was a wood shortage in our wood centre.

Mr Davis gave us a sob story about the economic running of the school and said wood was in great demand now that the rebuilding of the bombed areas was being attended to. It all flew right over my head, leaving me a bit disturbed and more than a little disgruntled at not being able to make a coffee table. So, with nothing to do but mope about my aspirations and their chances of materialising, I let my mind roam free to daydream. Of course it disappeared off into the only place that I really loved – those docklands – where it ambled for a while only to come rocketing back with a solution.

'Mr Davis, sir!' I exclaimed, disturbing him as he was trying to give another kid some tuition.

'What, Stockley?' he asked, with a look that said, 'No matter how you twist it, son, we ain't got the wood!'

By the time I had finished explaining my idea, he had a brighter look in his eye.

1. He would be rid of me for a while.
2. If my idea were to be a good one, it would be problem solved.

He must have thought it was worth a shot because he said yes. However, I had another request: donkeys.

'What for?' he asked, a slight suspicion in his tone.

'Rheumatic fever, sir.'

'Rheumatic fever?'

'Yes, sir – I had it, sir. Can't carry stuff far without stopping, that's why I need help, sir – to carry the stuff.'

'OK, who do you need?'

At first I was going to ask for Joe and another of the lads but then I thought that, if I got refused the wood I was going to beg for, I would have to nick it because sure as hell I did not want to come back empty-handed. And if that were the case then I couldn't have Holy Joe with me, so I nodded towards the class reprobates: Bow and Tommy.

It didn't take long before we were down by the wood yards, but we didn't go straight in. Before I approached the boss man first I had to find out a few things. For one thing I had to find out if he was Catholic or Protestant – no use asking an Orange Lodge fella for free wood for a Catholic school and vice versa. Made sense to me, so I waited until one of the worker fellas came by.

'Hey, mister!'

'What do you want, son?'

'Your gaffer, is he Cat'lic or Prod?'

'Cat'lic, I think – he's always callin' them Orange Lodge fellas fit to burn. Why?'

''Cos I need a favour. What's his name?'

'Tom – Tom Sheldon.'

I thanked the man, then waltzed on into the ganger's hut, one sock up, one down. Bow and Tommy were standing by the gate, waiting. I explained that we came from St John's School and we were having trouble getting timber for the woodwork class.

'Fuck off!' he told me.

I was shocked until he rambled on about the Catholic Church being bloody rich: 'Between them and the bloody Orange Lodge, this country is fucked! They bleed us dry, they do!'

At least I could understand that: I had often heard people moaning about the collection plate being stuck under their noses during church services. It even happened during the war when pockets were really empty. So I thanked the man anyway and then left.

'What's up?' asked Bow. He laughed when I told him. 'Because . . .' he began, 'the fence is down at the back. We can go and get what we like.'

'Naw, we'll leave it until we got no other options. Come on, there's loads of other wood yards, only this time we'll make sure what the gaffer is,' I told him.

The next one was – for sure – a supporter of the Orange Lodge, so I said we were from Fonny Road, which was a Protestant school. He gave us loads. Poor Tommy Connor: Bow O'Rourke loaded him up with most of it, but took only a lousy armful himself. As we were struggling up Sandhills (well, Tommy was) the sweat simply poured off him, so much so that I felt compelled to carry some myself because Bow thought it was hilarious. He kept saying that, should Tommy sweat any more, all the timber would float back down the hill and end up in the docks. Had I not jumped in to help, I'm certain that Tommy would have tossed the lot onto the floor.

Mr Davis was more than happy: he was ecstatic, and enthused about a chunk of hardwood that Bow had brought more by accident than design. Having felt a bit guilty that Tommy had the most to carry, Bow had stooped and picked up a piece of lone wood to go with his pile. That was the mahogany piece the woodwork teacher drooled over.

From that we learned even more as we digested the fact that this heavier hardwood was worth far more than softwood – ha, it was a knowledge that would stay with me for many years and help me to make a fair few pounds when I became a wagon driver!

Mr Davis was only too glad to send me for more timber, allowing me to choose whomsoever I wished to be my 'donkeys'. But the lads did not see themselves as such. To them it was merely the price of skiving off school with the best of excuses, should a truancy officer happen to pounce. However, it was with Bow O'Rourke that I found a gem that would stay with me for a long, long time: ebony. While passing Grumpy's timber yard, Bow nipped in for a wee behind the stacks and came out with a small plank of black wood.

'Never seen nothing like this, have you?' he said.

I took it and whistled at its weight. 'Is it wood or a piece of bloody coal?'

'Naw, coal will make you dirty, look!' He ran his fingers down it, but no black was showing. 'That's definitely not coal. There's the bark,' he said, pointing out a pattern on the surface.

Sure enough, there it was. 'Is there much more there?' I asked, but Bow merely shook his head.

'Dunno, didn't look,' he said, so we went back to his toilet place.

At first we couldn't see it, but then we did: all on its own it was, a largish pile up against the fence that was broken. Our eyes met, Bow's and mine. There followed a simultaneous smile that said everything that had to be said without saying a word.

Mr Davis ogled that piece of ebony, then rattled out the countries it came from: West Africa, India, Sri Lanka and Indonesia. It was the first time that a geography lesson had been held in his class and the most attentive we had ever been for one. He surprised us all by showing us how it sank in water owing to its density. It was something that we remembered for years afterwards, along with the fact that piano keys were made from it, as were many types of ornament that buffed up beautifully when polished.

'All wood is magical,' he used to say, 'but this ebony is the crème de la crème of timber.'

'Worth much, is it, sir?' asked Bow, thinking this to be a fast way to make some money.

'To someone who specialises in it, yes.' That put a grin on Bow's face. Then the teacher said, 'But . . .', which wiped it off again. 'But you have to know what firm does the specialising. Piano makers and suchlike, or top-quality furniture manufacturers, they're the kind of end users for that wood. When a firm uses a lot of it they normally order it before it's cut and have it delivered from the forest to their premises.'

'So, if you had a few planks, could you get rid of them?'

'Not really.'

'Would you buy some, sir?' asked Bow, with his fingers crossed behind his back after feeling disappointed.

'No good to me, young O'Rourke. That wood is prime stuff and needs time and much effort put into whatever's made from it. If I were to make anything from it, I would take my time because things like that have to be made properly or not at all.'

'What kind of things would you make, if you decided to, sir?' I prodded.

'I think . . .' Mr Davis said, then stroked his chin as if giving it great thought. 'I reckon I would make a decent-sized coffee table. The mirror effect would be marvellous – it would last a long time and would always be in vogue because of what it is.'

'Always be in *what*, sir?' Bow enquired, a twisted look on his gob.

'Vogue, never go out of date due to its perfect beauty.'

'Like a song always being in the charts, sir?' Tommy Connor chipped in.

'Not soft, after all, Connor, are you?'

'Never said I was, sir.'

'I know that, Connor, but you do really good impressions at times, don't you?'

Tommy smiled. He knew he wasn't soft but now he knew the game was up because he had always thought his teachers to be of that frame of mind, but obviously, he hadn't kidded them as he thought he had.

Before too long the woodworking stores were full of assorted timber, but I had lost my zest for woodworking. Now I was into the moochings that had been permitted me and I was beginning to feel the need to show off my capabilities. I had become slightly addicted to being in charge, or at least saying where it was we would go. However, I'd been a victim of my own success because now they no longer needed any wood. Although I tried to settle into the mundane once more, my mind so often galloped off into that world where the idle cranes and bogies stood, waiting. So much so that I began to skive off school on woodworking days just to satisfy the urge to be where my mind lay. I would begin by going to the woodwork centre and would then slope off once Mr Davis had marked me in, which was what the teacher used to do when wood was required. Being a joiner by trade, Mr Davis didn't have that teacher mentality that demands rules and suchlike to be rigidly adhered to, so, when he saw me sloping off, he turned a blind eye, knowing I was a competent street urchin.

That was how I came to be on those docks during one lunch hour with Mick Furlong and Bow O'Rourke, who were eager to learn how to drive the cranes and bogies. Now it wasn't Logger being the teacher: I myself had taken up that role. I was showing Mick how to drive one of the bogies when Bow shouted to me, 'Hey, Peter, how does this work?' He was sitting in one of the rigid-wheeled cranes that worked off electricity. There were two push handles, one on each side of the control panel directly in front of the driver. One moved from left to right and controlled the required power; the other controlled the forward or reverse motion: right for forward, left for reverse. It was a kind of safety thing: you had to select forward or reverse with one, then get the vehicle to move by adding the power with the other lever. However, those handles had to be pushed in the correct order. If you were to push the power first, it wouldn't work. You had to select the direction first and then add power. It was not rocket science, but confusing when you first got into the driver's seat, which Bow had already done, hence his call to me.

I could have been Mr Davis, Muff or Mr Thomas as I walked over to Bow – the teacher to the pupil. It felt good. As I stood by the crane, I pointed to the levers to press, explaining as I pointed. Somewhere between my telling and his digesting there must have been a blank space because he pushed on the wrong handle.

''Snot working!' he snarled.

I took a small step forward and pointed to the handle that he should have used first, saying, 'That one, that is the first one to press for forward or reverse, then that one for the power to make it move. OK?' I then moved back for him to try.

'OK,' Bow replied, then pushed the wrong lever again. Now I could understand why the teachers looked as if they were swearing under their breath because I had a few choice words being uttered under mine due to his incompetence.

I took another step forward and, just to emphasise my words, leaned right in and pointed a finger at the lever he should press first, then I moved that finger and pointed to the second lever and said, 'Then you press that one,' which he did. The soft bastard! Slowly the crane moved forward, trapping my foot. I could feel it pinching on my shoe as it did so.

'*Stop!*' I yelled. 'It's going over my foot!'

That solid, rubber-wheeled tyre had moved onto my shoe, trapped it and was squeezing my foot as if to say, 'Guess what's next.' But I had yelled just in time to get Bow to push the lever back into neutral.

'What?' he asked, sensing something was wrong as I glared at him for moving the crane before I had backed off. 'What's up?'

'What's up? You're on my foot!'

'Oh, sorry, Peter, here!' he said, then pushed the handle back to forward, sending the crane forward and pain rushing through me like a whirlwind.

'No, yer soft *twit*!' I screamed, causing him to turn the handle once more to stop it where it was, right smack on the full toe with all the weight, causing it to crumple and inject me with pain, pure pain, the likes of which I had never experienced. As I glared at him, he sat there almost in awe – maybe at my face, maybe at my anger, maybe because he was about to laugh because that was what we did whenever such things happened. But this was different: it was in progress, my foot was the victim and *he* had caused it.

That set him into a panic: 'What way shall I go, what way shall I go?' he screamed.

'*Any fuckin' way!*' I yelled. '*Any fuckin' way!*'

So he pushed the handle once more and I refrained from saying '*Stop!*' The pain rolled around my now-spinning head because it could no longer find a corner to reside in and cause me anguish. By the time Bow got out of the crane I was sitting on a pile of fades (rotting fruit) from the ship and attempting to take off my shoe. I had no idea what I would see but I was expecting something awful as I undid the laces.

'You all right?' said Bow.

I looked at him, then growled as my hand clenched around a mouldy orange, which I used as a missile to hit him with while he laughed, and laughed some more until I joined in the laughter, but still called him a stupid prick!

However, that was not the end of it.

A big docker walked over, saying, 'You all right, son?'

He began helping me with my shoe. I sat back and let him as I replied, 'Yeah.' As I looked around, not far away was a huge hunk of wood, like a railway sleeper. 'We were lifting that, and me mate let it drop and it landed on my toe,' I told him.

'Yer a fuckin' liar! I saw what youse did: youse were messing around on that crane.' He said that just as my shoe came off, then he removed my sock – and promptly fainted. I was astounded: there was that big galoot of a docker lying flat out, my sock in his hand and my knackered foot staring at me. My big toe was a mass of mangled flesh and nail, as if someone had pummelled it with a hefty hammer. But for all of that horrid injury I couldn't get the big docker out of my mind – he was still unconscious when the ambulance arrived, so they stretchered him into it and let me hobble.

For a few days I had a limp, but, as there is nothing you can do with a big-toe injury, I just had to get on with it. Of course I did not tell Mr Davis the truth. I merely told him and my parents that I had kicked something (which became true a couple of years later, when I did, and broke the bloody thing again).

Then, as if the gods were unhappy with me for doing nothing, Mr Wright, Mr Daybell and Mr Thomas came to see me. Metal was short, and there was an urgent call for a new goalpost – upright fixings, so the next season could be accommodated. I nodded, gleeful to be back in business, even though I didn't make a carrot, but could nevertheless ply my trade of ducking, diving and cajoling.

Look out, metalworking firms of the dockland, here we come! I thought to myself.

This time the same rules applied, but it was easier to obtain because those metalworkers were in and out of their factories by the minutes for fresh air, unlike the wood-yard wallahs, who had acres of grounds in which to wander while they dodged the boss to sneak a sly puff.

The very first one I sidled up to for advice on the religious denomination of his boss quickly filled me in that the guy was a Proddy Dog. So with the name of our Protestant adversary, Fonthill Road, on my lips, I began the (truer) sob story of a poor school with aspirations of having a good football team but with no goalposts for the coming season.

Hole in one! Bow and Tommy were soon secreting those pieces of metal in the rear of Grumpy's wood yard so we could take a rummage around the docks and warehouses before heading back to school with our booty.

We had a laugh at the way the grownups locked themselves into separate cupboards of religion, yet worked with one another without conflict in their jobs. It seemed so ridiculous. Often on those docks we heard discussions about 'Proddy Dogs' and 'Cat'lics', but no one fought over them, unlike 17 March or 12 July, when the stories of those groups being at each other's throats were rampant. Our enclave, the Billogs, was mainly Catholic and the furore resulting from the 12 July Orange celebrations had been a yearly comet of hatred towards the Protestants, which lasted only a day or so and was then buried in our minds for another year. Hardly worth the effort, especially to us kids, of burying the fact that you can throw a bottle at people on the 12th or thereabouts, but it was wrong to do so any other time – it just didn't make sense.

My dad had the best idea. When I saw him dickying himself up on 12 July, I would ask him where he was going. He would say, 'Up to Netherfield Road, lad. Those Orange buggers certainly know how to have a good party!' Then he would wink at me and try to console my rather perplexed face with, 'Ha, I'll drink anyone's ale, lad! I love the atmosphere of a good time.' It was like that down the docks. Most were liberal and therefore watery like their fellows, regardless of religion; it was the biased ones who were oily and didn't mix. As for us kids, we really didn't give a shit which side of God's arse people kissed.

As big and gruesome as those docks could appear to be as sweat holes, there was an air of flowery light-heartedness floating about in their canteens, and in particular the Stan Waters cafés, which we loved to visit. I'd first been introduced to them just after my mother died, when Ninny was the manageress of one such Stan Waters at the Huskinson Dock. I was seven years of age and sat beside her on the counter next to the till that she operated. The men would file past with their bacon or sausage sarnies (often referred to as 'dockers' doorsteps'). Ninny would smile at their banter as she took their money. Being an anomaly in such a place caused the obvious question, to which she would explain that Mum had not long died and that she was left holding the proverbial 'baby': me.

At the end of the day, Ninny put on her coat and said, 'Come

on, son' – meaning for me to get down from that high counter on
my own, which I slowly attempted but found myself stuck. With a
bit of effort I launched myself from there, only to stop at the floor
on my feet while my trousers carried on to my ankles due to the
weight of all those pennies and ha'pennies that had been given to me
by those kindly men, at least half being Cat'lics and the other half
Proddy Dogs. The only thing I truly remember feeling about that
day was embarrassment, due to standing there in my Y-fronts, clean
as they were because Ninny always said, 'Make sure you wear clean
undies – you never know if you'll meet with an accident!'

The lovely atmosphere of those Stan Waters cafés had never
changed; we even went in them just for a game of cards once we got
to know some of the men. Bow was always first there whenever we
got the chance, just as in the days when the metal would be left lying
in Grumpy's wood yard to be collected. We had learned that card
games were a little short-handed near to the end of the Welt. That
was the name given to the hour-on/hour-off system that had started
during the war when the men worked long hours for little pay and
were a bit disgruntled by the fact that their lungs were being starved
of oxygen down those deep hatches where they toiled nonstop for
hours and hours. Plus, most of the men smoked and would have
to take a break from the hatch, which took some time getting out
of. Naturally, there were a lot of complaints from those who didn't
smoke and felt themselves to be working harder, but then some
brainy peabody came up with the Welt idea, which was fair to the
nonsmokers because it gave them the same amount of time off.

Anyway, they would all pile into the nearest Stan Waters café,
where they rested, smoked, talked street politics, cracked jokes and
. . . played cards. Towards the end of the Welt the conscientious
worker would leave in order to get back on time and give his

opposite number a break, which left the still-running card school short on players.

Bow once sat there looking intently interested as the cards went around, so much so that, during one of those quiet periods (which lasted about fifteen minutes), he was invited to try a quick hand. He quickly threw in his penny and became hooked because he won a hand, which made him rich with two shillings

Thanks to that win Bow caught the gambling bug and played whenever he could. He borrowed a penny from both myself and Tommy, and soon found himself holding cards that could rake him in a half-crown or so if Lady Luck were to smile on him.

Alas, it did not this time, and ten minutes later we were all a penny poorer and rummaging through one of the dock sheds, looking for something that we could take and sell to get our money back. One tin of salmon each would do the trick, so we set off back, taking care to wait for the bobby to come out of his hut and take a pass-out chitty from a departing haulier before hurrying past with our booty while he was distracted.

The metalwork teacher was more than enthralled with the five bars of two-inch metal strips that we brought to him. Ha, he even bought Bow's salmon off him for threepence!

That ability of ours to acquire stuff for free had an enormous impact on the teachers, who often allowed us to go roaming on the days when we should have been learning about woodwork, metalwork and sometimes general schoolwork, if what they needed had an urgency to it. We knew the religion of almost every chargehand in the wood yards and metal-fabrication works on and around those docks and had the monopoly with them because – I think, no, I'm sure – we were the only ones to do such begging; we never, ever met anyone else who did it. And the beauty was, I got all the credit. It was the only thing that I was really noted for in the eyes of those teachers! By the time the beginning of that last summer came around the metal and woodwork shelves were full, the storerooms overflowing. I could drive a bogie and a crane like a natural, the lads had a good basic knowledge and so – except for my heart – the world was there for trespass. Now all that separated us from the final term was the summer of 1957, with its pea, bean and spud picking.

I shall always remember the final week of that term due to almost having my head knocked off by Jack Keaney Junior, or 'Little Big Jack' as he was known. He was Joe's older brother and the first son of Big Jack. I was on my way to call for Joe when I saw our Ann (Logger's sister) stepping out of Joe's house, so I dodged into a doorway to hide. The doorways of most flats were inset by about three feet, which hid me well as I waited for her to arrive so I could jump out and frighten her – or them, for by now I could hear a conversation, which meant she was walking with someone. It turned out to be Eileen Keaney, who was Ann's friend and about the same age, around twelve or thirteen. Out I jumped and scream they did, but young Eileen got more than a fright: she stood there screaming for ages while she wet herself there and bloody then! So I fucked off.

Can't take a joke, thought I as the idea of Big Jack being angry upset my jellybeans. I never gave a thought to Big Jack Junior; he must have surely done the same during his time roaming those landings.

Here's how it went a couple of weeks later: I'm coming down the stairs; Big Jack Junior's walking along the landing. I hit his landing as he's about to hit the stairs.; we meet; I smile; he growls. I'd forgotten that the sight of me presses the button for him to remember.

'Hey Stockley!' he booms.

'What?' says I (rather innocently, to be frank).

'You near scared our Eileen to death the other week!'

'I never!' says I truthfully, then I get on with the facts of it. 'I was scaring our *Ann*; your Eileen just happened to be with her.'

'Yeah, well, you shouldna!' he says, then lashes out with this frying pan he calls a hand and whacks my face as he would an annoying wasp hovering over his favourite cake. Wow! The last time I'd been hit like that was by my father on the night when I smashed those windows in Leamington Road School. The whole landing seemed to shake. He was eighteen, big and strong like his father, and I was wondering if my head was going to fall off or merely spin for a while until my feet could reaffirm that they were still on the ground. He spoke and I could hear him but it was as if he were an apparition. I'd been stunned into silence, although I felt I wanted to roar out – but to what avail? He was still standing there, fully loaded, with the ability to throw me over the landing if he wished. I merely looked at him, all the while saying to myself, You will pay for that! You will fucking pay for that! Over and over I said it to myself until he walked away.

I watched him go down the stairs without even a glance back, so cocksure he was and safe in the knowledge that he was so big and strong that he was able to suppress anything that should come up against him, as all eighteen-year-olds believe. It was then that I wondered: did the man actually hate me, or was he really that concerned for his little sister that such admonishment was deemed necessary? The throbbing of my face incited another rash thought: would anyone know if I were to drop a brick on him from the top landing?

My days were taken up with pea picking but my nights were spent watching him. Just like his father, Big Jack Junior loved a pint.

When he finished his drinking, he came home through the middle entry, into Owens Road, where he ambled across with his pals, then often stood talking in the opener leading to the stairs he'd climb up to gain the second landing, where he lived. Like clockwork, he stood in that opener bidding his friends goodnight before they would split: he up the stairs, they over to their homes elsewhere.

Yes! says that evil little mind of mine. You can!

Now all was set.

I remember the day well: 5 a.m. up, train out to the pea picking, fill three hampers, eat a half of one – those fresh peas were lovely. Travel home with the lads, all of us laughing, skitting and frolicking, but at the same time I'm thinking, Will he do the same tonight?

First, I go over to the Orwell to check if Jack Junior is there. He is. I know now he will be there until closing, so I go up to the olla at the top of the street and get me a big brick, a corner slab. I can hardly carry it as I struggle up Fonny Road because I want to go up the back stairs so that no one will see me placing the slab by Mike Kinsella's doorway. Old Mrs Kinsella won't see (she doesn't venture out at night) and Mick is at camp with the Cadets, so he won't be around to see it either.

There, that brick is safe; now all I need is Little Big Jack. In my haste, it never even occurred to me how dangerous my plan was.

Waiting, staying in the shadows, waiting; don't let anyone see me while I'm waiting. Is Jack still there? I worry in case he's not. The worry casts doubt as to whether he has stayed in the Orwell. Or is it possible he left and went down to the Roundhouse, or even the Melrose pub? He could've gone there. They do so often change, especially the younger ones – they like to get around more. As my doubts grow I go down the stairs. I have to convince myself that he is coming. I sneak over Owens Road, glancing back to look at the opener and then up at the landing, from where I shall drop that slab; it is bloody high. Then I carry on through the entry leading to the Orwell pub. They are beginning to leave now, saying their goodnights as they go. Quick peek. Yes, Little Big Jack is still there, smiling.

He won't be smiling for long! I think as I head back to take up my station. The entry tempts me to lighten myself due to the bubbling of the fresh peas that I have eaten during the day – buggers, they are, for working your bowels. But I won't have time if I have to get back up to the top of those stairs before Jack Junior comes.

Two flights of stairs to each landing, eight flights altogether; first up. Little way across left, then turn left and up again, four times. Soon be there, I tell myself as my tummy rumbles the warning that I have to go, and then sends that bloody pang before the pain that says, 'I *mean* it!' Another few ups, with two more to go, and the pain now says, 'Are you listening to me?' And I stop, as if paralysed by stomach pains. They ebb just enough for me to take the next two flights up to that top landing. Then I hear Jack's voice and loud laughter. I look over the landing and, sure enough, way down there he is standing, talking to his mates, just as he always does. Now all I gotta do is drop that bloody brick.

Oops, tummy tremor! Little Big Jack is laughing. I can hear him all the way up on that top landing.

Sod it! I tell myself, then reach down and unclip my waistband: trousers down, arse to the railings.

'Go, *go*, go and do the job of the brick!' I tell my defiant passenger as I forcefully eject it, where it freefalls as I quickly pull up my kecks, then turn and run.

He is halfway along that landing as he cries, 'What the *hell*? *Eugh!*'

'Betcha can't slap *that*, Jack!' I mutter to myself as I run and laugh and run some more until I get home, still chuckling as I go in, causing Mum to think I'd gone soft. I didn't get to sleep for many an hour once I lay down in my bed but then I did have a good sleep.

Joe was the bearer of points scored the following day on the train as we went pea picking.

Bullseye!

'All over the back of his suit . . . Bloody hell, Peter, it was *everywhere*! He thinks it was you, y'know, so be careful.'

'How could he think it was me?' I asked.

'It was full of peas!' Joe replied with a laugh. 'He looked like a pot of mushy peas!'

After that I stayed well out of Jack's way. But I think Mike Kinsella's misfortune had a lot to do with muddying the waters of everyone's clear memory, for he suffered a terrible accident that was the talk of the Billogs: while at camp with the Army Cadets at Altcar, he had lost an eye.

Apparently there was a lot of tomfoolery going on, with some cadets blackening the nether regions of other cadets with boot polish, which led to some in-fighting. Mike got himself into his dormitory to get away from it all because he wished to keep clear of trouble. He was looking out of the window at the rowdies being unruly when someone threw a bottle, which crashed into the window, causing it to shatter and some glass to penetrate his eyeball.

It hit us all hard, for we were like brothers now after all of those years as Scallywags. He was in hospital for some time and came out wearing a patch, and, although we got him a stuffed pet parrot and a crutch, really we found little enthusiasm to follow through in order to make anything frivolous out of his situation, so the whole matter was more or less left to die.

CHAPTER 11

THE MORGUE
PRANK

L ogger was now in his final year before leaving school, and his mother's prayers were close to being answered, as he became increasingly less interested in his pigeons and began to get more and more involved in the Army Cadets. All she ever wanted for him was a trouble-free and happy life with the ability to pay his bills and walk tall. Like most mothers of that neighbourhood, she sacrificed, strived and slaved for such an outcome for her family. Now it seemed that her efforts were finally paying off, especially when he came home in his uniform looking every bit the soldier, smiling, handsome and respectful to her as if she was his world, which she was.

But he also had his mates to tag along with and an array of things to follow up, as well as continuing to learn about the world he was becoming a part of. It was an education that he could gain only by doing, but being canny while he did what had to be done.

One of the things he had to do was pass on what had been passed on to him. It was a must, even though it was nothing and would not benefit him in any way other than to become a fruit in the bowl of yesterday that would always remain fresh to his taste buds and make him feel good: the 'Morgue Prank'.

He had often spoken with Tommy Keaney about it when they talked about the time the Morgue Prank had been played on them by my brother Johnny and the older brother of Tommy, who, being the first son, was named after their father, Big Jack. The Morgue Prank was played out in the actual mortuary of the Kirkdale Homes together with whatever bodies lay in there at the time.

Some years ago a group of kids came across a way into the morgue and then for some macabre reason found it fun to mess about in there, lifting the arms of the dead bodies and pretending they were alive. This became a prank to be played on anyone they could lure down there. Eventually, that became a kind of ritual, which, up to my time, had not been played on any of those Scallywags. Now Logger was seriously discussing it with his pal Tommy due to the news that the Kirkdale Homes were earmarked for closure within the following twelve to eighteen months.

'We'll use Betty and Ethel,' Logger said, during his layout of the plan to entice us down into the morgue.

'It might work,' said Tommy. 'But our Joe remembers the time when we got it done to us. I couldn't sleep that night and had him up because of it.'

'That was three years ago, Tommy. He'll have well forgotten that by now.'

'OK, but we're gonna need a good diversion to kid them, especially to get them over the Kirkies at night.'

'We'll get Betty and Ethel to help – they love to get up to

266

mischief,' Logger told him, causing Tommy's eyes to twinkle, for he well knew of the dabblings those girls got up to. 'Will you ask Betty? You know she'll do anything for you.'

'All right.'

As Tommy made his way to look for Betty, he remembered the time she first called to him from her bedroom window facing Joe Dodds's horseboxes. She had known the boys and most of their names and had soon clocked those who had visited the horseboxes most from watching through her bedroom window. Her eye had fixed firmly on Tommy, who was as cheeky as they came, but he had never met a girl who had approached him in such a forward way before.

There he was, that night, minding his own business while drawing on a cigarette as if he were King of the Teddy Boys, with his drainpipes and long coat, collar pulled up to meet his curly Curtis cut, when he heard a whistle; it was a low kind of whistle that caused him to look around. The road seemed deserted, so he started looking at the windows facing, and then saw the white of Betty's blouse, with her arm waving from her bedroom.

Who, why? he wondered as he dragged on his ciggy one more time before flicking it to curl the smoke skywards, and watched it land with a small explosion of sparks ahead of him but it was soon extinguished by his beetle-crusher shoes as he neared Betty's window.

Both being fourteen at that time, she hungering for it and he being a little more experienced than his friends, he took one look at what was on offer, then slithered through her window like a boa constrictor, almost losing one of his prized beetle crushers as she closed the window down a bit prematurely.

Betty told Ethel about it, making it sound so exciting that she felt very much inclined to go with her friend, who had made a date with Tommy and Logger to go over into Joe Dodds' yard. After that, all Tommy had to do was snap his fingers and Betty would come running. Being a nymphomaniac had its drawbacks, however. One fella can't really keep up, and so was born a legend of those buildings – at least as far as sex education was concerned – among the young up-and-comers who desperately wished to learn.

Tommy's journey soon came to an end as he met Betty and Ethel on the stairs, not far from where the Scallywags were chopping firewood.

With his curly hair spread out as if he'd just had an electric shock, Bandy looked more like a man possessed as he ripped up floorboards from one of the bombed-out houses. Tasker was down below, collecting the planks, which he put into bundles of three in order to carry them down Owens Road to the square, where Sylvester and Bullet were chopping them into fire-sized chips of about six-inch lengths.

Meanwhile I was out selling them around the landings.

'Threepence for all this, missus,' I said, as the lady eyed up the size of the bundle in my arms.

'They was only tuppence last week,' she protested suspiciously.

'No, missus,' I corrected her as I recalled the reason for her concern. 'You only got half as many because that's all we had left. Remember, you pulled us as we were brushing up at the end of the day, so we gave you what was left?'

'Oh, yes,' she agreed as she stepped back to open the door to the coalhole. 'Here, throw them in there. I'll go get my purse,' she told me. Thankful to rid myself of my burden, I unloaded the armful of wood into the space of that little cupboard, which had the remnants of a delivery of coal from the previous week on the floor.

'Getting more coal this week, missus?' I asked.

'Why?' she said as she returned, digging into the unclipped purse for my three pennies.

''Cos, if you do, move the wood 'cos it'll get buried by the coal otherwise,' I said, pointing down into the little cupboard.

'I will,' she replied, as she handed me the coins.

'Ta, missus,' I said and then fled as if my life depended on it to go and get another armful of chips.

She smiled as she closed the door, my speed reminding her of her own enthusiasm when she herself had been a child – only then her moneymaking efforts had brought a lot less than threepence to the table.

On my way back down the stairs I saw Betty and Ethel talking about what they had agreed to do with Tommy and Logger. Although they were seen as the local 'bikes', I had a respect for them because they shared out all their favours fairly.

'Who is it tonight, girls?' I asked with a cheeky grin.

'Ooh, look, Ethel, it's pencil dick!' Betty said, and then the two girls sandwiched me.

'All right, girls, I'm in a— Oi, stop that!' I demanded as Ethel's hand dived to my groin area.

She laughed, enjoying my protests, but spoke to me in baby talk. 'Ah, what's to do with the little fella, then? Doesn't he want to come out to play? If you can get it hard now, you can come over the horseboxes later, after we've finished with Tommy and Logger!'

'Gerroff!' I protested as she tried to unzip me.

Then Betty put her arms around me from behind, pinning my own arms to my side. 'Shall we jump him, Ethel?' she asked mischievously.

'Gerroff, *now*!' I demanded, as the thought of them debagging me right there and then on the public stairs brought a bit of colour to my face.

The girls laughed and then stood back, allowing me to move on.

'Youse should do that when I'm not working,' I told them before I sped off, their laughter hot on my heels, followed by Betty's voice reminding me: 'Don't forget the horseboxes tonight!'

When I told them about it Joe and the others wanted to go after the girls but changed their minds after Mick reminded them that nothing would get done if they did. He calmed them with, 'We'll go to the horseboxes later.'

They resumed their chopping while Joe loaded me up with my next armful of chips.

'Shall we go and spy on them?' I asked

'Never mind spying on them: we'll line up for seconds!' said Robby.

'I bagsy thirds!' Mick chipped in.

'Who's going last?' I asked after claiming fourth.

'Billy, he's a good swimmer,' said Joe with a smile.

And so it was that the lads smuggled themselves into the horsebox compound that night, waiting. But what they didn't know was that Betty had been watching and waiting for Logger to return from the Kirkies, where he had left Ethel and Tommy.

'This is the gear, innit, Tommy?' Ethel asked as they sneaked among the dark shadows of those Gothic-looking Kirkdale Homes.

'Yeah,' Tommy whispered, then held up a warning hand, having seen some old Kirky-Homers leaning out of a wire-netted window, blowing smoke into the night air and watching it swirl and then dissipate as the flow took it west. Once Tommy saw the men walk off, he waved Ethel on. 'We'll wait here for Betty,' he instructed her, knowing she would not be long once Logger had told her to hurry.

Meanwhile, Logger had gone to the horsebox enclosure and climbed over, from where he pretended to be calling for Tommy. His tall frame was visible as a silhouette to the boys as they squinted through the slats of their hiding place.

'It's Logger!' Mick whispered.

'Wonder where our Tommy is,' said Joe, sensing maybe something was wrong.

'Don't know. C'mon, shall we go and ask?' I suggested.

Logger smiled as we appeared.

'Where's your Tommy?' he asked Joe.

Joe shrugged. 'Don't know, Logger. He was having his tea in our house when I left.'

'The snidey git musta gone to the Kirkies. We've found a new den there, a great place it is, but we wuz supposed to meet here tonight though 'cos Betty and that lanky one was supposed to be dropping their kecks for us.'

'What's the new place like, then?' I asked.

Logger pretended not to hear as he put on a show of being deep in thought. 'You what, Nylon?' he said as if it had just dawned on him that I'd spoken.

'I said, what's the new place like, then?'

Larry knew he had us as we all gathered a bit closer for a listen. 'It's at the back of the Kirkies, just by the old rhubarb patch and where them goosegog [gooseberry] trees are.'

'Isn't the mortuary bit there, next to the old air-raid shelter?' Sylvester asked, hoping Logger would say no.

'Yeah, it's the old mortuary. They've got another one now so it's been left empty. Do youse wanna come and see it?' Logger asked.

'Shall we?' said Joe, as if putting it to the vote.

We all agreed except Robby, who voiced a little concern due to his fear of rats and creepy-crawly things and almost any shadowy places, especially those little nooks and crannies where the mortuary stood. 'What if – what if someone should come or anything? I don't wanna be getting into any trouble or nothing.'

'Don't worry, Robby, lad,' said Logger. 'We'll leave a window open and if anyone comes, you can spring through it.'

'All right then,' Robby reluctantly agreed. He said it sullenly as if someone had twisted an arm behind his back.

As they walked up Rumney Road the black outline of those massive buildings seemed to have a halo of stars and the distant light of the moon gave it a more eerie glowing background effect. Robby's tummy was rumbling a bit as his nerves acted like paddles in his digestive system. Bandy Billy stuck close to Logger as the tall lad strode through the tufted grass, which lay between the railings and the gooseberry patch. Mick and Mike kept getting under each other's feet, causing some friction between them as nerves began to tighten a bit around the neck of their bravado. Meanwhile Joe and I purposely stayed behind Robby to stop him turning back and running off – plus, if there was to be an offman, we wanted to be the first!

At the rear of those big Edwardian- and Gothic-style buildings among the bare gooseberry bushes and a few bare apple trees, Logger could see the open windows, with their wire-netting covers to prevent any of the hundreds of feral cats from leaping in. We carried on, with the smell of the place now in our nostrils – that lived-in but musty and pissy type of smell which the aroma of carbolic only seems to enhance. Nerve endings were now firmly attached to the running switch of our brains as we stood in the shadowy darkness beside the mortuary, the door of which Tommy had left open after climbing through the skylight window.

One by one we filed past Logger, who had pulled open the door for us and was now standing by to close it. Almost nose to tail, we stopped as the first of us, Billy, refused to go any further until Logger was back in front. As the door clicked shut and our eyes adjusted to the darkness a lighter flicked once, but failed to produce a flame. Then a second time, which produced a few sparks, then a third time before the shooting sparks caused the wick to catch alight. Now Logger's face looked haunting as the glow from his candle shadowed his features. Holding a finger to his lips, he murmured, 'Don't make any noise and only speak if you have to, but in whispers!' He then turned to lead the way along the short corridor leading to the mortuary's room of inspections and dissections.

The door creaked open to show a room lit only by moonlight afforded it from the dirty opaque skylight that Tommy had climbed through and no one ever closed because of the constant aroma of the place. There were three corpses covered in white sheets but nevertheless obvious, with pointed toes facing one way and bulbous endings where the heads were; two were on trolleys and the other one was on the inspection table. We all froze as Logger walked over to the nearest one on the table, then lifted up the end of the sheet to take a peek at the face: it was the cadaver of an old man who we guessed had no relatives, so his body was to be used for research. Already the top of his head had been removed for the brain to be taken. Logger had not known of his presence but had seen it all before, so he wasn't put off and thought it good to add effect to what he and Tommy had planned for the nosey upstarts who wanted to spoil their amorous adventures.

He beckoned us lads over to him and then, as we all stood around the table, he whipped off the sheet to reveal the body. Robby tried to head for the door but Logger quickly grabbed his arm, saying, 'Don't panic, soft arse! He's dead, he can't harm yer.'

'Looks 'orrible!' Robby said squeamishly.

'Looks dead 'orrible!' said Joe without even knowing that he'd punned it.

'Look, watch this!' Logger said as he put his lips to those of the dead man, then held the nose as he blew into the man's mouth, causing the belly to swell up.

'Eee! Whatcha doin' that for?' Mick Furlong asked.

'Watch!' Logger insisted then put his hand under the cadaver and lifted.

Suddenly there was an eerie sound as the body slowly belched the wind that Logger had blown in there, as if once more alive. Logger laughed as most of us looked sickened and scared.

'Thought we'd come to look at your new den,' said Mick, desperately trying to appear unconcerned.

'Yeah,' Billy added in a louder tone as he tried to tough it out.

Logger put his finger to his lips to get us to keep the noise down. 'It's through there,' he said, pointing to a door on the other side of the second corpse.

''Ere, thought you said this place wasn't being used no more!' said Joe suspiciously.

'It's the cold weather, Joe – kills the old ones off like flies. The Grim Reaper musta had a busy night last night,' Logger said, as he moved over to the second body. We watched as he lifted the sheet on it and looked in. 'Here . . .' He beckoned for us to gather round. 'Get a look at this one, it's like it's got two heads!'

That really seized our curiosity, so we all moved round to see and didn't notice as Logger moved back a pace or two. Suddenly the corpse sat up and raised its arms. All hell broke loose as shouts of 'Mummy! Mummy!' filled the air. Bandy Billy was pushed over during the stampede for the door. In the rush to get away Joe was pushed and landed on the old man's body. He let out such a yell. Tommy added to the confusion as he appeared from behind the second door with a white sheet over him and the lanky Ethel 'oohed' and 'oohed' beneath her own sheet. Meanwhile all Logger did was laugh and laugh, then laugh some more until his sides ached.

The light from the corridor behind him shone onto the grounds in front of the morgue, giving an old man a floodlit view of the boys as they virtually flew past, not caring that they had been seen. The Chief Constable himself could have been waiting with a posse for all they cared as they crossed the grounds like a bounding antelope escaping the clutches of a very hungry lion.

As for the Scallywags doing the hoochy-koochy in those horse-boxes, well, that was a nonstarter, although four people did end up in there, with a bottle of dinner beer, which Betty had snaffled from her mother's larder. However, they just couldn't settle to their normal antics thanks to the elation of having pulled off the best-ever Morgue Prank, which would doubtless be talked about for a long, long time to come.

CHAPTER 12

A SECOND CHANCE

Now that the Scallywags were in their final year, they felt good They could see the open gate at the end of their long trek through those fields of learning. Meanwhile, the feedback from Tommy and Logger was great: Logger had taken a job in Hansons Dairies in Long Lane, Aintree, while Tommy had a job in a factory that made steel oil drums. Both seemed much happier than at school and, besides, they now had a regular income, so did not have to rely on any of their usual moneymaking antics, which left the up-and-coming Scallywags to step into their shoes. However, due to my heart-valve problems taking a turn for the worse, I was increasingly left out of the run-of-the-mill stuff because I was finding it harder and harder to keep up.

A game of cricket finally brought it home to everyone that the glow within my dynamo was diminishing as I tried to run after warding off the ball and sent it rumbling away. I was so tired after that one that I held up my bat to indicate a walk back to the crease. Robby Jackson ('Jacko') came to my aid then by offering to run for me. His leg irons had recently been removed, thanks to his good response to treatment, and he was raring to take on anything and everything the world could throw at him.

Although I was more than happy for Robby, it made me feel sad that my life had come to this: having to have someone to stand in for the most trivial of things, a cricket run. It was a safe bet that any onlookers would be asking, 'Why doesn't Peter run himself?' Soon it would be a known fact that I was fast becoming an invalid and the very thought of that really bit into me as I found myself regretting not having taken the advice of the doctors when I first became affected by the rheumatic fever. That foolish stint of running round the square when I had tried to kill myself was really taking its toll now. The more I thought about it, the more I slipped into the 'if only' world that so many people regretfully find themselves in.

Meanwhile the opposite was happening for Robby as he emerged from that cocoon of invalidity with a zest for life that only such people can acquire. He wanted to do all that he had missed out on, heard in rapturous stories from his peers. Having seen them going on their adventures, he had often tried to follow them but could only ever get as far as his impairment would allow him to go. Now that was gone, there would be nothing high enough to stop him or far enough to keep him away, or dangerous enough to deter him.

Joe, Mick, Robby, Mike and Billy began showing Jacko the playground ropes they had been swinging on since they first trespassed on it and found his appetite to be insatiable as he scaled the high walls with ease now that he had no callipers; what he lacked in the strength of his legs, due to that long period of little use, he made up for with pure guts and determination. Everyone was filled with admiration as he strove to become a full and active member of those Scallywags.

However, for all of the efforts that Joe and the other lads put into bringing Jacko up to speed they couldn't instil those all-important rules they'd all been taught by Logger, Tommy and any of the older lads at the very beginning of their trespassing days: the rules of safety. The older lads had been nurtured by those before them and had passed these lessons on to the younger ones in their charge. Then there was no doubt that Joe & Co. would then pass all of their safety rules on to whatever young ones they decided to take under their wings, but, as far as Jacko was concerned, he was their age, so it came as natural for them to believe that he would already be aware of the safety advice they'd all grown up with. To them it was as simple as getting out of bed each morning, but they'd forgotten that what was natural to them was new to Jacko, who'd always had to put callipers on before standing.

The safety rules had been instilled in the older lads by their parents: in the early days it was mainly siblings you took on your travels because Mum and Dad had to work long, hard hours, scraping a living. Once a young kid could wipe his own arse he was set free to roam with the older youngsters, the only proviso being, 'Make sure you look after him!' Where you went was never an issue, but the safety of those in your care was always the number-one priority.

But Jacko proved to be a quick learner and he soon cottoned on to stepping daintily over the live rail lines, even though he had no idea how much power surged through them. When those Scallywags acted cautiously, so too did Jacko as he calculated the sums of their caution adding up to something dangerous. The noticeable drag of his leg became more of a limp as his muscles grew stronger, and it wasn't long before he was near to the middle of the pack when it came to doing an offman due to one prank or another misfiring, causing an irate person to give chase.

During the years we had known Jacko he had been nothing but a goer, always striving to get those callipers off, as well as to show that he was not any lesser person despite his disability, and we all admired him for it. However, one evening in the late summer of 1957, I left my house to go on a message for my ninny around to Joe Hills' shop. As I passed the side stairs that came down from the landings, I heard my name being called. It was a lady by the name of Mavis Wheelan – a pretty young thing she was, one of those whom you knew to be polite to. So I stopped and began to answer her enquiries as to my health and suchlike when suddenly she went wide-eyed, as if she had been injected with fear. Then she began to scream and carried on screaming. The noise was so loud that I felt deafened but also extremely curious as to what was making her act in such a scary way. I turned and caught something bouncing off the railings that surrounded 4a Owens House, the home of recent migrants into our area: the Campbells.

As I realised that falling object to be a person, the body impacted with a resounding thump onto the rails surrounding the yard of 4a, then rebounded off onto the service roadway, whereupon the realisation that it was Jacko made me go cold. I hurried over but could only watch, helplessly, as our friend twitched as if he were fighting for the right to live. He had fallen from the top landing via the rooftop, to which he had tried to gain access by using a hold some twelve inches above the gutter which had snapped off, sending him crashing, first, onto the top landing rails – which must surely have broken his back judging by the dent it left – then down those four flights. He hit the bottom rails before landing to the accompaniment of screams from Mavis.

Numbed, I watched poor Jacko twitch as if trying to move away from the pull of death that was tugging at him; and then old Mr Campbell came out of his house and covered my friend with a multicoloured eiderdown.

Eventually, an ambulance came, but by this time Jacko had stopped moving and the square had become alive with curious people. Meanwhile, Mavis was being attended to by a lady and Mr Campbell took his quilt from the ambulanceman and walked back inside his house as the emergency vehicle drove off.

I wanted to tell the world what I had just seen and there were plenty of people wanting to know, but my mind simply could not focus on anything other than the fact that this was a terrible thing to happen to one of my mates. Then, for the second time in my young life, a few hours passed that later I could never account for.

Such events always leave hoards of unanswered questions that attack you constantly and they all begin with that almighty word: 'If'. 'If' is the gateway to the unknown – 'If I do this, what will happen?' Many of us have said that and have then gone on to discover something or regret having tried. 'If only . . .' Boy, the number of times those two words have been uttered as the bitter pill of a mistake is swallowed! As far as Jacko was concerned, we Scallywags used the 'If only . . .' words so many times: if only he had not contracted that disease, would he still be alive today? But the main 'if only' that kept cropping up was answered by our Logger as he listened to us discussing the death of our friend: if only he had not climbed up that stupid pipe in the first place!

'None of us would have done that,' Joe had said before Logger butted in.

'Yes, but all of you have gone on to do even more stupid things. That goes for Tommy and me and almost all of the older ones before us. Jacko didn't because of his leg irons and therefore was never warned off. He was in too much of a rush to catch up on what he'd missed, but the main thing he missed was all those warnings. To us lot they came as natural as growing up – we learned from each other and hoisted our own red flags. Poor Jacko never had them drummed into him.'

That all sounded a bit long-winded but we got the gist of what Logger meant as we nodded our agreement. It was sad – so very, very sad – mainly because he was a mate, but all the more so because it put a grim face on everyone who knew Robby Jackson, which was almost every person in those Buildings as well as our school and the church. Maybe Jacko helped save lives because of the warnings given out after that by the adults and ourselves too whenever we saw younger people in precarious spots. It all made sense now, as did the memories of the times when the men and women of the neighbourhood had warned us off one thing or another. However, what had not really made sense was the number of times that we had *ignored* those warnings.

As the memory of that tragic event slowly began to fade, the exit of the educational tunnel was getting bigger and brighter. Robby, Mick and Mike were the first to leave in the summer of 1958 and had almost four months of ribbing us as 'schoolkids' before Joe and I joined them on the Christmas of that year. Billy Vaughan finally joined us in March 1959, when he left school on the Easter break.

Leaving school was not so different as we thought it would to be. As usual, it was like a game of follow-on: Logger and Tommy had followed those who left before them; Robby, Mick and Mike had followed Logger; and Tommy, Joe and me followed next; and then Bandy Billy followed us. Nothing really changed as we tried to choose where to work. We still looked for guidance or inspiration along the paths that the older lads had taken.

Basically, it was as if we were back in the juniors – in that line of follow-on – only this time we were not within the confines of a playground, so the boundaries of where we could end up were limitless. Although we did not know it then, those boundaries were endless but the limits would be the results of our own endeavours.

By this time Logger and Tommy were both working for Hansons Dairies, loading and unloading empty milk crates then shunting them around to the wash bays, where the bottles were set into the wash lines for sterilisation before they could be refilled with milk. Once filled, they would then be refrigerated until it was time for them to be loaded onto the wagons that would take them to the various depots for delivery. Though not a challenging job by any means, it paid well and taught them the true meaning of money.

In those days the employers looked kindly on those who showed initiative by looking for a job rather than being sent from the dole so, if you really wanted a job then you went looking. Robby Tully had searched and taken a job with a tailor's and had soon become the first of us to wear a Crombie – come to think of it, the *only* one. He became 'the puddy-cat with the coat'!

Mike Kinsella found a job in Reece's bakery in Hawke Street, Liverpool, where he worked for many years.

Mick Furlong took a job on a Norwegian boat and was subsequently ribbed as to whether he would bend down to pick up the soap if he dropped it.

Joe Keaney tramped the streets and visited many offices in search of a job. Finally, he walked into the Co-op offices on Walton Road, where he blew out a sob story that his dad had promised to throw him out if he didn't come back with a job that night. Maybe it worked and maybe it didn't, but he was sent from there to Marsh Lane in Bootle, where the manager of the Co-op shop there gave him a bike and filled the basket on the front with a typical grocery order, then watched as he rode it around the street, just to see if he was capable. He was, and so he got the job, which he stuck at for at least twelve months.

Billy Vaughan took a job in a printer's in Duke Street, not far from a club called the Pink Parrot. He was glad to get employment and put up with being a dogsbody for a while before he went in search of another job.

As for me, I was as envious as hell due to the fact that I could not take any of those jobs owing to my bad heart. Then, finally, I got a job in the Gaiety, a picture house on Byrom Street/Scotland Road, rewinding films. With its enclosed space and dark rooms, it was not what I wanted at all, but it sufficed because it was not demanding work and, if I'm honest, it was a bit on the interesting side, finding out how those films were shown.

That brought us to Easter, our first one as workers. Initially we were at odds as to where to go, then somebody mentioned Formby and the newts. A sense of nostalgia urged us to go. Although we were all working, the Scallywag side of us encouraged the idea of bunking, which most of us did, and so we were soon skitting the two who had paid their fares (Robby and Mike) as we hurried along the lane leading from the station down to the shoreline of sandhills, which held the many ponds that the newts and frogs used for spawning.

Somehow the width of the brook bordering the field didn't seem as wide that year as we walked along the lane. Mick Furlong tried to jump it casually but barely managed to land on the grass on the other side. He grabbed the fence wire to pull himself up but the aged post holding up the wire decided to call it a day and slowly gave way, causing him to be off-balance and end up leaning backwards over the brook while hanging on for dear life in case he should plonk into the stream. We just could not help but laugh at his predicament and ignored his pleas as he hung on for dear – dry – life.

'Ooh, look, Mick!' said Mike, as he stepped over him onto the other bank. 'This is easy, innit?'

That caused a round of laughter and prompted the rest of us to follow suit while poor Mick hung there, cursing us as we went by. It was during this period that five lads from Formby came by. Robby, at this point, was still on the road and heard one of them saying something ending in 'Scouse scruffs'.

None of us had heard so we were oblivious of the flaring up as Robby shouted back, 'Who the fuck are youse calling Scouse scruffs?' Within a flash all hands hurried to his side, including the unfortunate Mick, for whom I had to stand in the brook in order to lift him up. The alpha male of our group, Robby, felt it was his job to lead as he leaned right into the face of the lad who had voiced the insult. As much as he was in the lad's face, Robby was just not a violent person, though: he would skit someone and often take an argument to its vocal limits, but he was not a basher for the sake of bashing. However, that day was different and he got really angry. Whether it was what the lad had said or his attitude I don't know, but whatever it was he got a slap across the face for it. And that was that! His mates darted into a line-up and that caused our lads to line up too. It was on, though not for me, as in those days I gave more thought to my dicky heart, so I just watched.

It was four on four, with one of them standing back, like me, and merely watching, too. I kept my eye on that one to determine whether or not he was going to join in. I'd no intention of joining in but told myself that I should, if this other lad did. He moved a little towards the scuffling groups, so I headed him off and stood in front so as to block his path. Then, as if by way of intention, I raised my mitts like at the beginning of a boxing round to let him know that I was willing to get involved, should he try. It was at this point that he made a gesture: he dug his hand into his pocket, so I drew back my fist as if ready to strike, should he should pull anything out of the pocket – a knife or something. Then he totally surprised me and offered what he had in his hand, saying, 'I'll give you this, if you don't hit me!' I certainly had no intention of hitting him unless he joined in, but I took the threepenny bit anyway and told him, 'OK.'

Soon after, the scuffling stopped; there were no injuries so no one had been really harmed. The pride of those toffs was rather dented because, in the main, they were bigger and slightly older than we were, but the sandpaper on our backs was much coarser. Aside from a few choice words nothing, more happened, and so we resumed our journey, chirping a victory by laughing and such like, as you do when the possibility of getting hurt does not come to pass.

It was a long road down to those sandhills and soon we were back in our jokey mood, taking up with the Fishcake (Mick) and skitting him over not being able to jump the brook.

'Yeah, bastards, youse woulda let me sink into that water!' he blasted, then pointed to me, with my soaking feet and wet trouser legs from where I had had to stand in the stream in order to lift him upright. 'There, look at Nylon with his wet feet!' None of them had seen me lifting Mick up, so they had no real idea why my feet were wet, but it didn't take long before I became the target of their skits.

286

I think they were in the middle of giving me loads when a Black Maria screeched to a halt next to us, then policemen jumped out and bundled us into the back.

Formby police station.

Somehow Mike Kinsella had managed to skedaddle – actually, he told us later that he had gone behind a tree for a wee just before the bobbies drew up – so it was just the four of us who sat on that wooden bench in the cop shop. After a while Robby was called up for his particulars to be taken down by a highly belligerent sergeant who from his attitude seemed to be taking the situation personally, as if he were related to one of those Formby lads.

'Name?' he demanded.

'Robert Tully, sir.'

'Robert Tully, eh? Any other name?' he asked in a very demanding tone.

Robby mumbled something in reply but it was insufficiently clear to be understood, which caused the sergeant to reiterate his question angrily as he stood and then looked down at the now very distressed Robby. 'I'm only going to ask you this once, then I'll come around there and thump the answer out of you! Do you have any other name besides Robert and Tully?' he persisted.

'Sylvester, sir,' Robby said clearly, but quietly.

'What?' the sergeant demanded as he thumped the desk. 'Speak up, lad, speak up!'

'*Sylvester, sir!*' Robby replied loud and clear, his face turning red as a postbox.

We all wanted to laugh but refrained from doing so in case that big-booted copper should come over and kick our arses, but while Robby replied to the remainder of the questions we looked at one another and our eyes sparkled with glee. We had always known his secret, but now it was really out in the open: Sylvester the Puddy Cat it was!

By the time we had all been booked in and our parents notified, the story of that threepence surfaced and what had been charges of assault were swapped for those of robbery with violence. We were like lambs to the slaughter and all because those lads had called us 'Scouse scruffs'. The charge sounded terrible but it was not our usual style in any way. None of us would demand money of anyone and most certainly not offer violence for it, but there it was in black and white – an unpleasant stain on our characters that would be with us for ever, should anyone ever look it up.

When you have to live with something you get on with it or worry yourself sick, which is what our Robby did. The roasting he got from his father – and some of the family – caused him great stress. He developed alopecia, which resulted in lots of white circles of baldness appearing on his head. We all felt really sorry for him but were truly glad that we ourselves were not affected in that way. For a while, we even reneged on calling him 'Sylvester'.

It all ended on 6 May 1959 when we were each fined £2, with fourpence costs. Thankfully, for all, it wasn't reported in the local paper, but we didn't care really since we knew the exact truth. After that Robby's hair began to grow back, but with a slightly different tint. He had always been cautious, but Sylvester now became the most ultra-cautious cat you ever laid eyes on.

My job in the picture house consisted of three main duties: rewinding the films after they'd been shown and putting in and taking out the main fuses each night and morning. They were large fuses, so large in fact that my hand could barely grip one fully. Each night I would get a beer crate and put it by the fuse box, drop the switch and then take out the big fuse. Then I would take out the other big fuse before resetting the big handle into its 'red' position so the lights could be used. The fuses I took out were for the projection room, which, according to the projectionist, had to come out in order to comply with the insurance policy. Dull as it was, I did it with the intention of looking for something that would tax me more and invoke an interest for me to follow, which would help take my mind off the crippling effect of my heart murmur.

However, I had some fun with my mates by letting them in through the side door to see some of the shows. One time Mick Furlong had come to see the film *Dracula* but when we were going home a few buckos from Gerrard Gardens attempted to cause trouble simply because they were local lads and we were strangers. I tried to explain that I worked in their local cinema and we were merely making our way home after finishing, not really trespassing on their patch and especially not looking for any trouble. However, they were having none of it; they were bent on causing trouble and we just happened to be the only ones available.

I ended up with six stitches in my head due to a blow from an iron bar while Mick was stabbed in the leg and arm as he did his best to help me by getting in front and trying to protect me because of my bad heart. In the end I was so mad that I fronted them to try to protect Mick after he'd been stabbed twice. I don't know if they thought, 'This lad is crazy, we're going to have to kill him if we stay because he ain't gonna give up!', or whether it was the sight of me ranting and raving with my fists up, ready to fight as the blood from my wound poured down my face, making me look even worse than I really was. Whatever the reason, their departure was gratefully received as they all ran off laughing. Then we made our way to the Northern Hospital, where we were stitched up and inoculated.

Robby, Joe, Mike and Billy all wanted to go down the next night and look for the culprits, but it was as Mick Furlong had said: they were just local bullies and we had no names to go on. 'Anyone looking around would have no idea who to look for, or where, would they?' So it was left to lie; even going to the police would be no good. Apart from being sceptical as to who had caused the trouble, especially with our recent conviction, we had nothing to give them except our words and our battle scars, so their efforts would be zilch. Being a city dweller has many ups as far as having a choice when it comes to lots to do and places to go is concerned, but the downside makes such incidents hard to control and bring to heel when you have so many people to choose from as culprits.

Afterwards I began to carry a knife but was warned off this precaution by my dad, who said, 'Son, you're putting yourself in danger just by having that. Once you pull that out, it becomes a make-or-break situation. It only takes someone with a bit of bottle – or to be stupid enough – and try to take it off you, then you're faced with the do-or-die situation of having to use it and face the consequences, the short straw being, by law, you should not be carrying it!'

'I'd take a chance and stab them,' I replied, thinking of the night when Mick and I had been attacked. 'Just like they did to Mick.'

'Yeah, and what if something goes wrong and you kill them, then what?'

Confused, I couldn't see what was wrong with killing someone if they were about to do to you what those lads did to us. Not that I would purposefully kill anyone, or want to, but nor would I want another split skull for nothing, nor want to be stabbed, as Mick was. Those scars on his arm and leg looked horrible and the doctor said he was very lucky that his artery hadn't been severed.

Dad could see my dilemma and now spoke softly as if to put me at ease. 'I know what you're going through, son. I'm not a priest, I've been through the mill just like you, and there's been times when I've had to fight, but we did it with our fists. Admittedly, things are changing now and lads tend to go around in gangs more than when we were lads. Tell you what, I'll make you a rope cosh. Least that way you can have something to ward off danger without any chance of killing anyone if you were to hit someone with it. How about that?'

A bloody rope cosh! What a whopper! I thought to myself as I nodded my head just to please Pops and stop him worrying about me. He smiled as I nodded, and then patted me on the head, half the weight in thanking me for agreeing and the other half like a loving tap before he walked off.

He was a whopper, my dad. As the uncle he really was, he had showered me with more love than my own father and had also given up so much for me: his life at sea, the life that he loved. Like me, he had been a forsaken boy, but he found life, camaraderie and – eventually – love through going to sea. He had met his wife through his shipmate my uncle Larry (he was her brother), who became his friend, the consequence of which was to marry into the family, thereby extending his own family from nothing to plenty, hence the desire to help me when it was clear that I would be truly orphaned if he did not take me on. The fact that my mother was his wife's sister did not take precedence over the truth that he had been in the same situation but without the available help that I had, so at fourteen he was shipped off to a life he came to love: a life at sea. But to help me he had to choose: those arsehole do-gooders, known as council welfare people, totally ignored the fact that John and Ann Boylan had raised two kids, both hard workers, law-abiding and a credit to the whole of our clan in demanding that he give up the sea if he wanted to foster his nephew. Otherwise, the lad – I – would have to stay in an orphanage until the age of sixteen. What balderdash! The only ones who refused to think so were those welfare bods and their foolish bosses who sanctioned such stupidity.

Therefore, Dad was made to quit the sea and I was left to carry the burden of his sacrifice as a sorrowful bud in my heart which flowered each time Uncle Larry came home from his trips and I could see the distant look of regret in Pops's eyes. I did my best to live up to the standard that my cousins (his children) had set but sadly let him down often, and that hurt us both a lot. John Boylan never once raised a hand to me, although he often had just cause to do so. I honestly believe that his influence on me has saved the lives of many a bully.

As for that cosh, which I first thought was going to be a flop, well, it turned out to be a cracker! Pops made me promise not to take it out as a rule. I agreed to his wish and happily exchanged the knife for it as I vowed only to take it to and from work. I used to practise swinging it during the running period in work while the films were being shown, which left me with nothing to do. Sometimes I would be going home and actually wish for those lads to appear and try it on, but I soon realised that was a foolish wish and so I stopped myself from thinking that way. As the weeks went by I began to see the wisdom of my dad's words when he gave me that cosh: 'If you never have to use this, you'll have a good life.'

My pals came at least once a week for a free movie but spoke more about hoping to see those lads who had hurt Mick and me than the film itself. However, it didn't happen and I felt glad because of the chance that maybe one of them could get hurt and I would not want any such thing to happen on my account; Mick Furlong rarely spoke of revenge, so they got no pushing from us. All the same it was there, as a direct result of our closeness, every time they came to see a film.

As the weeks passed the expansion of our new world and its avenues came to us as stories from others such as Logger, Tommy and the older people we met in the jobs we had taken, because, during rest periods, their experiences began to be related across the tearooms. Then in the evenings, when we met on the street, we would repeat the various tales about what was out there as work and prospects. – such things as 'the stands', of which there were many as far as we could make out.

Stands were meeting places where men met and waited for employment each morning. They had wagoners' stands, shipwright stands, warehouse stands and stands down at the fruit market for men who needed work, and, due to the prevailing situation of there being much casual labour, many were gathered there. Even the dockers, who were employed by the dock board, still had to stand in pens just to catch the eye of hatch bosses needing men to offload the ships. Admittedly, there was plenty of work but it came in fits and starts and you would never know how long it would last before being struck by a slack period during which many men were 'broke' (finished up), then had to wait for the next ship to dock, which would start another busy time of employment.

Although we had watched our fathers weaving in and out of those periods of work we had never really taken the reality of it all on board. We had been blinkered from it all by being kids whose parents lived by the rule that children should be seen and not heard. All they ever really wanted was for us to stay safe and come in punctually for meals and bedtime – and no trouble. Now that we were on the fringes of this slippery slope of employment ourselves it was a revelation, a cupped hand being slowly opened by stories from those who had lived it. All the attempts by our teachers to instil some sort of knowledge had been somewhat wasted, but now our receptors were tuned in to being educated as the stories of those stands and the battles for work began to seep in: we wanted to know it all.

The stand most spoken about was the Hopwood Street stand, which was used for drivers, second men and standwagon men. 'Drivers' was self-explanatory and we already knew what a 'second man' was from seeing the wagons pull up in Owens Road, when the second man would get out and guide the driver back into the garage, where he would help unload the vehicle or tie on the sheets and make it safe for the night.

'Standwagon man' (or 'men') was the one we wanted explaining. Then, with the ease of an A B C book to a ten-year-old, it became clear that standwagon meant just that: a wagon standing still or parked up on the dock or place from where the load or freight would be collected. If you were a standwagon man, you loaded stationary wagons, usually four a day, with bags, boxes or bales. The bags were normally sacks of raw goods from abroad such as coconut copra or other kernels, whereas the boxes would be goods from the likes of China and the bales were usually made up of hemp, rubber or cotton. Once that was clear, we began to take more note of how to get the job. Simple, it sounded so simple, and yet the more we listened to the stories, the more complicated it became.

The wagoners' corner was where Hopwood Street joined Scotland Road. On one side stood the Parrot public house and on the opposite side was a chemist. Men would wait from about 7 a.m. until 8.30 a.m. each workday morning except Saturdays. Each man would keep a sharp eye out, looking down Hopwood Street towards the docks from where the wagons mostly came. Occasionally, a wagon would turn into the street from Scotland Road, but that was a rarity compared with the other way. Being uphill from the docks, the top of Hopwood Street was a good vantage point for seeing a fair distance, hence the agitation among the men whenever they spotted a vehicle heading towards them as it trundled up Lightbody Street from the dock area, then seemed to disappear before rising again as it clawed its way over the humpback bridge that crossed the Liverpool-to-Leeds canal before stopping at Vauxhall Road, then heading up Hopwood Street towards the waiting men.

As the wagon trundled towards them through every man's head ran the thought: How many will he want? Once level with the men, and to give a fair chance to all, the driver would holler out the number he wished for and then wait a short while as the battle for a place on the back of his vehicle began. Almost always there would be one or two over the quota, causing the driver to repeat his first total, to which came the reply, 'Carry on, driver, there'll only be that many on when you get there!'

So often would be the stories of the ensuing battles as the wagon drove along, heading for the company's yard, where the men would give in their dole cards and then be sent to the work site. A body gone flying off here or there would pick himself up and hurry back to – maybe – catch another vehicle wanting workers.

Upon hearing these tales the lads found them hard to believe, but gradually it got harder to doubt stories that don't change their makeup or consistency, and soon they were believing and fearing but looking forward to the day when they could battle for their own jobs in that field. The only drawback was that they would have to wait until their eighteenth birthdays.

Another avenue for them was the Isle of Man Steamships and the North Wales Ferries. The jobs spoken about for those ships were for people their own age: galley boys, pantry boys, deckchair lads and buffet boys or, as their paper discharges would show, 'catering boy'. This had the lads rather eager and now was the time to apply: it was the middle of May 1959. The Easter boats were already out, but the summer contingent was being readied for service after their winter lay-up, over in the Birkenhead docks.

Once again, as the lads enthused about the possibility of getting a job on those boats I was left to suck on the sour lemon of my bad heart. The reported hurrying-and-scurrying life of a boat-lad was not conducive to taking it easy and so it was back to the semidarkness of the projection room, where I would continue to rewind films and manage the main fuses for a meagre wage.

With the wild and famous enacting scenes on my screen as the thrill seekers sat and watched, slurping on ice creams or munching on popcorn, I moped around the projection room, occasionally swinging my rope cosh at the shadow of my miserable self or reflecting on my misfortunes as the clock ticked on towards my destiny. At the end of the night I got a wooden beer crate and placed it below the large electricity box, then stood on it to reach for the lever that I had to push up for 'power off'. Then I reached in and took out the big fuse that serviced the projection room. Job done!

Home now, I thought, after resetting the big lever so that early the next morning the other lighting could be used by the cleaners; then I left. I didn't care that I'd just missed the last bus – it was only a two-and-a-half-mile walk home and the weather was fair – so I plodded on up towards Mile End as if following the shadows of the street lights as they swung lightly in the gusting wind. I was just about level with Boroughs bathhouse at the top of Burlington Street when a group of lads appeared, apparently chasing a loner who was doing his best to ward them off as he tried to get away from them. Suddenly, he went down and the pack of about four lads pounced to kick and swipe at him.

My first instincts were to run over and put myself in the firing line to at least give the lad a chance to regain his feet but then that stop/start button in my head began to click in and out as if on its own, causing me to argue with myself as to what was right or what would be best. I reached for the cosh that my dad had given me, only to realise that I'd left it on the table in the rewind room. Still riddled with indecision, I looked over as the lad tried to get up but was booted down by a connection to his face. Then he shouted and it was his words that caused me to react: 'Argh, yer bastards, I was only seeing my girlfriend home!'

To me that meant the lad was an innocent victim, just as Mick and I had been. With the caution of a starving animal, I dived into that affray as if it were a meal that would disappear if I didn't eat fast enough. This onslaught gave the other lad a chance to regain his feet but, as I moved to get close so they could go back to back, someone caught me good and proper with a bar over the head. Suddenly, there came that familiar feeling of blood trickling down my face. I turned to see how close the other lad was, then my heart sank as I saw him running off as fast as he could go. The swap had been made: I was now on that altar – alone! I battled on but took yet another blow to the head, which left me somewhat reeling as they encircled me.

'What you get involved for?' demanded one.

''Cos youse was all onto one, and that's not right!' I replied, thankful for the short break the question gave me.

'Don't you know him, then?' one shouted.

'No, just told yer . . .' I paused purposefully to lengthen the break. 'Only got involved 'cos it was all youse onto one.'

'But he's a prick!' another shouted.

'How am I to know? Look, me and me mate got jumped by a gang a couple of weeks ago . . .' I pointed back to where I'd come from. 'By the Gaiety, after I finished work. I thought maybe youse were the ones who had done us.' Now I was glad of two things: one for the break and the other because they all seemed to be listening. I put my hand up to my head. 'I got a cut head then as well, had to go to the Northern with it. My mate got stabbed twice by them.'

'So you thought we wuz them?' said one, who stepped forward a bit.

'Yeah,' I replied as I looked closely into this lad's face. He looked a lot like Billy Vaughan, with a tight crop of curly, fair hair, but was as tall as Joe Keaney. As the fella looked me up and down I stood steady.

'Well, can say one thing for yer, lad, you got bottle taking us all on while you was thinking us to be those others who'd stabbed your mate. Ha, guess what.'

'What?' I asked, feeling more at ease, but still ready to repel.

'That arsehole you just saved is more than likely one of those who jumped you. He's from those tenies at the back of the Gaiety and he usually carries a knife. 'Mufta!' he called.

'What?' his mate replied.

'Have you got that knife?'

'Yeah, here!'

The lad came up and handed his friend a knife, which the main fella took and then handed to me. 'Here, we took that off him. He was threatening us with it so we took it off him, then he ran. You saw the rest.'

'Sorry,' I said, feeling so stupid but thankful that these were decent lads. Then, like a flash, I felt glad that I'd left the cosh at work, for I would surely have used it in that first attack.

''S all right, lad. what's your name anyway?'

'Peter. Peter Stockley.'

'I'm Ronnie, that's Mufta, he's Willie and that one is Paul.'

'Here . . .' I offered the knife back.

'No, you take it and give it to him back if you see him, right up his carsey!'

I grinned, then thanked them again and went on my way. I hadn't gone more than fifty yards when Mufta came running after him. 'Hey, lad!' he called as he got near.

'What?'

'That fella's name, it's Crillan, Jimmy Crillan, and he lives in the gardens behind the Gaiety.'

'Jimmy Crillan. OK, thanks,' I said as Mufta turned and ran off.

My dad shook his head. 'What we gonna do with yer? You'd get in trouble in an empty, darkened, locked room!'

'Wasn't my fault, Pops, honest.'

'But it *was*, lad, you should not have got involved. Look where it's got yer.'

'I don't know, I may have made some friends out of it.'

'Oh good, what have you got – four stitches, one for each friend? I remember when you tried very hard to become friends with those Scallywags you knock around with. You used to bend over backwards for them. Now you want to collect cuts for each friend, you'll end up getting beheaded just to have a fan bloody club!'

'Look on the bright side, Pops. You were right about carrying a knife, or any weapon for that matter.'

'Told yer I was.'

'Sure you did, but now I know it, don't I? First hand!'

That night I got home later than usual due to my friends having come down for a freebie, but made certain that they took the long way home via Fontenoy Gardens. Although that journey had been fruitless, I felt good that they had put themselves out for me – it sort of shored up my feelings for them by welding our bonds. So I fell asleep as a happy wanderer that night.

The following morning I arrived at work just as the cleaners were coming out. One of them was carrying the beer crate that I used for standing on.

'Where you goin' with me crate, Mary?' I challenged her.

She raised it as she smiled. 'I got lots of empty beer bottles in me yard, little man, one bottle a week I have.'

'Ha, a night she means!' her mate chipped in.

'Shurrup, you! Anyway, lad, I can fill this with the bottles, so not only do I get the money back on them, I get a shilling on the case also. Ye wouldn't deny me that, would yer?'

At this I smiled; how could you say no to that? After all, a shilling was a packet of fags to some. By the time I got up to the top floor to the electricity box I was so engrossed in the thought of those Welsh and Isle of Man boats that I'd forgotten about the cleaner taking my box and so I began to look for it, then I realised and called myself stupid, then looked around for something else. The only thing I could find to help me up to the required height was a metal mop bucket, which I turned upside down and then placed in position. Then I threw the switch and took hold of the big fuse.

With one hand holding that large fuse I stood on the bucket, then steadied myself while I raised my arm to push the fuse into its position. There were two lips on that mop bucket used as attachments for the handles; they caused the bucket to lean slightly forward towards the wall the switch box was fixed to. When I raised my hand to bring up the fuse to the height of the box, it caused the centre balance of my weight to shift just enough to cause the bucket to tilt the opposite way. Although it was only a small tip down by my feet, the impression that shot through my mind was that I was falling backwards. It was such a shock that I dropped the fuse to stop myself and shot my hand out to hold on, into the lower part of that fuse box, and directly onto the live connection for the fuse.

Wow!

Talk about a horrid shock! It was the scariest thing that had ever happened to me. The only way I can fully explain the happening would be to say this: it seemed as though two hands, as if belonging to a giant, came crashing down on my shoulders with such force that it felt as if I were being pushed downwards, then its tight grip lifted and shook me as I'd never been shaken before, back and forth violently, forcing my head to wobble, as if something wanted it off. The power being used made me feel like a rag doll in the hands of an angry child during a tantrum.

I do not know how long this went on for but the one thing I do know is I wanted it to stop but – and this was weird – I was not scared. I yelled for help, but it came out like an elongated, screechy yodel due to the violent shaking. It really was uncanny. No doubt this experience lasted only a few seconds but to me it felt as if I'd been projected through a barrier into a void, then held there while being shaken as a punishment for having trespassed in the first place. To me it was another kind of passing of time, as if I were on the outside looking in. Then, as quickly as it had started, that phenomenon completed itself then sent me crashing to the floor, where I lay, somewhat stunned, definitely shaken and, as the seconds ticked by, breaking out into a cold sweat.

Still dazed and uncertain as to what had fully happened, I sat on the floor and brought my knees up to my chest, then put my head down on my arms, which I had locked around my knees in order to keep them upright.

Thank fuck that's over, whatever it was!' I thought. Then, gradually, I accepted the fact that I had put my hand into the live side of the electricity box. The enormous power I had felt, was like nothing I had ever experienced before; it had been bloody awesome. I held my hand up, level, in front of me to see what effect the experience had caused me, expecting it to be trembling, but when I looked my hand was as steady as flat water.

How? I asked myself. How come there ain't no shaking? How? But I had no answer, and I doubted if ever anyone could. In the past I'd had attacks of nervousness during tight situations, even during a close game of darts in the community centre, the pressure of which used to make my foot twitch or my wrist tingle, but this time . . . nothing. It just did not make sense; then again neither had anything during that period of near-electrocution, which would become even stranger one day very soon.

For starters, I demanded a safe form of step-up to enable me to change the fuses from then on. The projectionist gave me an old chair, which wobbled. I told him to go fuck himself. He threatened to sack me. I told him to go fuck himself for the second time; he told me to take a week's notice. To this I said OK, but he would have to do that fuse thing himself until my quitting day came. He apologised, then said I still had my job, but when he came in the next day he had no film to show because I had cut them all up into bits, much too many for him to splice together and put the show on. I was – as expected – out of a job.

If you gotta die, then die you gotta. I had no intention of living like an obedient zombie in that place, and my bad heart could do one. From then on in I was gonna work like my mates and, if that meant they had an early funeral to attend, so be it! To date and by doing what those doctors said I had to, I'd had two beatings and eight stitches in my head, and little else to show for it. I would just as soon work myself to an honest death and die happy.

Forget it, Doc, up yours, convention! I told myself. Now let's get on with the show and be happy as you go!

The lads were surprised when I took a job in the 'shitty mill' on the corner of Boundary Street and Vauxhall Road. It was aptly named, with the clouds of dusty meal circulating like fog. It was where I learned to plough my nose and rake furrows in it so that I could breathe. The canal at the back doors acted like a target range for our yokkers to land in as we coughed and spat out just to clear our congested lungs. The phlegm would sail through the air and twirl in the breeze as it floated down to splash into the lazy waters below, sometimes to be snatched by an overzealous seagull due to its compactness. At least I was working manually, barrowing bags around, and that was all I cared about.

After a month at that job I had to take a day off to go for my six-monthly checkup at the hospital. The doctor put his stethoscope to my chest, then to my back and then to my chest again. He double-checked my notes, then left the room and came back with another doctor, who did the same. I thought the shit that I'd been breathing in at the mill was lying on my chest and causing funny noises, or something peculiar. Then the second doctor took me to a side ward and told me to wait there; he was gone ages.

Finally, the door opened and a man came in, dressed in a suit. At first I thought he looked like a detective or politician – in fact, anything but a consultant, which was what he introduced himself to be. He explained that they wanted to do some tests on me, which would require me to stay in the hospital overnight. Then he gave me a pen and paper and asked if I would write down my diet for the past few months, along with all the things I'd been doing: where I had worked, what it entailed, anything and everything that I had done. Just to be certain that I understood properly, I asked if I should put down the cuts and bruises I had received recently but he smiled and shook his head.

'No, basically, we want the unusual – anything you would normally not do, things you have eaten that, say, your friends would not, or have not. Even if you have been in an environment that you would not normally be in.'

'Like my new job?' I asked, thinking about the horrid dusty mill that sent me home looking ghostly each night and coughing up chunks of yuck during my mile walk back to the Buildings.

'New job?' he asked, then listened intently as I explained the horrors of that workhouse.

He shook his head. 'No, that wouldn't affect your heart,' he said thoughtfully.

'Heart?' I repeated, almost as if a thought had dropped down to my tongue and slipped out. Well that, surely, only left one possibility, which I duly recounted to the astounded doctor.

'You *what?*' he exclaimed. Upon hearing about my terrible experience at the hands of that electricity box, he slammed his pad down on the bed.

Apparently, electricity can be a powerful killer but it also has healing tendencies. That was my understanding of the doctor's hedging and filibustering, as he poured out fifteen years of advanced knowledge to try to account for the fact that the potency of that shock had somehow jolted my heart valves back into normality. A little could kill or cure just as easily a lot could, but there was no way of measuring who could take a little and who could take a lot. Yet, just as the permanently implanted electronic pacemaker was beginning to emerge as the de facto treatment for irregular heartbeats, here stood I, walking proof that one zap could do it – given a little serendipity and a sufficiently hare-brained approach to electronic maintenance.

As I walked out of that hospital I didn't give a monkey's as to what did it or how, for I was back to where I wanted to be: normal, *bloody normal*, with the clear choice to do anything, at any speed I chose and for as long as I wanted to. Once again, I could be a normal Scallywag; the fences were down and all the doors were unlocked.

Hello, world! *Hello!*

Now I was free to do it all, just as I'd dreamed for all those years. First stop, says I, the Isle of Man boats!